Raising Their Voices

Raising Their Voices

The Politics of Girls' Anger

LYN MIKEL BROWN

HARVARD UNIVERSITY PRESS

Cambridge, Massachusetts

London, England

1998

To my daughter Maya

Copyright © 1998 by Lyn Mikel Brown
All rights reserved
Printed in the United States of America

Library of Congress Cataloging-in-Publication Data

Brown, Lyn Mikel, 1956–
  Raising their voices : the politics of girls' anger / Lyn Mikel
Brown.
    p.   cm.
  Includes bibliographical references (p.   ) and index.
  ISBN 0-674-83871-8 (alk. paper)
  1. Girls—Maine—Psychology—Case studies.
  2. Girls—Maine—Attitudes—Case studies.
  3. Girls—United States—Psychology.
  4. Girls—United States—Attitudes.
  5. Girls—United States—Social conditions
  6. Sex role in children—United States—Case studies.
  7. Anger in children—Case studies.
  8. Anger in adolescence—Case studies.
  9. Women—Socialization—United States.   I. Title.
HQ777.R665   1998
  305.23—dc21   98-15216

Contents

97010

Preface

After the publication of *Meeting at the Crossroads,* Carol Gilligan and I were struck by the degree to which those who publicly engaged our description of girls' psychological development passed over the clarity and strength of girls' voices. Although they resonated with or challenged the *losses* the girls in our study sustained over time—the loss of voice, the narrowing of desires and expectations, the capitulation to conventional notions of femininity—they overlooked the fact that most of the girls resisted these losses in some capacity. Part of the reason for this representation of our work was that its appearance coincided with the publication of other studies of girls' experiences—most specifically, two reports by the American Association of University Women, one a national survey that found a dramatic drop in white and Latina girls' self-confidence and self-esteem, the other an educational report that connected this drop to girls' unequal treatment in school. Our attempt to trace the psychological development of a group of girls at the Laurel School, a private girls' school in Ohio, was quickly cast as another example of girls' loss of self-esteem. Although this interpretation of our findings provided additional evidence of the difficulties girls experience in their struggles to be heard and seen and taken seriously in school, it also buried what we considered to be a central finding of our study—that girls actively *resist* dominant cultural notions of femininity, particularly at the edge of adolescence.

As a result of this representation of our findings, and the fact that I continued to hear, in both scientific and popular accounts of girls' lives, primarily about the psychological trouble white girls were in,

I began to envision a study that would bring the resistant voices of such girls to the surface for consideration. I began to wonder how girls' resiliency and psychological health might be connected to their opportunity to know and express strong feelings, particularly anger, without being ridiculed or punished. The girls in the Laurel Study who stayed connected to themselves did so at the risk of disrupting conventional expectations of femininity. The sometimes loud and indignant voices of these "resisters," the clarity of their vision, and their willingness to stay with what they knew and experienced in the face of pressure to conform were inspiring and compelling. Their capacity to name the sources of ill treatment, injustice, and bad feeling freed them to deal with anger constructively and reasonably; this anger motivated their resistance and strong voices. On the other hand, the Laurel girls seemed most in danger when they became confused about the source of their strong feelings, when they could not name the objects of their anger. In such moments, when self-doubt and uncertainty about their interpretations of reality crept in, anger turned inward to self-reproach and sometimes to self-harm.

During our work at Laurel we found that active resisters, girls who carried their voices of protest into middle adolescence, tended to be on the margins of their privileged, predominantly white girls' school, owing to color or class. Partly because of a growing awareness of the significance of my own working-class background on my interpretations of the Laurel girls' voices and partly through my relationship with a white working-class girl from Laurel whom I will call Anna, I began to wonder at the struggles and challenges these resisters faced in their determination to remain in touch with themselves and their communities. Anna's movement from a smart, introverted, albeit somewhat self-disparaging girl of twelve to a sometimes cynical, often angry young woman with great self-awareness and capacity for social critique was both inspiring and troubling. The constant tension between Anna's love of school and her estrangement from the values and expectations of upper-middle-class life echoed my own growing up. In Anna I recognized the intense pain as well as the great promise of her outsider status. I wished to focus more closely on girls' active resistance to the often imperceptible forces that threatened to move them out of touch with their experiences.

The study I report in this book was designed to bring the resistant voices of girls like Anna, specifically white girls from working-class and working poor families, into relationship with white girls from middle-class families; to bring the similarities and differences between their experiences and voices to the surface and into the ongoing conversation about girls' and women's development, a conversation that still too often assumes that to be white is to be middle class and privileged and that to be poor or working class is to be of color. I listened intently for a year to two groups of white girls from central Maine—one poor and working class from the rural community of Mansfield; one middle and upper middle class from the mid-sized city of Acadia—as they discussed their lives and critiqued the world around them.

In our study of girls and young women at Laurel, we deliberately focused a great deal of attention on the strength and power of the younger girls' voices and spoke directly to the need to preserve their tendency to stay in touch with strong feelings such as anger and frustration. Through childhood these girls had a clarity and strength not often noted in studies of female development. At the edge of adolescence—at ten and eleven and twelve—however, something happened. As girls moved into the dominant culture, as people reacted to their changing bodies and as they confronted new expectations and gained new capacities for understanding, reality as they experienced it in childhood began to shift. What they once felt and thought no longer held the same meaning for others. As the names for things—relationships, feelings, actions—changed, girls struggled with the definition of reality.

The usual terms for such an adolescent shift seemed to us both inadequate and inaccurate. This was not a negotiation or resolution of the distinction between appearance and reality—girls were not simply experiencing the "normal" difficulties of moving away from childhood fantasy and accepting adult reality. As we listened we came to understand that girls were questioning the very terms of this reality. Their fight for voice and for their angle of vision called into question the stability of conventional femininity. Through their resistance they asked, both implicitly and explicitly, whose construction of reality was to be given legitimacy and authority. Thus at early adolescence girls seemed to see the patriarchal framework for the first time and name its effects on their lives: they would have to narrow their feelings and modulate their voices if they were to make a smooth transition into the dominant culture. Strong feelings like anger would push people away; full use of their bodies and their brains would make people uncomfortable.

Girls at this point in their development talked about knowing when they were being themselves and when they were pretending, performing, or impersonating the right kind of girl in order to maintain relationships or satisfy others' views of appropriate behavior; they spoke of the importance of being "discreet" if they were to pass as nice girls in their relationships; they told us they felt their thoughts and feelings were in "jeopardy" of being lost to them in such relationships. They became astute observers and judges of hypocrisy in themselves and others.

We were struck by the Laurel girls' capacity to articulate this process of dissociation and disconnection, and by their awareness of their own fear, sadness, and anger in the face of pressure to accommodate to conventions of white middle-class femininity. We were also struck by their capacity to appear as if everything was all right, as though nothing was happening. Although some were questionably thin, for the most part their good grades, high test scores, and smiling faces gave no indication of the struggle we were hearing in the privacy of the interviews. In fact, their performances would lead most to assume that they were eager to embrace the reality into which they were being socialized.

Thus *before* we heard a loss of voice or shift into idealized relationships, we witnessed an active struggle and resistance. We heard the curiosity and witnessed the disruptive behavior of the younger girls; we observed the sometimes cynical and angry resistance of girls on the brink of adolescence; and we experienced the political potential of the active underground as girls moved through adolescence. Here, in the girls' intense struggle against pressures not to know and not to speak, we thought, was the hope for a different developmental trajectory, and with it, the potential for societal change. Here, at the edge of adolescence, we argued, was the anger expressed, the resistant, knowing voices determined to be heard, the underground voices easily called forth by someone who would listen and take them seriously.

The study I present here begins with the knowledge of such struggle and resistance and is predicated on the possibility of healthy pathways for girls. In this book I document how a small number of outspoken white girls from two very different cultural communities fight for the life of their minds and the presence of their bodies. On the way, I examine the wider social climate in which such struggle takes place, reflect on the processes through which girls' voices are constrained and regulated, and explore the various ways the girls resist such regulation. I then consider education as a contextual audience for girls' development, addressing the inability or reluctance of those working within educational contexts, both women and men, to hear and respond well to girls' resistance. Throughout I attempt to show how the contradictions inherent in class-related notions of femininity can undermine girls' strong feelings, particularly feelings of anger, and contribute to their disconnection from themselves and from public life.

When women and girls protest the realities of their experiences, they are likely to be accused of contributing to a "cult of victimization" or "culture of complaint." These misnomers of political resistance reveal the depth of cultural denial, the covering over of girls' and women's psychological realities, particularly when these realities are painted with strong feelings and vivid illustrations, as they are in the case of sexual harassment, physical violence, acquaintance rape, and incest. I would suggest that such a response reflects on a much wider level the struggle for interpretation that girls coming of age experience every day.

In a dominant culture that has such difficulty with girls' straightforwardness, the question of creative resistance to stereotypes and various forms of oppression becomes central to girls', and ultimately women's, psychological health. Encouraging girls' strong feelings and taking seriously their social critique invite them to participate in the social and political world around them, a radical act with potentially transformative consequences.

Girls' open resistance to the psychological and physical denigration inherent in dominant cultural definitions of femininity is disturbing; it is disruptive and, to many, frightening. When women turn away from such anger, it is also, for girls, truly confusing. And when we, as feminists, concern ourselves solely with academic arguments about the one "right" course or form of feminism at the expense of the complex realities of girls' lives, the girls are left to find their own way in the world. To girls' great credit, what we see is not complete confusion but pockets of expressed, sometimes quite organized, grassroots resistance. These girls are listening to and fighting for one another, whether protesting under the banner "Revolution Girl Style Now" or whispering conspiratorially in the back of a classroom. They are actively struggling to sort out the meanings of their lives, contesting the pressures to align with a reality that devalues and dismisses them. This is a book, then, devoted to the resistance, to its emergence and existence, as well as to the appreciation of forces and events that threaten its visibility and effectiveness.

one

Stones in the Road

Not long ago a story in *USA Today* began by describing a shift in the weather, a sunny day turned angry: "It was a feisty day," the author observed, "perfect to touch off a revolution."[1] This particular revolution took place at the middle school in Ames, Iowa. For more than a year some boys had been wearing Hooters t-shirts to school —advertising the restaurant chain infamous for the tight, skimpy uniforms waitresses are required to wear—and two fourteen-year-old girls had had enough. In response to the boys' shirts, which sported owl eyes peering out from the Os in "Hooters" and carried the slogan "More than a mouthful," the girls designed their own: a profile of a rooster, his eye peering out from the O in "Cocks." Their slogan? "Nothing to crow about." The girls were denied permission to wear their t-shirts to school. They did anyway, and the ensuing uproar prompted the school to ban both shirts. The girls found this response disappointing and inadequate. Their goal, according to one girl, had been "to make people talk and think about it . . . We wanted [the Hooters shirts] to be socially unacceptable rather than legally unacceptable." One of the creators of the Cocks shirts, frustrated with the school administration's lack of appreciation for the finer distinctions at stake, put it this way: "Ours was a political statement and theirs was just sexism."

A year earlier, by a landslide vote of her classmates, seventeen-year-old April Schuldt, unmarried and five months pregnant, with shiny red hair, chipped black nail polish, and combat boots, found herself an unlikely homecoming queen at Memorial High School in Eau Claire, Wisconsin.[2] Students voted for April—the daughter of a factory-worker mother and a steel-worker father—because, in the words of one student, "she knows who she is . . . she's nice to everyone." But since April did not fit the ideal of the beauty queen, four school administrators and a teacher "arranged" for a more likely winner: a cute, bright swimming star. When she was tipped off, Schuldt said, "I wasn't sad, I was angry, like what can I do? What can I do?"

April and her friends chose an upcoming pep-rally as their stage. "It sounds easy," Schuldt said, "but it wasn't, 'cause pep-assembly's a real big deal, especially at homecoming; the whole school gathers."

The band was playing, the football team was there, everybody was filing in and this little clump of us went out and sat in the middle of the gym floor. Now that's taboo 'cause the floor belongs to the cheerleaders and the pom-poms. We sat there and our hearts were pounding; we were expecting to be dragged out by our hair, but then something else happened. Students started coming down from the bleachers, people came out of the band, teachers came and sat down, the whole floor was covered. The pom-poms were all cramped together trying to do their thing in this little amount of space—it was unbelievable the support I was getting.

By the time the superintendent launched an investigation and the truth came out, Homecoming Day was long past. But for April it was the principle of the thing: "I'm not someone who wants to be Miss America," she explains, "I want to be an English teacher. I'm different, but I'm real. I don't think all women and girls nowadays want to see someone totally without flaws standing up as queen—not everyone's perfect. We have a daycare center at our school, we have a parenting program. There are pregnant people in the world. Even though I'm pregnant, I'm still me. So why are we making believe ordinary, nonperfect people don't exist or are less deserving?"

I find myself thinking of these two accounts of girls' resistance as I sit in a school classroom listening to a blonde, blue-eyed eighth-grade girl from rural Maine describe the way she stood up to her English teacher, refusing to take his persistent denigration of her and the other girls in her class. She is part of a panel of five girls participating in a day-long workshop on gender equity, and so perhaps she should not seem as alone as she does. In many ways she is familiar —tall and slender, willowy even, her shoulders pulled forward, her voice wavering as she begins her story. But it's what she says and the compelling, focused way she speaks that pull her away from the other girls. Determined, resolute, her voice gathers momentum. She is freshly angry and hurt as she tells the room full of teachers and administrators how she pointed out the sexism to her teacher in class, and then, when he wouldn't listen to her, reported his behavior to her parents, who helped her negotiate a conversation with the principal. She is mad at the teacher, yes, but mostly she is hurt and disappointed at the response of her classmates. It was not the boys in her class who turned away, but the other girls, who she thought would hear what she heard, feel what she felt. Although she is still stunned at the girls' meanness—the way they ostracized her and called her names—she is no less certain that she did the right thing.

I begin with these stories—each told by white girls living in predominantly white areas of the United States—because they focus on girls' feelings of anger and indignation, their critique of unjust authorities and social structures that do not account for the reality of their experiences, and because they illustrate the girls' creative, organized action on their own behalf. The intense feelings and expressions of anger characteristic of such stories also resonate with the voices of the Mansfield and Acadia girls reported in this book.

Much attention of late has been given to girls' invisibility in schools, to sexual harassment in public spaces such as cafeterias, hallways, and on school playgrounds,[3] to gender bias in classrooms,[4] to losses in self-esteem and self-confidence, as well as to signs of psychological trouble, such as eating disorders, negative body image, and depression.[5] We know and understand very little, however, about girls who resist these losses and retain their psychological resilience and invulnerability. Indeed, Michelle Fine and her colleague Pat Macpherson argue that the writings of feminist academics "have been persistently committed to public representations of women's victimization and structural assaults and have consequently ignored, indeed misrepresented, *how well young women talk as subjects,* passionate about and relishing their capacities to move between nexus of power and powerlessness. That is to say, feminist scholars have forgotten to take notice of how firmly young women resist—alone and sometimes together."[6] Such attention to the psychological losses many girls experience, while certainly pointing to the effects of injustice, may inadvertently contribute to the privileged capacity of whiteness to name the experiences and outline the developmental trajectories of all girls, regardless of social, racial, or material status. In addition, a focus on psychological losses, even specifically white girls' losses, may inadvertently contribute to an over-emphasis on passive indoctrination and an under-emphasis on girls' resistance that might inform strategies for encouraging and sustaining their voices.

Grrrls, Grrrls, Grrrls

Reports outside the academy, however, would lead us to believe that we are living with a radically different generation of girls—white and of color—willing to fight for the right to their own space, demanding to be heard and seen, card-carrying members of a generation that is, as one *Utne Reader*'s cover proclaimed, "Dissed, Mythed, and Totally Pissed."[7] "Are girls turning meaner?" a young writer for *YO!* asks. Increasingly at her school, girls are suspended for fighting. Says one girl, "They want to say 'Don't mess with me.' They want to be seen as trouble-makers. They want to be just like the guys and stand out too."[8] "Girls will be girls," *Newsweek* announces, reporting that female gang members "are every bit as ruthless as the boys."[9]

No longer necessarily offshoots or subordinate members of male gangs, those girls—whether white girls from smalltown Maine or Mexican-American girls from Los Angeles—who have joined girl gangs seem thirsty for self-definition, power, and control, as well as for a sense of belonging and a need for loyalty and group support.[10]

And yet to make such a superficial equation of female and male gang identity is to ignore the girls' understanding of themselves as young women. After a two-year study of Puerto Rican girl gang members in New York City, Anne Campbell found neither a total rejection of femininity nor a total desire to be like the boys, but a complicated feminine identity grounded in their cultural communities and developed against the backdrop of prejudice and poverty. "The girls accept the desirability of some aspects of femininity, class, or ethnicity but reject others," Campbell notes. "Essentially they are saying, 'I am not *that* kind of woman,' which is very different from saying, 'I am not a woman.' "[11] By listening to their talk, Campbell hears a contradictory discourse of femininity that contains deep concerns about mothering, an acceptance of early sexual experimentation along with a rejection of "loose" sexual morality, pride in their autonomy and their ability to fight, opposition to any view of themselves as passive or subordinate, with a particularly strong rejection of female compliance to male control.

A few years back, the emergence of confrontational "angry girl bands" such as Bikini Kill, Bratmobile, Hole, and Babes in Toyland led to the Riot Grrrl movement, a largely white, middle-class network of young women rallying under the slogan "Revolution Girl Style Now." Appropriating an in-your-face, working-class, punk-inspired do-it-yourself ethic, Riot Grrrls have adopted an attitude of self-sufficiency and use their anger as a source of power. Grrrls meet weekly to discuss political, emotional, and sexual issues. Their basic credo—that young women should take care of one another—is spread through self-distributed alternative music and a plethora of underground fanzines such as *Girl Germs, Bikini Kill,* and *Sister Nobody.* Here, in Xeroxed pages delivered by hand or through the mail, young women create the space to rant and rave and rage about personal and societal abuses and spread "a fierce reclaiming of things girlish, a push for girl love, unpolluted by competition and male domination, and an insistence on being heard."[12]

Not unlike girl gangs, the angry girl movement thrives on contradiction and the reappropriation of conventionally feminine images and language historically used against women and girls. As Kathleen Hanna, the lead singer of Bikini Kill and deemed by *Spin* magazine "the angriest girl of all," puts it, "Because I live in a world that hates women and I am one . . . who is struggling desperately not to hate myself . . . my whole life is a contradiction."[13] Contradiction is manifest in Riot Grrrls' appearance—baby-doll dresses with lace peter pan collars worn with black boots, shaved heads, and cat's-eye glasses—and in the spectacle they create. When Hanna roars on stage, "Your world not mine your world not mine" in a halter top with the word "slut" written in large letters across her stomach, she epitomizes the movement's attempt to disrupt worn-out dichotomies by connecting femininity and rage.

The complexities of these girls from different social and material locations disrupt a dominant culture wedded to discrete, abstract categories and dependent on metaphors of duality and polarity.[14] Within such a construction, Helen Haste argues, "we are drawn to map masculinity and femininity onto the other deep polarities of the culture," such as activity and passivity, rationality and chaos, public and private, thinking and feeling.[15] Moreover, as Elizabeth Debold explains, "The categories *masculine* and *feminine* imply norms of behavior for each sex that are related to male and female identity within white and middle-class culture, which is the dominant discourse within the United States."[16]

Throughout their lives, girls from diverse cultural, racial, and class backgrounds and with different sexual identities encounter and negotiate the voices, stories, fantasies, and explanations that regulate and maintain the dominant culture's polarized discourse of gender. They hear about and witness what is deemed appropriate behavior; they learn how girls should look and sound if they are to be acceptable. Girls are either initiated into or, with the support of their families and local communities, encouraged to actively resist this dominant social construction of reality.

In part because young girls are not taken seriously in this culture, they are more or less free to break the rules of the gender game; they can blur the boundaries, be creative, boldly explore possibilities.

Although their play is readily mapped onto the cultural polarities of male and female—for example, girls who are active and athletic are still not girls but tomboys—they move more or less fluidly between masculinity and femininity.[17] Thus, although girls are certainly aware of the lines of demarcation, well rehearsed in the dichotomy of gender relations, and knowledgeable about what is expected of girls if they are to be called girls, they are not yet strictly pressed to comply with such expectations.

Even if younger girls *were* pressed, Elizabeth Debold argues, it would not "be enough to stop them from becoming more 'masculine' in their activity preferences." Although school-age girls know that in the white middle-class world a hierarchical distinction is made between active males and passive females, until adolescence they do not know it in a way that could deeply affect their behavior. That is, they have not yet gained the capacity for abstraction which, although a significant cognitive advancement, also "makes them vulnerable to internalizing impossible ideals and images as they shape their gendered identity as young women," and which moves them to understand and embody the dualisms of the dominant culture. While younger girls are certainly not pre-cultural, they do not yet have the capacity for abstract reasoning that would allow them to know and desire as enculturated subjects.[18] And this, more than anything else, is why preadolescent girls are not bothered very much with the discrepancy between the dominant definitions of femininity and their own daily lives.

Early adolescence, however, heralds dramatic physical changes, intense social scrutiny, and new cognitive capabilities; it is, as Jerome Kagan explains, a unique developmental moment when the child is disposed "to examine the logic and consistency of [her] beliefs." This move toward examination is "catalyzed by experiences that confront the adolescent with phenomena and attitudes that are not easily interpreted within [her] existing ideology."[19] The rich language of childhood relationships comes up against the vernacular, the ways of interacting and gendered knowing, of the dominant culture and the pressure to be either one thing or the other—to be, for example, either pure or sexual, passive or active, feeling or thinking selfless or selfish, good or bad—in essence, feminine or masculine.[20] Such intrusions nudge the preadolescent to reconsider the way the world works and relationships go. For girls who have lived rather fluid lives, moving between the categories of masculine and feminine, and whose childhood understandings have been constructed in relationship with their families and local communities, the increased pressures to fall in line with narrow notions of white middle-class heterosexual femininity can seem, quite understandably, disturbing and problematic.

As Haste observes, our dominant cultural theories of gender, and, I would add, their unmarked relationships with class, race, and sexual orientation, are "made explicit when there is a threat to the status quo, a questioning of what has been deemed normal—something that is likely to spark off predictions of dire consequences."[21] Adolescent girls' frustration and anger at the impossibility of bringing their rich and varied life experiences into relationship with such a narrow social construction, their refusal to map neatly onto the existing social and psychological landscape, to fit easily into the dominant category "woman," is one such threat. Their resistance creates anxiety, not only because they are disrupting conventional sex-role socialization, but because they are disturbing the dominant culture's polarized construction of social reality.[22]

One can hear the white working- and middle-class girls in this study struggle against such polarization as they try on and reject, pull and push against, attempt to reframe and reinterpret the culturally inscribed and socially sanctioned notions of womanhood that specify the normal, the good.[23] In their conversations about who they are and who they are not, who they desire to be and who they wish never to become, they reveal their problematic relationship with conventional definitions of femininity. When they ventriloquate, or speak in and through voices that reverberate dominant expectations, stereotypes, and images of girls and women—most often during moments of gossip and disparaging talk about others—even as they struggle to like themselves as girls and to resist the pressure to contain and constrain their own voices to fit such expectations, they reveal the contradictions that catalyze ideological conflicts. Their anger and frustration at the limits imposed on their experiences and desires point to the heart of the matter: not only is there no way to fit their varied experiences and understandings of themselves, the range of their feelings, and the complexities of their relationships into the dominant cultural construction of gender, but there is also no adequate justification for the attempt.

The girl gang members and grrrl activists, like the "Cocks" t-shirt designers, April Schuldt, the eighth-grade resister from rural Maine, and the other girls presented in this book, different as they are, bring into focus the limited and limiting discourse of conventional femininity—how it serves to render incoherent the complex and contradictory realities of young women's experiences today—but also how such limits trigger an outrage that intersects with race, culture, and the different circumstances of girls' lives to create openings, new possibilities, and sites for successful struggle. These young women, within the boundaries of very different social and structural constraints, use the subversive power of body, sexuality, and language to challenge conventional meanings and expectations of femininity. As living contradictions, they represent stones in the road toward idealized femininity, causing those of us who listen to them to ponder the usual or "normal" paths toward womanhood, to reconsider our assumptions about the way things go. With their questions and observations, their basic need to name their experiences and to say what is happening, they pull us along the rough terrain, along roads we could not discern without their guidance. The twists and turns, the bumps and bruises they sustain along the way remind us vividly, if only momentarily, that there is no original way to be, no decidedly right way to move forward.[24]

Developing Anger

While most girls identify with neither gangs nor Riot Grrrls, such demanding voices underscore the desires and struggles, anger and resistance most girls, to some degree, experience at adolescence. And yet there is little to be found in the psychological or feminist literature about girls' anger or about the benefits and costs of its expression. Indeed, after an extensive literature search Fine and Macpherson concluded that "young women's political outrage simply does not exist as a category for feminist intellectual analysis."[25]

Writings on *women* and anger, however, are more plentiful.[26] Most explore white middle-class women's genuine difficulty and discomfort with anger and their need to recover the psychological and political power of this emotion. "For women," Jean Baker Miller argues, "the problem is a situation of subordination that continually produces anger, along with the culture's intolerance of women's direct expression of anger in any form."[27] In fact, for many white middle-class women, anger falls into the category of what the philosopher Allison Jagger terms "outlaw emotions."[28]

Although anger is more culturally acceptable for white working-class women and certain women of color than it is for white middle- and upper-class women, it does not necessarily translate into constructive action or effective social change. For example, listening to young urban women of many colors, Pastor, McCormick, and Fine discovered that, while the girls developed a critical consciousness in response to the sexism, classism, and racism they endured, and while they were more likely than their white, privileged counterparts "to assert themselves within white, often male dominated institutions," they did not seek one another out for collective action.[29] They often found themselves caught in a "cycle of resistance and accommodation," whereby their individualistic resistance strategies would "more often than not reproduce the very oppressive culture they think they are resisting." Thus their justified anger was unlikely to be an effective response to political injustice or a catalyst for social change.[30]

It is not surprising that white middle-class women in particular have difficulty with anger. At odds with a lifetime of socialization to attend to the needs of others, anger, as a self-protective response to hurt and bad treatment, focuses attention on one's self. Anger reminds us that we are in disagreement with another and thus, in a sense, separate.[31] Moreover, powerful social sanctions make the expression of such strong feelings unacceptable and often dangerous. As Elizabeth Spelman argues, while women and other members of subordinate groups "are expected to be emotional, indeed to have their emotions run their lives, their anger will not be tolerated." Such anger is likely to be called irrational, "redescribed as hysteria or rage." This is so, she argues, because the expression of anger is intimately tied to self-respect, to the capacity to realize and author one's life fully. For this reason women's anger is often considered not only inappropriate but also an act of insubordination. Anger is threatening to those in power "not only because the subordinates' anger might be followed up by action, but because it surely signals that subordinates take themselves seriously; they believe they have the capacity as well as the right to be judges of those around them, even of those who are said to be their 'superiors.' "[32]

Self-respect is dangerous, Spelman points out, because "dominant groups surely know at some level that good clear thinking on the part of people in subordinate positions [about their situations] is likely to make such people angry." Because it is tied to self-respect, a sense of entitlement, and lucid thinking about wrong-doing, anger is "the essential political emotion,"[33] and thus "to silence anger may be to repress political speech."[34] Reasoned anger is critical not only to the healthy psychological development of individual women, but also to their capacity to recognize injustice and organize for change.[35]

Young girls, white and of color, seem capable of experiencing and expressing anger as a natural part of their relationships.[36] The capacity of the younger girls in the Laurel Study to be openly angry— "really mad"—to be disruptive and resistant, gave them an air of authority and authenticity, and revealed a simple desire to speak and to be listened to.[37] Girls at seven, eight, and nine assert their strong feelings when they are hurt or treated unfairly. These are the hallmarks of healthy anger, an emotion distinct from more destructive, controlling forms of aggression.[38]

As we might expect of young children, girls follow their impulse to respond, and this impulse seems intimately tied to experience and self-righteous demands that their hurt be taken seriously, that unfairness toward them be addressed. Such a sense of entitlement and personal authority, as yet unchecked by adolescent propensities to hold themselves to, or feel threatened by, ideal standards or internal comparisons, surfaces as girls name and address what is wrong in their relationships.[39] As a result, their anger often quickly dissipates; relationships have a free-flowing quality—girls move together and apart, between harmony and conflict, almost daily. In this way, young girls appear to have a healthy resistance to those experiences and messages that would pull them away from their feelings and thoughts, and thus have a basic protection from psychological trouble.

But girls gradually learn that anger is a complicated emotion for anyone in this culture, and especially for women. From watching and listening to the way the world goes, they learn that their expressions of anger are inappropriate and unacceptable within the narrow framework of the dominant culture.[40] Over time, then, what was once a sign of girls' strength and resiliency—their capacity to feel their anger, to know its source, and to respond directly—becomes a liability, at least in those places where white middle-class values and conventions of femininity prevail. In these arenas girls learn what to say, how to speak, what to feel and think, if they want to be the right kind of girl, if they want to be listened to, accepted, rewarded, included. With these messages comes voice-training from those adults who, themselves, have uncritically bought into this fiction: good girls are calm and quiet, they speak softly, they do not complain or demand to be heard, they do not shout, they do not directly express anger.[41]

Anger, *because* it is tied to self-respect, must be excised if a girl is to move seamlessly into today's culture, that is, if the culture is to welcome her and remain unchanged by her presence. In other words, anger and conventional femininity are subversive of each other. To understand the "social introjection" of the feminine ideal, Teresa Bernardez argues, is to understand "the inhibitions that prevent rebellious acts."[42]

The pressure for girls to split off their anger is enormous and the rewards are clear. The girls who do so, however, risk losing the capacity to locate the source of their pain and thus to do something about it; they risk losing the potential for a once ordinary, healthy resistance to turn political.[43] Without anger there is no impetus to act against any injustice done to them. If we take away girls' anger, then, we take away the foundation for women's political resistance.

In a climate that forbids or overly regulates the expression of angry feelings, frustration and fear often lead to aggression. Not surprisingly, then, girls express a good deal of aggression, though it is likely to become increasingly indirect as they move through childhood. Researchers define indirect aggression as "a type of behavior in which the perpetrator attempts to inflict pain in such a manner that he or she makes it seem as though there has been no intention at all. Accordingly, he or she is more likely to avoid counter-aggression and, if possible, to remain unidentified."[44] Oddly, such behavior, rather than understood as problematic, as an adaptive response to narrow and oppressive expectations of femininity, is offered as a sign of girls' greater emotional and psychological maturity, a consequence of increased social intelligence.[45] And yet "anger," as Naomi Scheman notes, "is 'object hungry.' "[46] Indirectness will not only contribute to confusion and make it more difficult for others to respond directly to one's feelings; it will, over time, make it difficult for girls to identify their angry feelings.

While girls' aggression becomes gradually more indirect through childhood, researchers also find, like an unidentified blip on a radar screen, a rather surprising rise in direct aggression around age 11. Aggressive behavior, both direct and indirect, "has its highest 'peak' at age 11," a trend "more clearly seen among girls than among boys."[47] As a study of boys and girls in urban Finland concludes, "the social life of 11 and 12-year-old girls is more ruthless and aggressive than has been suggested by previous research . . . [and] gives a rather cruel picture of the social life of girls."[48]

Indeed, researchers studying display rules—guidelines for controlling and expressing emotional behavior—in school-age African American children from urban, low-income families discovered a "striking" gender difference in the expression of indirect aggression, specifically in masking or hiding anger. Masking, the authors explain, can occur either when a child expresses no emotion at all or expresses another, more acceptable emotion. Although in this study, as in other studies of girls, black and white, masking generally increased with age, girls at early adolescence report such behavior *less* than younger girls. A similar pattern occurred for the expression of sadness. "Pre-adolescent girls," the authors suggest, "seem to place less value on this social form and may be more direct about their expression of felt affect. Our observation is that girls in this age group are often quite formidable in their assertiveness with peers and teachers."[49]

Researchers have begun to identify and explore the significance of middle-school girls' expressions of anger and forms of aggression, suggesting that we have not fully appreciated the intensity of feeling or understood the meanings of girls' interactions with one another. Redefining aggression as it relates to girls, for example, a number of recent studies report that girls in early adolescence are more likely than their male counterparts to exhibit "relational aggression," a form of aggression "characterized by the threat of withdrawal of affiliation for the purposes of controlling the behavior of others."[50] Donna Eder suggests that the aggressive ritual insulting and teasing she hears among white and black working-class girls are, in fact, a way girls support one another, protect themselves from male ridicule, and distance themselves from dominant gender roles. Girls, she found, used teasing to socialize others into group behavior and norms, to learn and practice self-defense strategies, and to solidify their group relationships, even to dissolve or mitigate competition over boys. Expressions of anger and distrust were directed at girls who did not comply, and their expression served as a reminder to such girls of the consequences of disloyalty.[51]

Don Merten, exploring "the meaning of meanness" among a junior high school clique of popular girls dubbed "the dirty dozen" by their teachers, described girls' struggles with popularity, friendship, and isolation. Meanness, he explained, was an effective strategy for maintaining popularity for these girls in the face of expectations to be super nice. Girls who were not nice to everyone all the time risked losing their popularity by being called stuck-up, but girls who transformed the support and power of their popular position into meanness side-stepped such accusations or feelings of envy. Their "reputation for meanness acted as a deterrent to both competition *and* suggestions that one was stuck-up." Thus, in a social context in which direct expressions of feelings and open competition among girls was unacceptable, meanness became an effective "discourse about hierarchical position, popularity, and invulnerability."[52]

Findings from studies conducted with diverse populations in dramatically different contexts thus seem to point to a rather similar finding—that girls at the edge of adolescence feel a good deal of anger and express a good deal of direct and indirect aggression. As noted, one might interpret such increased indirectness and masking of anger as a sign of girls' greater maturity, indicating a gradual increase in their capacity to control irrational impulses and mitigate aggressive behavior. On this view, girls' heightened anger at early adolescence may represent a reemergence of Freudian drives and impulses that need to be controlled, repressed, or sublimated for girls' healthy development and the smooth continuance of the culture.

I want to suggest a somewhat different interpretation, however, one that reasserts rationality and connects adolescent girls' heightened anger and aggression to their observations and experiences. I contend that girls' increased anger and assertiveness at eleven and twelve reflects their emerging comprehension of the culture they are about to enter and their place as young women in it. On this view, new cognitive competencies of early adolescence, catalyzed by pubertal changes that identify girls physically with women and that invite more intense pressures to accommodate to the dominant cultural ideals of femininity, awaken girls to examine their childhood assumptions about what it means to be female and to reflect on their past and present experiences as girls.[53] Early adolescence, in other words, disposes girls to see the cultural framework, and girls' and women's subordinate place in it, for the first time. That their reaction to this awakening would be shock, sadness, anger, and a sense of betrayal is not surprising. Moreover, since these strong feelings emerge just as girls move into the dominant culture, at the very moment when their anger is most disruptive to the social order, proponents of the status quo have much invested in covering or pushing these feelings out of public view.

The inner edge of adolescence may thus mark girls' first full-blown and, in some cases, most powerful open stand against cultural oppression and repression. As alternative voices and interpretations conflict with their experiences of childhood, girls struggle openly with questions about how to feel and think, how to proceed, how to be in relationship with others and with a culture that both devalues and idealizes women. Because in the course of this struggle girls lay open to scrutiny the category "woman," because their outrage points to the hurt and injustice inflicted on those who stand outside the dominant framework, because their conflicts and struggles, their questions and their state of uncertainty create openings and challenge the social order, it is important, particularly for women, to listen to and engage girls at this developmental juncture, to appreciate and to learn from their outspokenness and creative forms of resistance.[54]

Class, Culture, and Race

The expression of anger and aggression in adolescent girls is greatly affected by their social and material status, by the definitions of appropriate femininity communicated to them through their immediate communities, through their families and friends. Such cultural contexts define the contours of anger, as well as the degree and form of its expression.[55] While the expression of direct anger may be strongly discouraged in girls from white middle-class families, for example, Miller and Sperry suggest that anger is valued in girls from low-income white communities "because it prompt[s] children to act quickly and forcefully to protect themselves."[56] They found that parents in such communities encouraged their children to respond aggressively when provoked by peers and were more likely to value anger as a call to action.

I am aware, however, that venturing into a class analysis of such issues is fraught with difficulties. The political discourse on class in the United States is woefully inadequate and almost always feeds an oddly specific stereotype of poor urban, black, unwed mothers. To be sure, being black, urban, and young exposes one to greater risk of poverty, but there is great diversity among the poor, and most officially poor people are white.[57]

Certainly the psychological literature on class in the United States is sparse, on white girls and class nearly non-existent. Perhaps this is so because there is little that can be said about the subject in general terms, so culturally varied, complicated, and full of contradictions are class experiences and struggles.[58] Indeed, Robert Stevenson and Jeanne Ellsworth argue that, unlike either the working-class "lads" Paul Willis described in northern England[59] or working-class and poor African American and Latino students in the United States,[60] white working-class youths in the United States are unlikely to develop what the anthropologist John Ogbu terms an "oppositional culture": a "cultural frame of reference [that] gives them a sense of collective or social identity and a sense of self-worth" in opposition to white middle-class society.[61] White working-class culture, Stevenson and Ellsworth explain, "has been described as 'fractured': historically along regional, racial and ethnic lines, and more recently by the displacement of industrial workers and the erosion of the labor union as a social and political collectivity." Therefore, they argue, "the working class has lost any form of collective consciousness that is distinct from the dominant culture."[62] White working-class youth in the United States do not have a shared cultural history or social narrative from which to draw or with which to identify.

Carolyn Kay Steedman notes that what *has* been written attributes a fraudulent, uncomplicated "psychological sameness to the figures in the working-class landscape."[63] This is partly because, she explains, "delineation of emotional and psychological selfhood has been made by and through the testimony of people in a central relationship to the dominant culture, that is to say by and through people who are not working class."

In this book I hope to show that understanding cultural and class differences is critical to a genuine appreciation of girls' resistance. The working-class and poor girls from Mansfield are not, as one might say, "bad off"—they are not cases in the extreme; they are, in fact, quite ordinary. And yet the differences between them and their middle-class counterparts are very real. The Acadia girls have parents who are highly educated and enjoy secure, well-paying professional careers; they have access to a wide array of opportunities. In contrast, the working-class girls do not have enough of what they want—money, opportunities, possessions, the simple luxury of not wanting. Despite reports of economic recovery, they live in a Maine county devastated by mill closings and down-sizing. Because they live close to the economic edge, they are dramatically affected by shifts in the local job market and unforeseen tragedies, such as illness or fire, for which most are uninsured. There is palpable anxiety around jobs, money, and the future. While they have the support of family members and their local community, in material terms, to borrow from Steedman, "there exists a poverty of experience to which [the middle-class Acadia girls] have no access; structures of feeling they have not lived within." This difference in experience and feeling has an undeniable psychological and social impact.

One of the consequences of exploring the impact of class and contextual differences on the girls' understandings of themselves and their views of femininity is an appreciation of cultural variations on what it means to be white. Increasingly, feminist theorists are acknowledging that "whiteness" is a cultural identity, and that past accounts of white women's and girls' experiences "were missing its 'racialness.' "[64] Listening to the two groups of girls in this study reveals a complex braiding of race, class, and culture that underscores their different understandings of white femininity. Although I did not directly ask about race—and because all the girls are white and whiteness is the unmarked norm, they do not offer their views about race spontaneously—I look to the girls' class-related struggles with identity, their relationship to power and privilege, their constructions of Otherness and their views of the normal and acceptable

two

Privileging Difference

Accounts of working-class life are told by tension and ambiguity, out on the borderlands. The story . . . cannot be absorbed into the central one: it is both its disruption and its essential counterpoint: this is a drama of class.

CAROLYN KAY STEEDMAN[1]

Driving the narrow, winding road to Mansfield to conduct year-end interviews, I find myself thinking back to my own girlhood in Vanceboro, a small border town in the far northeastern woods of Maine, the place where three generations of my father's family were born and raised. Mansfield is much like Vanceboro, though a bit larger. Its population of about 900, spread over a wide expanse of farm and woodland, which also includes a nucleus of houses, a few combination grocery store–gas stations, a bait and tackle shop, a post office, two small wood mills, a volunteer fire department, and a school, carries a similar sense of community and also of isolation. Here thirteen of the girls in this study live their daily lives, more than half of them on farms or, as we say here in Maine, "in the woods."

As I enter Mansfield's town limits, I consider the events of the past year and how it is that I came to be here. Many research studies, I imagine, are initiated by a fortuitous convergence of people and possibilities. I met Diane Starr, an educational technician at the Mansfield School, when she contacted me about her desire to listen to a group of outspoken and opinionated poor and working-class girls with whom she had a close relationship as a basis for her Master's thesis.[2] She wondered if this might be a project that would engage to reveal their cultural and racial positioning. This analysis, then, contributes to broader attempts to mark out differences within whiteness; to understand how the construction of whiteness varies across lines of class.[65]

This book is grounded in the belief that listening to girls at early adolescence will break open heretofore unexamined notions about gender, class, culture, and race. I hope that, in the chapters that follow, the voices of the girls in this study will re-awaken awareness of and appreciation for the personal power and political potential of girls' and women's anger, widen our understanding of girls' creative resistance to the pressures they feel to voice and enact patriarchal views of femininity, and complicate our current understanding of the impact of class and white culture on female subjectivities.

me and my current concerns as well, and asked if I would join her in this venture. Soon after, I spoke about our developing plans with Valerie Pettit, a seventh-grade English teacher at the junior high school in Acadia—a mid-size city by Maine standards—whom I had met when she enrolled in a course I teach on women's and girl's development. Excitedly Valerie told me about a group of girls she taught and knew well who sounded, in spirit, very much like middle-class counterparts to the Mansfield group. The three of us, together with a student of mine, Hollis Rendleman, decided to videotape the two groups over the course of a year.

The nineteen girls who participated in these two groups met weekly or, in some cases, bimonthly in their public schools to discuss their relationships with one another, their families, their teachers and the schools, and to explore their views on subjects rarely discussed: their strong feelings, particularly of anger, their critical opinions about the way things work in their schools, their conceptions of what it means to be female, and their critique of pressures to meet dominant societal expectations of femininity.

Despite sharing similar topics of conversation, the two groups were radically different from the very beginning, particularly with respect to social class. Although this exploration was never meant to be a "quasi-experimental" study of class, we found that social status—theirs and ours—had a profound effect on this study at every level, directly affecting our initial approach to the girls, the formation and final composition of the groups, and the nature of their relationships with us, with one another, and with their schools and communities. Rather than bury or attempt to explain away such differences, we hoped to see where they would take us, hear what they might tell us about the complicated, interwoven relationships among gender, race, and class and the ways these relations are affected by and play out in two very different rural and suburban cultural contexts.

I have deliberately chosen not to detail the Mansfield and Acadia girls individually. Although I provide a somewhat general index of the girls in the study, I do not include defining characteristics, such as age, family makeup, parental income, and the like, because I do not want to jeopardize the confidentiality I promised.[3] While I have gone to great lengths to disguise *all* the girls by changing their names, physical features, and details of their stories that do not influence the larger picture of their lives, I have taken particular care with the working-class girls because they live in such a small community and because they speak in such detail about personally painful experiences. While this may have left gaps here and there for the reader to endure, my loyalty remains with the girls.

Mansfield

Mansfield, like Vanceboro, like many small rural Maine towns, boasts residents with deep family roots. Indeed, generational claims, more than financial or material wealth, are often the measure of one's social position. People who lack such claims are considered to be "flatlanders" or "from away," whether they are new to the area or have lived here for ten or twenty years. "Although there are a few people in town who 'have money,' " Diane Starr elaborates, "most feel lucky to scratch out a living and support their families" with low-paying or part-time jobs. "This puts everyone more or less on equal economic footing."[4]

Such social stratification, or lack thereof, is reflected in the small school that serves the town's approximately 120 kindergarten through eighth-grade students. Popularity based on material resources does not play a large role in Mansfield School's social hierarchy, as it does in large-town and city schools. Rather, popularity is a more complex attribution, influenced by such things as individual personality, old loyalties, and family ties. Students, in fact, are likely to find it difficult to escape the burdens of established reputations constructed from personal or family history. "If you were a girl in Mansfield," Diane explains,

you probably would have known your classmates since kindergarten, some since birth. You would know your friends' grandparents, histories, family trees. Almost every house in the town would hold a story for you; each resident, a memory . . . You would know everyone and everyone would know you. Change comes hard under these circumstances; it is especially difficult to change your image in others' eyes. You might be remembered for something you did in first grade. You might even be remembered for something your parents did or even deceased family members. There is no being invisible or unnoticed in Mansfield, except inside yourself or in the isolation of the country setting.[5]

As in other rural communities, the boundaries between family, work, and school have always been fairly fluid in Mansfield.[6] Because of its central location, the Mansfield School has been a community meeting ground for generations. The white clapboard building is quaint and inviting, its three stories lined with windows brightly decorated with construction-paper art, its rooms bright and airy. A small gym doubles as a dining hall for students who want or need a hot lunch at noon. The modest teachers' lounge, equipped with a few amenities such as a refrigerator and microwave, an overstuffed couch and chair, is as likely to be occupied by a student as by a teacher. With roughly fifteen to twenty students per multi-age classroom, Mansfield students receive a good deal of individual attention, making it difficult sometimes for them to submerge themselves in "the crowd." But in spite of occasional desires for privacy, the students seem to enjoy the school's homey atmosphere and flexible schedules; many of them arrive early in the morning and remain long after the last bus has left. The school is the hub of the Mansfield community, supplying meals, friends, sports, entertainment, and recreation in the town.

Diane worked intensively with a multi-age classroom of about twenty girls, ages eleven to fourteen. These girls thus had a personal closeness with her well before the project began in any official capacity. They would seek her out for counsel and support during tough times; they considered her trustworthy and loyal, someone who would speak to them straight and not sell them out. Although I was introduced to the girls and they knew that I would be watching their tapes and interviewing them individually at the end of the year, it was very clear that Diane should be the facilitator for this group.[7]

When Diane told the girls about our hopes for the study, they were excited. Every girl in the sixth-, seventh-, and eighth-grade classroom was welcome to join the weekly conversations. The girls who participated volunteered, with parental permission, to spend their noon recesses having their discussions videotaped. In the beginning fifteen of the girls decided to join the group, although attendance was fluid; girls came when they felt like it, and usually any one session consisted of four to six girls. While the number of girls varied on any given day, the group formed a fairly solid core of thirteen—two eleven-year-olds, Cheyenne and Patti, six twelve-year-olds, Brianna, Amber, Sarah, Stacey, Corrine, and Nina, two thirteen-year-olds, Susan and Rachel, and three fourteen-year-olds, Dana, Sherie, and Donna. Cheyenne and Amber are sisters, as are Brianna and Donna. The girls all knew one another quite well before the study began, but there were many variations of friends, best friends, and peer groupings among them. Donna and Cheyenne were especially close during the year of taping, as were Rachel and Stacey. Dana, Sherie, Corrine, Rachel, Stacey, Amber, and Sarah were a rather tight group of friends, and often attended the weekly sessions together.

Thus, unlike Jay McLeod's "Hall Hangers" or Paul Willis's "lads," the Mansfield girls were not part of a gang, nor did they form a distinctive subculture in their school.[8] They did, however, embrace the opportunity to express their opinions and strong feelings to one another and to us, and so they do not represent all the girls in Mansfield any more than they represent all white working-class girls their age. But again, our intention in listening to these girls' voices was "to shed light on the problem of interpretation rather than to generalize" about either group of girls.[9]

The Mansfield girls met in an upstairs classroom after lunch. They were eager to begin each week. "Usually the girls would be ready and waiting for me at the door," Diane recalls. "They would have already gone into my room and gotten the camera and the tape and sometimes might even be taping by the time I got there."[10] They began their sessions jockeying for position, some grabbing chairs, others sitting on desks or on the floor in a relaxed manner. Videos of their interactions reveal a lively, physical, and often boisterous group of outspoken girls vying for the attention of the camera, shouting, often pushing each other before settling into more concentrated conversation. Although Diane knew individual girls well, "the physical aspects of communication within this group were surprising to me," she reports:

Tough, rough, slapping, grabbing, and pushing were all actions that one might see at any time in any session. In fact, a [playful] "slap up long side the head" was an effective and accepted way to tell the person sitting next to them that they were ready to speak. There were also the kind, grooming activities that one might see in the classroom—hair braiding, hair brushing, back rubbing. At recess the girls are often kicking, tripping, or rubbing [one another's] faces in the snow. At first these activities might look like angry ones; physical fights between warring factions. But, in fact, they were loving activities from girls who were not afraid to show their physicalness, their strengths, girls from a tough environment.[11]

On camera and in individual interviews the voices of the Mansfield girls carry the language and culture of working-class Maine, with its attention to self-protection and survival, its directness, suspicion of authority, and disdain for government intervention or outside regulation of community or family life. These "rural adolescent girls speak to the isolation of the wilderness," Diane reports. "Their lives revolve around many kinds of relationships within the security of the small community. But their lives balance this security with the rugged individualism that is highly respected in the Maine woods and the Northeast. Being a girl among these oppositional contexts creates complex, yet common experiences."[12]

Most of the Mansfield girls are from working-class families, although a few move in and out of poverty, depending on seasonal job opportunities, such as wreath making or fruit picking. Mansfield's economy, like that of many small towns in Maine, relies heavily on local paper mills. Some of the girls' fathers work part-time or full-time in the woods cutting trees for the mills; others drive trucks or haul gravel or wood; one is a self-employed mechanic; another is unemployed because of a physical disability. More than half of the girls' mothers work part-time—one as an L.P.N., another at a wood mill, and others in local stores or as waitresses in town. Nine of the girls live with both parents, three live in single-parent homes, and one lives with a step-parent.

The range and depth of the Mansfield girls' experiences forbids any simple rendering of their early adolescence. Of the thirteen girls, six have experienced physical abuse at the hands of a father or other male relative. At least one girl is intimately familiar with the court and child-welfare systems, having testified against an abusive parent. A number of the girls in the group are sexually active, and two are on the pill. Some speak fondly and with excited anticipation of their sexual and emotional relationships with the migrant workers who come through the Mansfield area during the summer months. Three of the girls smoke, and some of them drink. Two girls, sisters, understand the dire consequences of being uninsured, having experienced homelessness after a flood destroyed their trailer; others know the poverty that lies just beyond their parents' unstable jobs and meager benefits.

Such private information about the girls' lives emerged often in their group sessions and in their interviews. They spoke at length about their relationships with their families—sharing moments of genuine pleasure as well as experiences of pain and violence. These family stories moved in and out of relationship with stories of failed connections, anger, and hurt feelings in school. This associative, seamless quality of the girls' conversations reflects the centrality of relationships and care-taking activities in their lives, as well as the lack of clear boundaries or borders between home, work, and school in their rural community.

Acadia

Less than an hour away from Mansfield sits the city of Acadia, with a population of roughly 18,000. As with many U.S. cities of its size, the downtown area struggles to survive in the wake of strip malls, fast-food restaurants, and the ubiquitous Walmart. Still, Acadia's small art gallery, popular cafes, restaurants, and shops draw sufficient numbers of people to the familiar old brick buildings that line the main street.

In Acadia, unlike Mansfield, there are fairly clear distinctions and divisions between upper-class, middle-class, working-class, and poor sections of the city. Much of the large working-class community is or was employed by the local paper mill, now in the process of closing. Symbolically, many of Acadia's elite—the professional community of lawyers, doctors, and businesspeople, as well as academics teaching at the private college in town—own houses on the streets that criss-cross the hill leading to the college; the middle-class residential areas spread out next, while the working-class and poor tend to locate on the low-lands, closer to the river that borders one side of the city.[13]

Acadia Junior High is situated on a flat, open expanse of land just inside the town limits. The elongated single-story modern brick building, flanked by a parking lot on one side and playing fields on the other, enrolls about 450 sixth-, seventh-, and eighth-grade students. In contrast with Mansfield School, Acadia Junior High is structured conventionally. Announcements begin and end the day, students are closely disciplined by the required hall and library passes, and things move according to schedule. The teachers' lounge is strictly off-limits to students.

Like the community it serves, Acadia Junior High has clear class divisions based on individual wealth, parents' education, and family social standing. Popularity, with a few exceptions for star athletes, falls to those on the higher end of the economic spectrum. Of the "three major cliques," the six Acadia girls in this group identify explicitly with the "middle class," a term that evokes some, but not all, of the characteristics of the middle class in society at large.

Whereas Diane opened the Mansfield group to any and all interested girls—an approach appropriate to the small, rural school and its multi-age classrooms—Valerie approached six girls she knew and thought would be interested in the project. She explained our plans and hopes for the study, and the girls liked the idea. Kirstin, Elizabeth, Theresa, Robin, Lydia, and Jane were all seventh-graders when the project began.[14] Kirstin, Elizabeth, and Jane, all twelve years old, knew one another well; indeed, they had been friends for years. Lydia, also twelve, was fast becoming a close friend of Jane's, while Theresa, thirteen, and Robin, soon to be thirteen, were more recent additions to their peer group.

Valerie facilitated the girls' group conversations. Although they clearly felt they could trust her, the Acadia girls had a somewhat more formal relationship with Valerie than the Mansfield girls had with Diane. They knew she had identified them for the study because of their open critique about the social climate and happenings around their school, but they had not fully tested the limits of this relationship outside the confines of their student roles. And so the first few videotaped sessions have an air of both caution and uneasy anticipation as the girls negotiate among themselves how they will speak and what they will say. Their initial uncertainty was also heightened somewhat because they didn't all know one another well before the group began.

A short time after the project began, I visited the Acadia group. The girls seemed to enjoy my presence, and so I increased my visits until, near the middle of the school year, I began to co-facilitate the group. At the end of the year, as with the Mansfield girls, I interviewed each girl individually, highlighting many of the issues we had covered in the group, often with reference to specific incidents that had come up during their videotaped sessions.

Unlike the Mansfield girls, the Acadia girls talked almost exclusively about the trials and tribulations of their school lives and very little about their home lives, except for the not unexpected complaints about their siblings. Certainly their evolving relationships with Valerie, with me, and with one another impacted what they chose to say—although the focus of their conversations did not change much over the course of the year, even when the girls were most at ease during the sessions. This split between their public and private lives most likely reflects raced, classed, and gendered norms of appropriate speech and behavior.[15] The Acadia girls carefully patrolled the borders of public and private, conveying in their well-practiced speech and physical movements the relationship between such boundaried expression and power in the dominant culture. Such surveillance is reinforced by institutional boundaries between home and school inherent in their suburban school. For these white middle-class girls on their way up, public accomplishments and social and political interactions at school are of primary concern; there is little room for the private pains and emotional residues of family relationships or crises that undoubtedly do exist. Indeed, the working-class girls' attention to personal relationships and their more expressive and associative ways of knowing disadvantaged them, even in their progressive rural classrooms.[16]

The Acadia girls do not experience material want; they are firmly grounded in the privileges of white middle- or, in some cases, upper-middle-class culture. Their fathers and mothers are mostly professionals; the majority have four-year college degrees, and many have attended graduate school: among them are a few teachers, a doctor, an engineer, a lawyer, a state representative. In each family both parents work, although in some cases the girls' mothers have returned to part- or full-time employment only as their children have grown. Five of the girls live with both parents, and one lives with a step-parent, though over the course of the year two of the girls' parents began divorce proceedings.

These girls are what they themselves would describe as "good" girls—they tell me that they do not smoke or drink, are not sexually active, in fact, do not have romantic relationships or even date. They dismiss these activities as irrelevant to their present lives, although their close surveillance of the "popular" girls' preoccupation with boys suggests that dating, at least, has more relevance and produces more anxiety than they readily admit.

The Acadia girls met after school in Valerie Pettit's seventh-grade classroom. The large windows that line one wall look out to the soccer field; the front and back of the room are covered, floor to ceiling, with chalkboards. Usually upon my arrival one or two of the girls would be in the room chatting with Valerie, and others would wander in as we set up the camera and tripod. The girls were friendly but aloof in these first moments. Because of their busy schedules—filled with sports, drama, band, or photography—one or two of them would sometimes leave early; during other sessions we had the luxury of hour-long conversations.

The girls pulled up chairs or sat on table tops; sometimes they sat in a row facing the camera, other times they formed a semi-circle. During the early sessions each conversation was punctuated with long moments of silence, but as the year unfolded the girls became more animated and outspoken. Even when the discussion was most lively, however, the girls usually waited for one another to finish speaking. With their legs crossed or swinging in concentrated rhythm, their hands in their laps or holding the sides of their chairs, their eyes focused on one another or on the camera, they appeared strikingly different from their Mansfield counterparts. Even as the girls became less self-conscious, more excited and loose, and also more direct with one another, they never reached the physically and emotionally charged level of the Mansfield group; instead, occasional ardent disagreements and quick-witted humor gave this group its liveliness and texture.

Because white middle-class women have defined the categories of analysis when it comes to the lives of adolescent girls, it was important to us that the girls in this study take the focus groups and interviews where they wanted, so that they might break out of narrow elitist categories that have circumscribed girls' and women's experiences.[17] Although Diane, Valerie, and I discussed issues we wished to address before beginning the study, we talked at length with the girls about the issues they considered most important, and all together we agreed on the direction we would take. We began each group session with an issue or question; the girls either responded or introduced new issues for the group to consider. More often than not the girls veered away from our queries and toward more personally pressing concerns.

Throughout the year both groups of girls questioned, often rejected, and moved beyond the categorical limits of passivity, depression, negative body-image and eating disorders, low self-esteem, and indirect expressions of feelings so often associated with white female adolescence. Instead they found space to boast and brag, to tease, to critique, to be brazen, proud, and strong, to be angry and aggressive, even at times to be outraged with one another; they imagined their futures and talked about getting what they wanted out of life. Yet the form these conversations took, the issues that captivated and focused their energy, the nature of their experiences and the expressions of their thoughts and feelings, differed dramatically between the two groups of girls.

As my analysis will show, there is nothing simple or transparent about the expressions of either the Acadia or the Mansfield girls. Given the pressures and expectations of adolescence, and the prevalence of sexism, racism, classism, and homophobia that too often leads to emotional, psychological, or physical trauma, reading girls' lives and interpreting their voices is always complicated business. Drawing "truthful" conclusions on the basis of surface performances or simple responses is not possible, because in the face of pressures to not know and not speak, adolescent girls develop and employ subtle and creative strategies of resistance. Even as the Acadia girls whisper in soft voices of female perfection or the Mansfield girls speak in tough, invulnerable voices of determined survival, their facial expressions, gestures, and bodily movements reveal the boundaries and limits of these personas.

Speaking and Listening

In order to understand and interpret the meaning of a person's words, one has to ask (and answer) two interrelated questions: "Who precisely is speaking, and under what concrete circumstances?"[18] In addition, it would seem, one must also ask: "Who is listening and what is the nature of her relationship with the speaker—especially with respect to power?" Such questions acknowledge the complicated social landscape in which discourse occurs and the various forces, personal and political, that move one to speak and act in certain ways.

Responding to such questions demands a method that is sensitive to the polyphonic nature of voice, the nonlinear, nontransparent interplay and orchestration of feelings and thoughts, as well as to the issue of power and to the fact that "positionality weighs heavily in what knowledge [and in what ways of knowing] comes to count as legitimate in historically specific times and places."[19] In trying to understand how the girls in this study negotiate early adolescence, I rely on a voice-centered "Listener's Guide" that illuminates my own positionality and power with respect to the girls and then offers a way to trace the movement in girls' understanding of themselves and others as they take in the voices around them, both appropriating and resisting different perspectives on relationship.[20]

My choice of a small, select sample was deliberate and necessary for such an interpretive, dialogic approach. I wished to bring to the surface the often subtle psychological associations the girls made during their conversations, particularly between femininity and anger, and to use their physical movements and facial expressions to elaborate and complicate my interpretations. The Listening Guide approach allows such close, in-depth analysis and is designed to accommodate different research questions. My goal was not only *not* to generalize to the wider population of white middle-class, working-class, and poor girls, but to explore the significance and highlight the impact of local understandings and constructions of self and femininity that make overly simplistic generalizations problematic.

My choice to conduct and report primarily focus group conversations rather than individual interviews alone was also deliberate. While personal case studies can be a powerful medium, providing psychological depth and offering a level of intimacy, it has been my experience that girls have too little opportunity to share the realities of their lives with one another and to consider the sources, as well as the political implications, of their strong feelings. I wanted not only for girls to experience the power of their collective voices, but also to represent those voices to others and thus to disrupt the tendency of psychology to over-individualize, to miss the relational and societal contexts through which individual selves emerge.[21]

The Listening Guide requires one to attend to a narrative or, in this instance, a conversation, at least four separate times, each time listening in a different way. In this study, I listened to (and watched, in the case of the videotapes) each interview and group session five times. First I attended to the overall shape of the dialogue or narrative and to the research relationship—that is, I considered how my own position as a white middle-class academic with a working-class childhood affected the girls' perceptions of me, our interactions, and my interpretations of their voices and behaviors. I documented shifts in voice, movement, and gestures when the girls spoke with me or became obviously conscious of my presence, and I tracked my feelings and thoughts, my questions and confusions, as I interpreted the girls' voices.

The second time through the videotapes and interviews I attended to the girls' first-person voices, to the ways they speak for and about themselves. Since, as Anne Campbell has illustrated, much of our sense of who we are arises from who we believe we are not—"The words and typifications we use to characterize our enemies are often an important guide to the ascriptions we most reject in ourselves"— I also listened to the girls' gossip and put-downs of their peers and siblings to establish whom they considered "Other" and why.[22] In the third "listening" I attended to the girls' discussions of personal anger and social critique: what people, events, or experiences provoked their anger and criticism? How and to whom did they express their strong feelings? What form did their anger take? Who or what forces constrained their expressions of these strong feelings?

The final two times through the videotaped conversations and audiotaped interviews, I focused on the ways the girls define and speak about appropriate feminine behavior and, in particular, the ways they accommodate to and resist conventional or culturally dominant (that is, white, heterosexual, middle-class, patriarchal) constructions of femininity. More specifically, in the fourth listening, I identified ventriloquized voices of conventional femininity. As I explore in more detail later, Mikhail Bakhtin defines "ventriloquation" as the very natural process "whereby one voice speaks *through* another voice or voice type."[23] My hope in this listening was to document the girls' verbal and behavioral expressions of feminine behavior idealized or denigrated by the dominant culture and to understand the ways in which the girls appropriate and struggle with such voices. In other words, how are we to understand the girls when they denigrate other girls because these Others are too "feminine," that is, because they are "naturally" deceitful or too emotional or too passive? Who is speaking? Where have these voices come from and what do they mean for the girls' emerging sense of self?

In the fifth listening, I attended to the ways in which the girls resist dominant cultural constructions of femininity; that is, I documented voices and gestures of strength, fluidity, irreverence, and creativity—voices that are often grounded in local understandings of white femininity in tension with the dominant ideal. I explored the ways these voices and gestures interact to attenuate the pull of convention. Here class and culture, relevant throughout the various listenings, took center stage as the voices and values of the girls' immediate communities came into conflict with those of the dominant culture, particularly as the latter is inculcated in the school classroom. Here also any notion of identity development as continuous, unitary, or linear was called into question as the girls struggled with different voices, some clearly more publicly legitimized than others, and as they learned the power of context and audience and the necessity of performing conventional femininity or impersonating the "right" kind of girl. In other words, such an analysis assumes that context and power relations affect girls' interactions and conversations, such that the selves they present to one another and to the camera are not the only selves available to present.

With each listening or viewing, I used a different colored pencil to trace the girls' voices through typed transcriptions of the videotapes and audiotapes. This allowed me to follow the movement of their group conversations and individual voices and provided a visual orchestration of the five listenings. I documented each listening on worksheets, recording in one column the girls' voices and in another my interpretation of their words. From these worksheets I created interpretive summaries, and from these summaries generated my analysis. Since I watched the videos as well as worked with the transcriptions, I was able to document gestures and movements that greatly enhanced my interpretations.

In addition to recording evidence of the five listenings in the group conversations and individual interviews, I constructed a matrix for each girl, noting in brief form her local constructions of femininity and her expressions—her ventriloquation or performances of and reactions to—dominant constructions of femininity.[24] This approach not only aided my analysis of the groups' conversations, but also allowed me to conceptualize how individual girls differed from one another with respect to the five listenings.

The Listener's Guide thus provides a way to chart the overlapping relationships among identity, anger, culture, and conventions of femininity in these working- and middle-class girls' conversations and narratives and also a way to elucidate the struggles these two groups of girls experience as they negotiate and contest the contradictory voices and visions vying for their attention and allegiance. Listening to all five voices, I hear at different moments an indecipherable cacophony, a patterned rhythm, an improvised beat. Attuning to the girls' voices and movements in this way reveals not only the "fragmented and reactive nature of their self-definition[s]," but also the contextual and community voices inherent in their different material and structural positions—voices that undergird their understandings of themselves and encourage a struggle for personal integration.[25] Listening to their expressions of anger and resistance, in particular, points to the tensions and ruptures in the moral fabric of their daily lives, to their refusal to accept without question narrow definitions of appropriate feminine behavior, and also to their self-respect and belief in their capacity for lucid judgment.

These working- and middle-class adolescent girls speak to a growing comprehension of, frustration with, and at times resistance to the demands and the contradictions of "female impersonation";[26] that is, to the expectations and images and voices of idealized femininity that narrow girls' experiences and pull them away from themselves and their astute perceptions of the world. They struggle with, critique, and resist what passes as feminine expression and behavior, *even as* they come to speak through culturally sanctioned, patriarchal voices of femininity, and publicly perform, at times even judge other girls, along the same narrow standards. And not surprisingly, girls' resistance to pressures to narrow their behavior, modulate their feelings, and check their desires, while certainly heightened at early adolescence, is rarely, if ever, unmediated by the conceptions of femininity that they have taken in over their girlhoods.

Speaking for and About

Dorothy Allison begins her moving collection of essays entitled *Skin: Talking about Sex, Class, and Literature* with a story of the time she brought her upper-middle-class lover home to North Carolina to meet her working-poor family. On their journey south Allison slowly realizes just how anxious she is, not about her family's reaction, but about how her lover might respond, about "the distance, the fear, or the contempt that I imagined could suddenly appear between us. I was afraid that she might see me through new eyes, hateful eyes, the eyes of someone who suddenly knew how different we were."[27] Her partner does respond, but not as Allison expects: "Her features were marked with a kind of tenuous awe, confusion, uncertainty, shame. All she could say was that she hadn't been prepared." "I don't know," her lover said later in the privacy of their room. "I thought I understood what you meant when you said 'working class' but I just didn't have a context."[28] "Context," Allison concludes, "is so little to share, and so vital."[29]

Over the past year, as I have listened to the voices and witnessed the interactions of the girls in this study, I have had to confront my own preparation, or lack thereof. What context did I have for their lives? How far is it possible to speak for and about these girls? I ask these questions knowing that I sit uncomfortably between two groups of girls who echo not only different periods in my life, but also complex and contradictory class factions and voices that have existed within my family throughout my life. These girls both represent and contest the ordinariness of my own journey from working-poor to working-class to middle-class: from a child born into a family of seven living on a father's part-time work in the Maine woods and on the railroad, to a school-age child of a railroad engineer and a nurse, to an adolescent of an economically middle-class family with a working-class core.

"The problem of ethnographic work," indeed qualitative research of any sort, Valerie Walkerdine warns, "is how to adequately account for the psychic reality of both observer and observed." Because so much in these girls' lives was familiar—because, like them, I grew up in both rural and smalltown Maine, went to public schools, felt the distance between my experiences and those of girls both more and less advantaged than I—knowing, understanding, and respecting the differences between my past and their present was a constant challenge.

I was affected, then, in quite different ways by the working- and middle-class girls in this study. I identified with the working-class girls' experiences and knowledge, their mistrust of authorities, their forms of resistance, their cynicism, frustration, and anger. I was thus struck by the disappointment and loss I felt knowing they perceived me as a middle-class academic. "No amount of humanistic seeking," to quote Walkerdine, would move these working-class girls to recognize or "see in me a . . . girl 'like them.' "[30] I also identified with the middle-class girls' efforts to be seen and heard, their struggle to negotiate and integrate limiting constructions of femininity with their new-found language of autonomy and individuality. I was aware that these girls perceived me to be like them and that, although I felt my difference from them quite intensely at times, the relationships we forged were often easier and more open than my relationships with the working-class girls.

Throughout this project I have tried to keep in mind how the "fantasies and fictions embodied in academic accounts [are] inscribed in the daily lives of ordinary people."[31] Because so few working-class and poor people speak and write for themselves, fictions and fabrications of their lives abound. Representations of their speech by academics all too often reinforce their silence or pathologize their anger, further marginalizing their voices when they do speak and write. Middle- and upper-class authors create a psychologically bland under-class voice that is linked to characteristics such as laziness, stupidity, unruliness, dirtiness, sexual promiscuity, and violence.

I have wanted to believe that my childhood and early-adolescent experiences would prevent me from contributing to these stereotypes or to the larger cultural silencing or effacement of these girls. And yet, throughout the course of listening to and interpreting the girls' thoughts and feelings, I remain conscious of the fact that, as an observer and a narrator of their lives, I too become, in Foucault's terms, a "Surveillant Other," not simply listening, watching, and describing, "but also producing a knowledge that feeds into the discursive practices regulating" girls' voices and class consciousness.[32] As Walkerdine notes:

"Our" project of analyzing "them" is itself one of the regulative practices which produce our subjectivity as well as theirs. We are each other's Other—but not on equal terms. Our fantasy investment often seems to consist in believing that we can "make them see" or that we can see or speak for them.[33]

Because of the power I hold as a social scientist and educator, my account of these girls' lives is always a regulatory reading. The knowledge I produce will inevitably differ from the meanings ascribed by the girls—meanings they produce as they live out the practices in which such meanings are formed. It is thus not whether I, as a white middle-class woman with a working-class core, can adequately represent these white middle- and working-class girls, but the quality of my efforts and the ethics and politics of doing so. As silencing or speaking on behalf of the Other has been used in patriarchal culture to mute or shape feminine experience, so have these same strategies been used by academics to mute or shape the experiences of the poor and the working class.[34]

My struggle has thus been against a temptation to either idealize or pathologize these girls, or to give them, attribute to them, knowledge, desires, or wants that are more about my experiences, my thoughts and feelings, my fictions and fantasies, than about theirs. My hope is to widen the scope of understanding—to portray the ways in which the girls in this study are aware, awake, curious, smart, and bold, if not also complicated, contradictory, limited in some cases by material resources, regulated by and resistant to others' fictions of who they are and what they are capable of being.

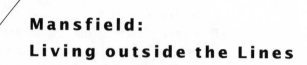

three

Mansfield:
Living outside the Lines

I was not raised to subtlety.

DOROTHY ALLISON[1]

In their upstairs classroom, closed to the outside world, the Mansfield girls gather and their talk inevitably turns to unfairness and anger. They are, at different times, angry at teachers, at parents, at one another, and at themselves. They are angry at those who do not listen, do not understand, do not pay attention to what they know and what they want for their lives. As Diane points out, they "cherish" their time together, seeing it as an opportunity to "swear, call names, vent, and be heard."

And yet this outer toughness often covers over the girls' vulnerability; it belies the sadness and sense of loss, the desire for relationships, and the wish for understanding and support that I sometimes heard in individual interviews. Their desire to be heard and taken seriously, however, was clearly visible in their interactions with one another and with the camera. Each group session brought a fresh intensity. The girls appealed to the camera as a recorder of their insistence, their sincerity, and their humor; it was capable, they seemed to believe, of rendering and fairly judging the truth of their observations about one another and the world around them. The Mansfield girls would often look straight into the camera lens and shrug their shoulders as if to say, "See, this is how it is. Do you now understand what I have to deal with?" The camera also became witness to their aggressive play, to their impertinence, their audacity. Meetings usually ended with the girls crowding the lens, laughing and pushing. Analyzing the videotapes in my office, I watch as individual faces peer in, the camera jostles, more faces squeeze into view, many hands appear, a peace sign becomes a middle finger, then raucous laughter is followed by the gray-white noise of the tape until the next session begins.

Whether speaking with their friends, recounting the stories passed down through their families, or traversing the complex and often contradictory terrains of home, school, and community, the Mansfield girls challenge the unmarked and thus seemingly natural order of white middle-class ideals of femininity—a "reality" in which passivity, silence, subordination, selflessness, and purity are mapped onto women's bodies. These are admittedly strong, tough girls—fighters who are at various moments sarcastic, brazen, loud, loving, responsive, and kind, who are generally distrustful of authorities, outspoken in their relationships, sometimes hopeful, more often than not anxious and uncertain about their futures.

The issues that surface and resurface for discussion over the course of the year, as well as the girls' constructions of these issues, complicate conventional distinctions between good girls and bad. The girls' voices, developed in a rural working-class community, disturb established patterns, revealing a complicated notion of white femininity not voiced or legitimized in the dominant culture.

Sexuality and Desire

Nothing makes this disruption of taken-for-granted definitions of femininity so apparent as the way these girls speak about their experiences of sexuality and desire. The conventional distinction between the "good" girl who is pure, without desire, chaste, innocent, and passively receptive and the "bad" girl who is tainted, sexual, knowing, and aggressively or openly desirous makes no sense to them.[2] Although they may talk about girls who are "sleazy" or flirtatious or boy-crazy, they do not dismiss such girls solely because they are sexually active or experienced; neither are such girls rejected for their self-interest or their outspokenness. Twelve-year-old Stacey, for example, complains bitterly about a girl who she claims "is sleazy," "always flirting with everybody," who, "if she sees a guy, just goes wacko." But what really angers her about this girl is not her sexual desire and experience, but the fact that her attention to boys translates into ill treatment of her girlfriends: "She doesn't really care if she's friends with anybody," Stacey explains, her dark eyes flashing, "she talks about who she does have for friends like they're nothing . . . she treats her friends bad."

For Stacey and her friends, a "slut" is not someone who is sexually active per se, but rather someone who is disconnected from her partner or from other girls. She is a girl who, as thirteen-year-old Rachel puts it, "don't care if the guy likes her or not, she just goes out with 'em," who "teases," "plays hard to get," "plays games" with her boyfriend's head, uses boys for money or attention. Thus a number of qualities besides sexuality distinguish the bad girl from the good, the foremost being her treatment of her friends.

The Mansfield girls draw clear boundaries around what is acceptable behavior with boys and also around female friendships when boyfriends are involved. They are not the kind of girls, they say, who would steal other girls' boyfriends or do things or say things that would cause a boy to break up with another girl. Such girls are "bitches" and "hos" and "sluts" and are not to be trusted. And yet, as twelve-year-old Brianna explains, though it is a problem when "girlfriends get into their other girlfriend's boyfriend's issues," the girls are not hesitant to offer their strong opinions about one another's boyfriends or to argue about the way relationships should go.

The Mansfield girls speak often about sex—voicing both a critical discourse and a language of pleasure.[3] "Take it from me . . . from experience," twelve-year-old Amber announces one day, referring to the "bad experience" she had with an older guy. "[Boys] aren't everything . . . Guys. All they want is . . ." "Sex," Donna, fourteen, interrupts. "And someone that looks good," Amber responds. Later in the session, when Nina can't think of anything that makes her feel good about herself, Cheyenne, one of the two eleven-year-olds in the group, teases her: "Well, Aaron might make you feel good." "Shut-up. Shut-up," Nina responds, laughing. And when asked to talk about a time when she felt good about herself, Rachel, fourteen, replies immediately—her tone of voice, like her story, rich with suggestion:

Rachel: OK, I have one Mrs. Starr. I have a wicked good one . . . This is, like, right before I started to go out with Derrick, like . . . like, like, a couple weeks before . . . Ty asked me out, [*to Stacey*] remember this? I was over to Stacey's house, oooh, and he [*lowers her voice to an inaudible whisper*] . . .
Stacey: What!?
Rachel [whispers to Dana, then speaks out loud]: He was just there, and he kept coming over and it was just awesome and I loved it, because he was like, he just kept trying to be around me, and it was so awesome because I liked him so much. He kept coming over.
Diane: So that's one time when you felt really good about yourself?
Rachel: Wicked. I felt *so* good . . . I felt so good.

Rachel rolls her eyes and shudders as she whispers to her friends, her face, body, and voice announcing the pleasure she experienced with this persistent boy she "liked so much." Stacey responds with her own intimations:

Stacey: Sarah knows what I really liked. I loved it. Right Sarah?
Rachel [laughs]: When she was in back of the school trailer with Bobby.
Sarah [looking over at Stacey with a knowing smile]: They were ridinnnnn'—
Rachel: Each other.
Dana: Each other.
Stacey [seemingly distracted]: Bikes!

Rachel: They were ridin' bikes.
Stacey: It was awesome. It was after the dance.

Although they are reluctant to say anything too explicit, the Mansfield girls clearly enjoy these "awesome" moments. Intimate encounters can make them feel, as Rachel says, "wicked" good. Such moments are thought about, talked about, practiced, and prepared for. "Check this out," Stacey shouts at one point during a session, as she puts her hand over her friend Sarah's mouth, throws her back, and pretends to give her a long kiss on the mouth. Rachel, on cue, grabs Dana and does the same. As Stacey comes up for air, dramatically panting, Dana shouts, "Now what do you think that looks like?" "That does not look like anger," Diane responds, referring to the topic for this session.

Dana: That ain't anger, believe me!
Rachel: It's a fad, that's what Miss Damon said. It's like a fad and we're being foolish.
Stacey: We're being faggy. We're being faggots. Ha, ha.

The girls' performance points to the explicitly heterosexual nature of their expressions of desire. Their practice seems to be a parody of long kisses one might see on the cover of romance novels or in action-romance movies. Stacey grabs Sarah, dips her, controls the embrace and the kiss. When Stacey sits up, Sarah remains in a passive position, a stunned, somewhat sheepish look on her face. While Stacey's allusion to "faggots" points to the boundaries of appropriate sexual expression, it also implies a resistance to these boundaries; her laughter and tone of voice suggest that she and her friends are themselves just a little out of line.

Any serious alternative to heterosexuality is unspeakable, however, as the girls quickly confirm. While girls who show physical closeness are accused of being "lezzies," by far the most damaging insults are reserved for boys and men. During one session the girls complain about their brothers, their fathers, certain boys in their classes, and certain male teachers in what they consider the most pejorative terms imaginable: "He dresses like a fag!" "He looks like a faggot," "He's being faggy." "My dad's a queer anyway," "What a pervert . . . What a fag." There is a striking difference here between the teasing nature of their comments about "lezzies" and the hostile tone of voice, the antagonistic facial and bodily expressions that accompany these remarks about boys and men. Such hostility underscores, indeed, polices the parameters of appropriate sexual desire and behavior. The girls' conversations about who they find desirable and sexy further solidify these boundaries. Fourteen-year-old Dana describes her ideal boy:

Dana: OK. Tanned complexion. Oh baby!
Stacey: Yeah.
Dana: Green eyes. He has to have like dark hair, brown eyes are the best . . . dark, fudge-brown hair [*runs her hands through her hair and down her neck*].
Rachel: OK. Like average . . . not really tall and not really short. Average, you know, with dark hair, dark complexion . . . muscle-bound.
Dana: Muscle-bound, baby!

When Diane complicates this physical description by suggesting that it seems terribly close to a portrait of a local boy known to hit his girlfriends, the girls quickly adjust by adding other, less tangible qualities. It is a construction they do not sustain for long:

Dana: OK. Listen. Nice and sensitive. That's another one.
Diane: OK.
Dana: Yeah. Because we like people who are like—
Rachel: Caring—
Dana: Nice and kind and don't treat you like crap.
Rachel: And they care, they really care, they want to be with you.
Sarah: How about Tim?
Rachel: He's wicked nice . . . He's muscley and he's tanned.
Dana: And he's *so* nice.

Rachel: Have you ever seen him without his shirt? Oh my God!
[*others laugh and make sounds of admiration*]
Dana: He is *nice!*

With refrains like "He's a babe" and "Oh man! Oh, gorgeous!" the girls together outline the physical objects and emotional contours of their desire.

Romance weaves in and out of the Mansfield girls' expressions of desire, disrupted often by their actual sexual and relational experiences. In nearly every conversation that turned toward romance, someone, often standing alone, insisted on bringing her reality to bear on the ideal. For these girls, it seems, friends don't let friends delude themselves about what's really going on. As Stacey and Rachel begin, in wistful voices, to imagine their futures with the right guys, Dana, the oldest of the group, interrupts with a reality check:

Stacey: They say, like, that there's a person for everybody in this world, but I don't know about that.
Rachel: I keep looking, is why I feel good about that. I'm still looking.
Dana: Then why are you back with Kenny, he ain't the ideal. I'd ditch him fast.
Rachel: Actually, he isn't. I'm just stupid.
Dana: Oh yeah, he tells you you're not worth anything and that you're too immature to understand him.
Stacey: He said that?
Dana: Last year he said that.
Diane: He told you that you weren't worth anything?
Dana: Too immature, she don't understand, she's stupid.
Rachel: No, he goes, "You know, you know, a lot of guys wouldn't put up with your shit." You should see some stuff he's done to me.
Dana: She's so stupid, she keeps going back to him . . . I wouldn't put up with it.
Diane [to Rachel]: Like what?
Rachel [looking at Dana knowingly]: Like what?

Dana: He got Anita Chase pregnant while he was going out with
Rachel. That is *the* most slimiest thing . . . [*sheepish smile*] Isn't
that disgusting? Yeah, yeah it is . . . I wouldn't put up with it.
Sarah: I hate him. He's such a jerk!

For Dana, in this moment, things are what they are; her directness
holds Rachel accountable for her decision to stay in a relationship
with Kenny. When Rachel begins to protest that no one knows for
certain that the baby is her boyfriend's, Dana will have none of it.
She argues with Rachel, whose expression has turned stony:

Rachel: They still don't even know for sure. It could be Blair's,
Jonathan's . . .
Dana: But there's always a chance that it *was* [his], and if it is, he
still did it. You know, he doesn't say he didn't do it, so there's
always a chance that he did do it.
Stacey: He just won't get tested for it.
Dana: Yeah. He won't get tested. He already said he wouldn't.
Why? Because he probably thinks he did do it.

The varied experiences of these girls, their mothers, sisters, and
friends stand in stark contradiction to sweet stories of romance and
idealized relationships. Along with often unromantic family situations, the girls witness the all-too-real consequences of unplanned
for, unprotected, or forced sex. They talk about the girls they know
who have babies, often by older boys or men who refuse to take
responsibility for their children.

Dana: Betsy Johnson had a kid. I mean, I don't know how she
could do it. I couldn't have a kid right now.
Sarah: She's had two . . . the other one got taken by the state.
Rachel: Oh my God!
Dana: Imagine that. She's the same age as me. Imagine me, fourteen years old, having a kid. I think I'd puke. It's too young. It's
ruined her whole—

Stacey: Reputation.
Dana: Teen life.

These girls are well aware of the potential costs and dangers of unprotected sex, whether or not they have, themselves, engaged in sexual activity. Some of the girls see having a steady boyfriend as protection against a bad reputation, while others negate the primary importance of boyfriends, focusing more on the personal consequences of sexual activity for their "teen lives" and their futures. Yet though the girls say they are too young to be mothers, individually and as a group they see motherhood as an important and valued experience, and not an altogether implausible one at their age. Given this, they find it incomprehensible and inexcusable that other girls they know could and do abuse themselves or their unborn babies by drinking or taking drugs while pregnant. Although these girls do not wish to have children in the near future, some have sisters or cousins who had babies as teenagers, and there is much animated talk about adopting babies at a later date. During these discussions of future motherhood, the girls' faces soften as they imagine their small babies—"they're so cute," they exclaim, "so adorable." Interestingly, few of the girls mention a husband or boyfriend as necessary to their family lives, and others make it clear that they want to live alone. Conversations initially about desire, love, and romance thus take an interesting turn when the realities of having children and making it in the world enter the discussion. At these moments the girls speak in determined voices about survival and also about hope for their children's future.

Voices of desire, danger, and responsibility weave through the Mansfield girls' narratives of sexual relationships, echoing the voices of young Latina and African American women that Michelle Fine heard in New York City sex-education classrooms.[4] As Fine notes, "The adolescent female rarely reflects simply on sexuality. Her sense of sexuality is informed by peers, culture, religion, violence, history, passion, authority, body, past and future, and gender and racial relations of power." For the Mansfield girls, class is central to "their struggle to untangle issues of gender, power, and sexuality."[5] Like the girls Fine listened to, they express anger at boys, alluding to the dangers of intimate relationships with them, even as they seek the pleasure and comfort of such relationships.

Danger, Daring, and Invulnerability

"I've got something that makes me feel terrific!" eleven-year-old Cheyenne shouts in session one day, sounding every bit the energetic kid she looks in baggy denim shorts and a t-shirt, her close-cropped black hair accentuating her round face. "I've got something that makes me feel awesome! When my dad, well, we were driving the moped . . . and I used to drive it everywhere . . . and we wrecked it, like, a million times and everything became broke on it, and he fixed it and it made me feel really good. And then I get to go Vrmmmmm all the way up to Donna's house." "How does that make you feel good about yourself?" Diane asks. "It's the thrill of it," Cheyenne says, smiling broadly. "The thrill of it."

The Mansfield girls take great pleasure in announcing their love of danger and daring and their invulnerability to such emotions as fear or pain or sadness.[6] When Dana announces one day to the other girls that she will soon get her driver's permit, Stacey throws up her arms and shouts, "Oh my God! Off the streets!" "I'm not walkin' on the sidewalk no more!" Rachel exclaims as she pretends to duck, veer off the road, and honk the horn. "Be safer in the middle of the road!" Corrine adds, to the laughter and nudges of the other girls. This scene initiates a series of stories of danger and daring from Sherie, fourteen, and Rachel, thirteen. "I drove my mother's snowmobile once . . . real fast, right into a swamp," Sherie begins, to the laughter of the others:

Sherie: We were driving in the fields, right, and [my mother] goes, "Sherie, slow down!" so I slowed down—I was going about fifty right toward the water . . .
Diane: And she wasn't on there with you?
Sherie [shakes her head no]: And all of a sudden the front end

went down . . . [*laughs*] It was so awesome . . . And my mother
got in trouble for it, 'cause dad yelled at her, and she said,
"Sherie was going too fast." And I was trying to wind it out.
'Cause we were racing, right? And that looked like the way to
go . . . it looked frozen to *me*. And we had to have it dragged
out.

As the stories of danger and physical injury escalate, each situation
seemingly more reckless and hazardous than the last, so too does the
girls' laughter, until they are doubled over, breathless and barely able
to speak.

Rachel: You know what was wicked funny? I was racing down the
road with Wanda on bikes and her tire was already so flat and
she was racing, okay, and all of a sudden her tire goes boom,
and she flew off.

Sherie: You know what hurt? When we lived, when we were camp-
ing out on Pleasant Pond? I was riding my bike . . . and it
flipped over and the handle jabbed right in my stomach. It hurt
so bad, it was awful . . . it hurt wicked . . .

Rachel: [My sister] pushed me into the road so I got run over.

Sherie [laughing hard, as are the others]: She had a broken arm in
third grade.

Diane: She pushed you in the road?

Rachel: Yes! I was on my sled and she pushed me in the road.

Diane: Oh well, she didn't mean for you to get run over.

Rachel: She was mad at me that day anyway . . . Hey, I was on *her*
sled so I didn't care. It got totaled.

These stories of danger and daring provide some of the most fun
and most funny moments I witness—the girls seem to take genuine
pleasure in one another, in the power and strength and fearlessness
they share. Their faces are wide-open, their laughter the hard, breathless kind reserved for rare moments and close friends. Such apparent
invulnerability has a more serious side, however. Over the course of
the year, for example, as twelve-year-old Corrine's experience with

an abusive cousin weaves in and out of the group sessions, her fear and pain are buried under layers of toughness and hostility.

During one session Corrine explains to the others in a defiant tone how she received the bruises on her face: "My cousin's not very nice," she says sarcastically. "He has a big-assed attitude problem and he hit me." French-braiding Rachel's thick red hair as she talks, Corrine tells the group that her cousin denied his actions by laughing at her in school and telling everyone she walked into the door.

Diane: So you did not run into it, like he said?
Corrine: No, I did *not* run into it. He goes, "You're pretty stupid running into doors." . . . He kept saying that when everyone went by and laughing. He goes, "It takes a person with a lot of brains to run into a door."
Rachel: He goes, "You gotta stop hurting those doors, sweetums."
Corrine: Dickhead.

On another occasion Corrine and Rachel together explain the large bruise on Corrine's arm:

Diane: Did your uncle see the bruise? Had it come yet?
Corrine: Um, hum. It came as soon as he did it.
Rachel: I saw it right when he did it . . . it was like worse than this.
Diane: Did it hurt?
Corrine: Yes! I ran home. I just started crying . . . Isn't he a jerk? I think he's a jerk-off.
Diane: I can't believe he would do that to girls.
Corrine: He would!
Dana: You don't know what he does. You can't even touch him without him pounding on you.
Corrine: Especially to me. He's so bad. I don't do anything. I was just sitting there.
Rachel: She just says some little thing to him and he'll kick her and punch her right in the head. He's so dumb . . . I cannot stand him.

While Corrine admits that she cried after her cousin hit her, this moment of vulnerability is fleeting. Quick to point out, even brag about, her many persistent, though ineffective, attempts to fight back, she comes across in the group sessions as either tough and aggressive or simply indifferent and aloof. In stark contrast to Rachel's animated character, Corrine, her long blonde bangs nearly covering her gray eyes, remains impassive as she lists the occasions of her cousin's abusive treatment.

Corrine: [Once] I told him to shut up and he came over and kicked me and I have, it was like, I don't know, I had this big black mark right there [*pointing to her shin*] . . . and it's still there . . . [Another time] me and Rach leaned on his car and he punched me for it.

Rachel: He punched me too, right in the head! I go, "What a jerk!" He goes, "I'm a jerk? You're a little—something I won't say." God, he punched us in the head!

Corrine: He punched me in the shoulder.

Diane: So you have bruises all over your body from him?

Rachel: Yeah. She's got a huge bruise on her leg. He just pounds her and don't even say anything.

Later, when Corrine recalls examples of her cousin's behavior, her tone is alternately hostile, sarcastic, and matter-of-fact. "He took my baseball hat from my locker," she tells the others off-handedly. "He goes, 'Oh thanks. I always wanted this.'" When Diane suggests that she go to her cousin's locker when he's in class and get her hat back, Corrine scoffs at her.

Corrine: He'd pound me.

Rachel: He'd pound her. He'd pound her right up.

Diane: But when he's not there?

Corrine: Yeah. And what am I supposed to do when it comes up missing?

Rachel: Get pounded. He'd pound her. He don't care.

Diane: Lie.

Corrine: Lie? Ummm, right.
Sarah: You should get a big bottle of mace.
Corrine: Yeah, you can get me mace for Christmas.
Sarah: Get a restraining order on him.
Rachel: He'd kill her.

Even though, as Rachel says, "it *is* bad," Corrine remains defiant, relaying her insolence to the group. When Diane expresses concern for her safety, Corrine shrugs it off, seemingly so disinterested she can't follow the conversation. "What happens if he breaks your arm someday?" Diane wonders.

Corrine: I don't know.
Rachel: Same thing that's happened already.
Diane: Nothing?
Corrine: What's the question?
Diane: What happens if he breaks your arm someday? That's my
    fear, that he'll hurt you; I mean hurt you real bad, Corrine.
    Aren't you a bit afraid of that?
Corrine: No.
Diane: You aren't—
Rachel: Corrine, you are *afraid* of him. She's always running away
    from him.

On the one hand, her cousin's abusive treatment seems inevitable to Corrine, since the school's repeated attempts at interference have had little lasting effect. On the other hand, the lack of parental response outrages her. Noting with disgust that her mother and father get "pissed" and would like to "kill him" but do nothing, and that her cousin's mother "favors" him—"it shows and it's sick"— and believes his explanations, Corrine tells the group defiantly that she's "getting ticked off." And yet, in spite of such defensive posturing, Corrine takes such abandonment hard and, by association, seems angry at and distrustful of most of the adults in her life, particularly the women, calling them names like "cheap ho," "pain in the butt," "cow," and "bag" throughout the group sessions.

Corrine *can,* however, count on her friends, who respond with outrage at her bruises and the incidents she recalls for them. "He's so cruel and mean," Dana says. "I betcha he beats his wife when he gets older . . . I betcha." Together the girls imagine all sorts of retaliations. They could throw a chair at him, as Susan suggests. Or they might turn Rachel's tough older sister on him: "[She] would end up shooting him! She'd beat on him," Stacey says. "She would," Rachel agrees. "She would kick his butt." "Or maybe," Dana suggests, referring to Rachel's story about breaking her arm sledding, "we should . . . put [him] on a sled and run him out in front of the cars." In the context of these and other suggestions, the girls occasionally abandon their expressions of concern and join with Corrine's hard, impenetrable toughness. "Na," says Rachel finally, dismissing Corrine's cousin as a problem. "He don't really bother me."

Corrine's bold posturing and heightened emotion are reminiscent of the earlier stories of danger and daring that the girls shared with one another. But though Corrine joins her friends in recounting stories of invulnerability and toughness, her stories are radically different from the others'—and it is the girls, her friends, who carefully, protectively, point this out.

Although, like the others, Corrine responds to hurt and danger with a kind of fearless bravado, unlike the others, she does not have control. Her story is not about a bike or a snowmobile, and she is not making the irreverent decision to be daring or to negotiate a dangerous situation. She *does* have control over the story she tells of the abuse, however. Like her friends, she would be the hero of her story—arriving at each denouement physically hurt, perhaps, but emotionally unscathed, her fearless spirit intact. Corrine's toughness is also, in part, for Diane to hear and for me to see.

Discernible between the lines of such a bold offense, however, are feelings of sadness, abandonment, and fear. At different points Corrine alludes to these feelings. Moreover, her body speaks of the effort it takes to hold such feelings in or perhaps down—the tight braid she inflicts on Rachel, her frown, her body stiff even as she feigns carelessness and disinterest. Picking up on these clues and drawing on their own knowledge of her situation, her friends break into her story to remind her of the danger she is in. When Rachel, in particular, interrupts to remind Corrine that yes, she is afraid, she suggests a more troubling, more painful reality out of deep concern for her friend. In so doing, she and the others dissolve their usual collusion in toughness to stand with Corrine's anger, but not with her invulnerability or disinterest.

But it is also clear that Corrine does not want to be seen as a victim. The other girls are aware of information Corrine chooses not to make public in the sessions, and their response is protective and also respectful of her right to choose what she feels it is safe to say in public about her circumstances. Rachel's comment—"Corrine, you are *afraid* of him"—alerts Diane to the level of danger and fear involved even as it creates an opening for Corrine to speak of her fear. When she does not, Rachel and the others join her where they can—in her outrage, in shared visions of retaliation.

This series of incidents underscores the layered nature and multiple meanings of the toughness the Mansfield girls portray and also their ever-present awareness of their audience. It is in response to Corrine that I am most conscious of the girls' scrutiny of Diane and me, and of the book that will be written about them; most conscious of the individual and group choices they are making about what to say and how to present themselves.

"She's Got Muscles": Fighting Back and Fighting For

The Mansfield girls talk with angry intensity about abuse they have heard about, witnessed, or experienced first-hand. In so doing they collectively reject any portrayal of themselves as passive victims. In response to Corrine's situation and also Donna's experiences with family violence and abuse, for example, they talk excitedly about taking self-defense classes, imagining with visible pleasure the day they will surprise the bullies and batterers with an incapacitating kick or throw. "Kick him in the ass," Stacey imagines. "There *are* groins," Sarah reminds the others.

These girls are justifiably outraged by such mistreatment and find it incomprehensible that anyone would voluntarily or passively stay in an abusive relationship, even though as the year unfolds it becomes clear from some of their own circumstances that "choice" is a cloudy concept, overlaid with various constraints and obligations, and that clarity most often comes with hindsight. Talking about a teacher they read about in the newspaper who had physically and sexually assaulted a number of female students at the near-by high school, the girls are furious first and foremost that this man could remain hidden in the system and that the school would be deluded into hiring him.

Sarah: He has that same thing in [another state]. When he got the job the people from [there] didn't even say nothin' about it . . . They didn't even tell the [school] about what he did up there.
Sherie: That school is so screwed up . . . They could have prevented it.

But their anger at the school soon turns to confusion about the role of some of the girls victimized by the teacher, at least as the story is told in the newspaper.

Dana: I don't understand that. Did they do that? Did they do that on their own will?
Rachel: Yeah, it says they used to go over there.
Diane: Well maybe they were just friends and he took advantage?
Dana: But why would they go over there after he did it the first time, unless they really wanted him to? That really gets me, because I don't really understand. I mean, if they didn't want him to do it, then they could have stopped him the first time and told on him . . . If someone ever did that to me they'd be sorry they ever did it.
Rachel: That's disgusting. It says they had bruises all over 'em.

The girls openly struggle to make sense of what appears on the surface to be another newspaper story of female victimization. The facts and the evidence, and their own grounded reality, however, make this simple portrayal incomprehensible. Both anger and genuine concern register on their faces as they admit their confusion and pose their questions: "Why? . . . Why would they?" The girls want to understand what lies beneath the surface of such a terrible event; what is it about these people—this man, these girls? How could he do such a thing? What prevented the girls from staying away, from telling? Their intense scrutiny of this story and their questions seem to underscore their own struggle against either being or being seen as victims, their wish to fight back, to remain in control, to believe that they would have the courage to break free and that someone would listen to them and believe them.

A number of the girls see in their mothers examples of such complicated, aggressive, nonvictimized white femininity. Here, in their families, resistance to passivity, to physical and emotional weakness, is nurtured. When Susan suggests that someone hit Corrine's cousin back with the same chair he used to hit Corrine, Rachel tells the group, "I told my mom we were gonna do that . . . She says that's a good idea." Fourteen-year-old Dana, known to the others as a fighter, describes an ongoing battle between her father and her step-father. In response, Diane comments, "So that's where you get your roughness from, from your—." But before she can finish, Dana cuts her off. "Mother," she adds quickly. Then, after describing a dramatic fight between her brother and her mother, she admits her astonishment at her brother's behavior: "Because *I* wouldn't [fight her]," she confesses. "You should see her arms, she's got muscles!"

Sherie then explains that her mother's toughness derives from Sherie's grandmother, who grew up as the oldest in a large family and had to learn to "stick up for" and protect her younger siblings, "who could only run, [but] couldn't stop and defend themselves. So like, my grandmother would stick up for them and beat up everybody that would beat them up." For Sherie, then, fighting the fair and good fight, protecting and caring for herself and those in her charge, is a legacy passed down from her grandmother to her mother to her.

Such toughness and self-protection fall comfortably within the discourse of white femininity for the Mansfield girls, who talk in the next breath about clothes and shopping, and engage in animated talk about the boys they like, their personalities, their physical appearance, and their appeal. To be tough, then, at least in their conception, is not to be mistaken for acting like a boy. Mingled with talk of their mothers' strength and toughness are descriptions of them as nurturing, loving, and devoted to their families, as women both in control of the house finances and willing to sacrifice for their children. "See that's one thing about my mom," Dana explains with obvious approval.

> She'll buy for us before she buys for herself . . . My mom deals the money in the house, to pay the bills, 'cause we really don't have nothin' to spend on anything else, so what we earn is what gives on the bills and what we really need.

Dana's mother is not selfless in the conventionally feminine sense, however. She protects and cares for herself as well as for her children. While sometimes "she'll buy something new [for us] and take somebody's old stuff," Dana says, "she'll go out and buy something [for herself] if she really, really needs it."

Although these girls are care-givers and nurturers, they reveal, often with pride, that part of themselves that is outspoken and direct, that knows and expresses deep, passionate anger, even that part of themselves prone to uncontrollable rage. They also reveal their struggle for self-control, their wish not to hurt people they care for, their desire to avoid irreparable damage to their relationships. While their experience of themselves and their perception of relationships contest the selflessness and purity typically associated with white middle-class notions of motherhood and femininity, care-taking, nurturance, and responsiveness hold a central place in their lives. "I don't want people to think of me as being mean, only thinking of myself," Susan says, echoing the concerns of other girls in the group. "I want them to think that I care about other people."

Longing for More

Tracing the "I" statements in the Mansfield girls' conversations, I was struck by the girls' expressions of longing, which tended to cluster around two topics: the ideal girl and their visions of the future.[7] In the first case, an air of playfulness and performance prevailed as the girls fantasized about how they wanted to look and dress, what they should weigh and how they would act; in the second, feelings of anxiety and uncertainty pervaded the girls' conversations as they struggled to reconcile their desires with the reality of their lives. Significantly, these issues remained distinct; contrary to what one might expect, the girls' fantasies about being beautiful, fitting the ideal body image, desiring to look and be like "Cindy Crawford or Niki Taylor," were largely unconnected to their concerns about having a life in which material wants were taken care of, in which education and a good job and a maybe a family were possibilities.[8]

Although the girls describe the ideal in supermodel terms, they pretty much agree that beauty matters less than strength, perseverance, and independence or the quality of one's relationships with others. In fact, they go to great lengths to describe the "real" women they personally admire and count on as outspoken, able to say what they really think.

In three separate sessions, at Diane's urging, the girls discuss their futures. Because we did not talk with the girls' families, I cannot know how their parents' experiences and longings may have shaped the girls' adolescent desires. And yet, the girls hint at the significance of working-class values and constructions of selfhood as they speak over and over again, with a mix of hope, anxiety, and helplessness, about a future of hard work and a desire to have enough money, a comfortable place to live, control over their lives, and a few special relationships.

Thirteen-year-old Rachel sits at a small table, head down, preoccupied with the notebook in front of her. Stacey, twelve, the only other girl who shows up this day, sits down briefly and then, perhaps picking up on Rachel's dark mood, walks aimlessly around the room.

After a few moments, and at Diane's invitation, she sits again. Diane begins: "What is one thing you foresee . . . one thing you think may happen to you in your future, that you wish was different? Does that make sense to you, Rachel?" In an uncharacteristically low voice and without looking up, Rachel responds:

Rachel: Yes. I think that . . . I don't think that I'm gonna have a lot of money, so I'm gonna want a lot of money. I mean, I don't want a *lot* of money, but I would want enough money. Of course I would *want* a lot of money, but that's not going to be possible, so I would want enough money. That's what I want in the future, but I don't think I'm gonna have it. I really don't.

Diane: Do you think it's going to be hard finding a job; is that what it is?

Rachel: Yup.

Stacey [in an animated voice]: Yeah. A job and money for me. And then I'm gonna get what I want!

Diane [to Rachel]: Because of your training? You think it's going to be hard because of your training or because of the economy, or because you're a woman, or what?

Stacey: All those reasons.

Rachel [still looking down, pointing to her head]: Because I'm kind of stupid . . . basically.

As the conversation continues, Rachel's voice carries the weight of her self-doubt and uncertainty. When she glances at the camera her face is expressionless. The thought of not having money, she admits, makes her "so freaked out . . . because I need money, of course. And I'm just afraid I'm not gonna have it."

Diane: Because you're not going to be able to find a job?

Rachel: A good enough one.

Diane: If you were sure you were going to go to college, would you feel like that?

Rachel: I don't know. Not as much.

Diane: Are you planning on college now?

Rachel: Nope.

Diane: So you're not planning on going? Why not?

Rachel: I just don't think I'm good enough.

Stacey: That's one reason why you're not gonna get a good job.

Rachel: It's not my fault; it's just not going to happen. I know it's not.

Diane: Why?

Rachel: Nobody in my family's ever gone to college!

Throughout the sessions in which the girls discuss their futures, Rachel remains resolute. Despite the other girls' sometimes lively talk of college and money and possibility, she finds it hard even to imagine her future. "The reason I can't think what I want to do," she explains, "is because I don't think what I want to do is going to happen." What she does know, however, is that "I want to go it alone." Knowing that "the money part" will be harder "without a man," Rachel imagines a relationship in which she is in control. "I don't know," she says. "I don't want to get married. I want to get my own job and do it all myself, have everything, just for me . . . I want a boyfriend, but I don't want to get married." In another session, Rachel elaborates this plan. She would adopt a child "that needs to be" adopted: "I want a black baby boy . . . They're so cute. The boys. The little curly hair. They're so cute. Oh, they're so adorable!"—but she would not marry: "I want a good job, and maybe one kid. And I want to be able to, like, party once in a while on the weekends."

Diane: But no husband? Is that what you mean? One kid but you don't necessarily need a father?

Rachel: I need a boyfriend who is the father.

Diane: But he doesn't live there?

Rachel: Sometimes, most of the time, but he has his own house.

Diane: So you want control of your own place, no matter what?

Rachel: Control of everything myself.

For Rachel a good future entails "a car," "enough money so I can get a baby-sitter," "enough to pay the rent." She hopes her sister-in-law will find her a job where she works, "an office thing." But Rachel's anxiety is never far from such imaginings. When Diane asks the girls one day whether they think that the future seems rosy or dim, Rachel is the first to respond.

Rachel: Dim . . . I want it to be . . .
Stacey: You want it to be dim?
Amber: Both, in the middle.
Rachel: I want it to be rosy. I want it to be . . .
Diane: How come you think it looks dim if you want it to be rosy?
Rachel: 'Cause I don't believe that what I want is going to happen.
Diane: I don't think you're asking that much.
Rachel: I know. It just sounds like too much for me.
Diane: A job, a place to live, a kid?
Rachel: Money.

Rachel's doubts and anxieties, her wish for control over her life, her longing for enough money to pay the bills and maybe have a little fun now and again are shared by the other girls, although, unlike Rachel, most of them swing wildly between their fantasies of an unencumbered life of success, travel, and money, and their concern about having "enough" to get by. How will they pay for college? they wonder. Who will hire them? Will they make enough to afford clothes and an apartment, to support a child? They talk in animated voices about becoming marine biologists, lawyers ("That's what I would love to do," because, twelve-year-old Amber says, "I love to fight!"), oceanographers, photographers, veterinarians, or perhaps joining the air force or the marines (the only problem there, Sarah, also twelve, explains, is that "they yell at you . . . and I'd probably smack them"). But the bottom line is money, and they agree with Amber when she says, "I'm all for [working at the mill], if I can't get anything else. I don't care where I work as long as I get money."

In a voice that sounds rehearsed, Stacey announces her most fervent desire: to be "financially secure for the rest of your life." Money, they all agree, is their main concern, and they want "a lot" of it. Money is an issue their families constantly struggle with, argue about, something that has narrowed their parents' options and taken away their control. They talk about the tension-filled family negotiations at bill time, the battles with their mothers for new clothes, the hard decisions to be made during the holidays or on birthdays. "Sometimes," Dana says, "we just don't have the money and it's really hard to buy stuff, so—that's just kind of the way it is at our house." The girls punctuate these discussions with their desires and strong feelings. "I just want a lot of money so I can buy clothes," Rachel says. "Money," fourteen-year-old Sherie comments, "makes me feel good." "[My parents] shouldn't have had us if [they] couldn't get us what we need," Stacey complains.

The gap between what these girls believe is going to happen and what they hope for is never far from the surface. Amber underscores the distance between what she expects from her life and her hope for a "real job" by shifting from the active "I" to the more general "you":

> Well, my future—I'm going to graduate . . . well, when I'm sixteen I'm gonna get emancipated; then I'm gonna live by myself, in my own apartment. And I'm gonna have a part-time job and I'm gonna go to school . . . I'm gonna drive a car and I'm gonna go everywhere and never be home . . . but what I *want* my future to be like is all that, but then *you* go to college and be a lawyer, get some money.

Apprehension about the future surfaces and resurfaces in these sessions—it is sometimes revealed when the girls make fun of one another's fears, as when Susan puts her arm around a deeply troubled Rachel and says with mock concern, "That's OK. You can always get a job as a sewer worker. Scrubbing toilets with a toothbrush." At other moments anxiety surfaces more directly in the form of self-doubt and self-deprecation, coloring the girls' capacity to envision and plan the future.

Diane: How about you, Brianna? What does your future look like?
Brianna: Black.

Diane: Black? You said black. Why black? . . . Because of the state of the world, or because of your . . .

Brianna: Because I'm stupid.

Rachel: That's exactly how I feel.

Diane: You feel you're stupid? You're not. You feel like that?

Brianna: If you looked at my future now and you looked at my future then, you'd see a big difference.

Diane: If I looked at your future now . . .

Yeah, and then . . . what it will be then, you'll see a big difference.

Diane: What difference will I see?

Brianna: Um, black . . .

For these girls, genuine hope and possibility come not from fleeting images of escape or flights of fancy, although they certainly entertain both, but in the form of women they know who have made it against all odds. When asked to talk about role models and ideals, these girls talk about older sisters, aunts, cousins, or friends who are "good" people and who have, through hard work, crafted decent lives for themselves; they have good jobs, nice husbands, children. For Rachel, it is her sister-in-law who is "nice," "really smart," "has initiative," "lots of friends," "a good job" and "a child," who didn't go to college but who, through persistence and determination, has made herself indispensable at work; for eleven-year-old Cheyenne it is an older cousin who "takes me places" and "always listens," who is "healthy . . . don't smoke or use drugs . . . don't really drink that much at all"; for Susan, thirteen, it is her older sister, who went to college, married a nice man, works hard, has a child, and "cares about everybody." For Donna, fourteen, it is an aunt who gives her advice, who is "there for me and I can talk to her." Because (as Donna says, and the others agree) "there aren't too many people out there like that," these girls place a high priority on their relationships with such women.

All these role models share qualities and life-styles the girls want for themselves. Like these women, the Mansfield girls long to be responsive and caring and loyal, but also self-sufficient and direct and in control of their lives; they want the initiative, smarts, determination, and sense of humor to make it on their own, perhaps with a child but not necessarily married or dependent on a man. Here their hopeful voices echo the American Dream—they long to pull themselves up by their bootstraps, so to speak. Like the women they admire, the girls want to be treated with respect, to enjoy their work, to have choices, to be healthy, to have a little extra money. Most of the girls say they won't be able to afford college—some are certain they won't—although they long to go and are willing to work two or more jobs for the opportunity.

The Mansfield girls' constructions of longing, particularly their expressions of deep feeling and anxiety about their lives, disrupt classist assumptions that still prevail in psychological and educational circles—particularly, that the children of the poor and working class live concretely in the present and reflect little on their futures.[9] Although the girls talk a good deal about what they're "gonna" do and be in the future, their concerns and fears provide clues to the prevalence of this myth. As listening to Rachel, in particular, underscores, what might be termed a concreteness in thinking or a lack of planfulness may more accurately reflect intense anxiety about future prospects and a sense of vigilance and wariness that keeps her focused on the present, in spite of her many longings and desires.

Anger, Class, and Femininity

The Mansfield girls' understandings and expressions of anger are greatly affected by their beliefs about human nature and their definitions of appropriate femininity. Anger permeates their conversations; it is an important emotion galvanizing them to collective action on their own or their friends' behalf, protecting them from hurt and injustice.

These girls define anger as emotional and physical energy that somehow must be expended and exhausted through expression or physical activity or dissipated with loud music. "When I'm at home," Donna, fourteen, says, "I usually go for a walk or I sit in my room and I crank my radio." When I'm angry, twelve-year-old Stacey, who likens anger to "getting tense," says, "I just go for a bike ride because I love riding my bike. Or I just go to my room and listen to my radio." "If I get really mad at somethin'," Cheyenne, eleven, exclaims, "I just take off [on my dad's moped] and keep drivin' and drivin' and drivin'!"

Anger with no place to go speaks through the body and bursts into the world of its own accord. "Sometimes I usually just get a headache first," Donna explains, "or I just start swearing or something . . . and then I get in trouble for it . . . It goes through [my head and body]. I start . . . it's like a really bad headache. If I've had a bad day or something . . . I get like really pushy or something . . . I take it out on other people and I know it's not right but they say something and it just comes out."

The Mansfield girls clearly see the constructive side of expressing anger, even as they allude to its overpowering potential. Donna finds the expression of pent-up feeling "a relief," though it is likely to get her in trouble at school. As if she had read the psychoanalytic literature on the consequences of suppressed emotion, thirteen-year-old Susan explains that "it's important to express feelings, because [if you don't] then it just builds up inside you and you get really stressed out about it . . . It'll just bother you even more if you don't express it." Patti, eleven, agrees: "[If it really builds up] I think you wouldn't know what to do about it and you would kinda think it's all your fault . . . I say what I think and it's because if you keep holding things in, you'll just get more upset over it. That's what I think." Stacey admits that "if you don't [express your anger] then it can just build up and if it's just that one time and it's really bad then that wouldn't be good." Sarah, too, sees the value in expressing anger as a way to "feel better" by getting "everything out that I've been holding up inside":

I say what I think most of the time. Most of the time, I'll just come right out and say it 'cause I don't hold anything back . . . because if you hold it all up inside then it gets worse and I start thinking about it more and if you tell someone about why you're hurt, or why you're angry, then they can sometimes help you and try to take care of the problem.

But while the Mansfield girls conceptualize anger this way and express a good deal of rage toward those who dare to hurt or "mess with" them or with those they love, they are careful to control their anger with one another. Knowing the intensity of their feelings, and in a number of cases, knowing from personal experience the physical violence or relational damage that can occur when anger or rage goes unchecked, the girls struggle to hold in or contain their feelings, afraid, as Donna puts it, that they might "go over the edge" and risk ruin or irreparable damage to relationships they count on for protection and support. And yet holding back this built-up tension is extremely difficult and takes practice, as twelve-year-old Amber can attest from her personal experiences in a violent household:

Amber: If you let it build up inside, it's just like you get angrier and angrier and it's like all built up and you just get so mad— just get really mad . . . You have to control it. I'm pretty good at that sometimes . . . I just do it because I don't want to lose my friends, so I just control it . . . I'll be mad at somebody; I'll want to say something to 'em . . . but I don't. I hold it back. Because usually what I have to say is mean and I just don't want to say it.
Lyn: If you were to say it, what would happen?
Amber: They'd probably be very mad, and I want to stay friends with them so I don't say it.
Lyn: What do you feel when that happens?
Amber: Angry! Frustrated.

Indeed, if these girls are evasive or indirect about their strong feelings, it is most likely with their girlfriends. "They say that it's good to express your anger," Cheyenne, Amber's younger sister, says,

to get it out of your system, but I don't. I just keep it inside of me because I know that I'll say something that I don't want to say and then the next day I'll be like, "Hi," and they won't talk to me because I said something bad to them . . . If I'm talking to a teacher, I'll like tell them what I think. But if I'm talking to Donna, my friend, or somethin', I just won't say anything to 'em. Like you want to be careful not to get too angry or show them that you're angry or you'll totally lose a friend.

With friends, Stacey reveals, "I usually just walk away from it really. Sometimes I say something, but I don't usually." Susan, one of the most opinionated girls in the group when it comes to teachers and the school, explains, "If I get mad at a friend, then I'd just go find somebody else and just not talk to them and if it's like a real— more serious, then I'll just go talk to one of my friends that I can trust."

Thus anger, as these girls describe it, is an inevitable, necessary release of built-up tension, frustration, and anxiety, part and parcel of daily life, especially for those whose families are isolated, under financial stress, or in crisis. While the necessity of keeping anger out of their close relationships with friends makes the Mansfield girls sound on the surface strikingly similar to white middle-class adolescent girls, they do so, not because anger is a culturally inappropriate emotion, but because they need their friends. Whether good or not, constructive or destructive, anger is perceived as a justified response to ill treatment, hurt, and injustice and a defense against psychological pain, loss, and vulnerability. Maintaining control over such intense feelings is a challenge, and the girls struggle with how to express their feelings to one another and to adults they care about in such a way that they will be heard and responded to.

Noticeably absent in their discussions of anger, however, are the Mansfield girls' expressions of outrage over material want and longing. Perhaps I notice because it is their anxiety, uncertainty, and self-denigration that most enrage *me* as I watch and listen to them speak, with eyes averted, of their "stupidity" and "dim" futures. It would seem that anger is an appropriate response to such an unfair scarcity of resources. Its presence in this arena, however, is little more than a whisper.

Stevenson and Ellsworth suggest that this whisper has as much or more to do with the girls' class identities as it does with the fact that, at eleven, twelve, thirteen, or fourteen, they have yet to appreciate the wider structural constraints on their lives. Their work on white working-class drop-outs suggests that the girls' self-denigration, their tendency to blame their poor prospects on their own stupidity, and their lack of anger at wider institutional and societal injustices may reflect an identification with "the culture of individualism, which . . . dominates the social fabric of white America" as well as the internalization of the dominant societal fantasy of a classless society. If these Mansfield girls believe "that everyone has an equal chance to succeed irrespective of their personal or family circumstances," they can attribute failure only to their own deficiencies.[10] Growing up as part of the "fractured" working class, trying to make sense of themselves and their struggles without a "coherent cultural frame of reference" that would give them "a sense of self-worth," the girls find it difficult to articulate a compelling challenge to the prevailing view that those who do not succeed are simply not trying hard enough or are stupid.[11]

The gendered and classed lines the Mansfield girls draw between and around the desired, the likely, and the possible once again disrupt white middle-class constructions of femininity. Femininity, for these girls, includes toughness, a self-protective invulnerability to sadness and fear, an often direct and unapologetic expression of anger, as well as a deep capacity for love and nurturance toward those who need them. Like the urban working-class girls Niobe Way listened to, the Mansfield girls know "the importance of speaking one's mind, expressing one's opinions, daring to disagree, and speaking the truth in relationships."[12] They readily and openly express their anger toward perceived injustice, admit their love for fighting and debate, admire those who do not take abuse, who stand up for themselves, and sometimes aggressively lash out at those who inflict pain. And yet they struggle to admit their own vulnerability and carefully control their expression of anger toward one another. In addition, their harsh constructions of themselves as "stupid" and their futures as "dim" and "black" support Way's finding that speaking one's mind does not "necessarily suggest self-confidence," as it might in more privileged white girls.[13]

These often contradictory strands of selfhood are indelibly colored by the material and social realities of the Mansfield girls' lives. Their aggressiveness, toughness, and invulnerability allow them a certain degree of protection against the contradictions they experience between what they long for and what is available to them. Their special attention to relationships with their girlfriends suggests that these friendships provide a measure of support in what often feels like a hostile environment. The gap between their fantasies and genuine possibilities allows them both to imagine escaping to the glamorous life of success and wealth and to draw strength and sustenance from women in their lives who have held their own in difficult circumstances. Such deeply classed voices and experiences weave together desire, danger, self-effort, anger, love, self-denigration, hope, anxiety, doubt, and determination to create distinct constructions of self and white femininity.

four

Acadia:
The Conventions of Imagination

Anger is a wide chapter of our book.

LYDIA

The lessons of culture, class, and femininity come into bold relief when we compare the conversations of the Mansfield girls with those of the middle-class girls from Acadia. The latter struggle intensely with idealized voices of femininity, with the polarizing metaphors that threaten to disconnect them from one another and from themselves. Such conventions are everywhere, seemingly in the air they breathe. These are the girls for whom such cultural constructions are meant, and they, in turn, are attracted to the promise of attaining purity and perfection, even as they realize the limits that such ideals place on their feelings and thoughts.

On the most basic level, these middle- and upper-middle-class girls, in comparison with the poor and working-class girls from Acadia, live a life largely free of anxiety over material want.[1] They talk about trips to Florida and the Caribbean, make passing references to their houses and camps and boats, to horseback-riding lessons and shopping at the mall. Their days are filled with sports and band practice, music lessons, outing club trips, play rehearsals at the Opera House, advanced math or language courses, all of which offer them a social and cultural currency that will assure their place in the upper-middle-class life to which they aspire. They anticipate college and successful careers; those who want families imagine husbands who respect their careers and interests and who share child-care. And yet the Acadia girls live this privileged life, at least in the way it plays out in school, with deep ambivalence—acutely conscious that where they and others fall along the social and economic continuum affects how they are listened to and whether they are taken seriously.

Both Ends against the Middle

Whereas the Mansfield girls' potential class consciousness centers around their longing for enough and the anxiety of knowing they will most likely have to settle for less, the Acadia girls are preoccupied with where they fit into the social and material hierarchy of school and society. These middle-class girls not only are aware of their position vis-à-vis the other groups in their school, but are also in a constant process of understanding, explaining, justifying, and defending against that position.

"There are three major cliques in our school," twelve-year-old Lydia carefully explains one day in our group session.

> One's the popular kids, and the second is like our group, which
> is the middle class or whatever; and the third is the, like, the
> bummed-out, troublemakers, all that stuff . . . We're like in soci-
> ety, you know, the popular kids, the middle class, and then the
> ones that are kind of . . . pfttt, cast out.
>
> *Jane:* Scrubs!
> *Kirstin:* We're in the middle class.
> *Lydia:* I mean, you have some friends that—
> *Lyn:* What does that mean, middle class?
> *Kirstin:* I'm cast out.
> *Lydia:* Us, you know, like—
> *Elizabeth:* Regular people.
> *Lydia:* Yeah, regular people. You're not popular, like the talk of the
> school or anything, and you're not like cast out, spit upon, or,
> well, [jokingly referring to the spitball barrage Jane endured
> from a "higher-up" boy just the day before], *you're* spit upon . . .
> in Language Arts.

The anxiety the girls feel about the class arrangements in their school surfaces in the way they tease one another. Are they really "regular people," the norm, or are they a slightly more privileged version of the "cast-out," the "spit-upon"? They are not "bummed-out" kids or "troublemakers," but neither are they part of the in-group in their school.

According to the Acadia girls, such class divisions have a long history. Their mothers tell them that little has changed since they themselves attended the junior high. Although the names for the three social groups will change at various times during the year—Lydia, for example, likes to refer to them as "the royals, the knights, and the peasants" because this classification bestows on the Acadia girls, as the knights, an obligation valiantly to protect those who are badly treated—the clear lines of demarcation remain constant.

When I ask what makes the Acadia group middle-class, as opposed to upper-or lower-class, the girls respond in quick succession:

Jane: Because we're too smart.
Kirstin: 'Cause we're girls—
Jane: And we're too smart.
Elizabeth: And we don't play all the sports.
Lydia: We're smart and we're different . . . We don't wear GAP
    jeans all the time; we wear homemade clothes.
Others [laughing]: We do?

This particular *combination* of being a girl, being smart, and being "different" keeps the Acadia girls from being in the popular group and yet also protects them from lower-class status in their school. Although the girls admit that money is an important factor, they suggest that material wealth alone does not determine class position; after all, as Theresa, thirteen, observes, some people, like the "wig-gas," who have "a good family and a good income," simply choose to "dress poorly and stuff," and so are "cast out."[2] And yet, acceptance into the upper class or popular group is about attaining an insider's understanding of language, dress, and other forms of social presentation—all closely tied to educational and material privilege.

While the popular boys "gotta be tough and biceptical," laughs twelve-year-old Kirstin, and put other kids down because "it makes them cool," "the girls in the popular group" are, according to Elizabeth, who is also twelve, "pretty, and play sports, and—"

Jane: Aren't smart.
Elizabeth: Wear the right clothes and—
Jane: Aren't smart.
Elizabeth: —stuff.
Valerie: What makes them popular?
Kirstin: Looks.
Lydia: Yeah, looks and how they're—
Kirstin: It's totally looks, I think. Clothes.
Lydia: Clothes!
Kirstin: A lot of what you wear.
Valerie: So, would you girls include yourselves in this group?
All: No!
Theresa: You know, they have name brands, like Umbros and stuff. Well, I don't have a lot of Umbros because I have, ummm, [lots of] brothers and sisters, so I get a lot of hand-me-downs. And people look at you and laugh, but all you're wearing is like shorts and . . . some no-name shorts and a t-shirt.

Their own social location, as they see it, is a result of the activities they "choose" to engage in, their "smarts," and their refusal to conform to the social expectations of the popular group—their resistance to being the kind of girls who act dumb or obsess about their appearance to please the popular boys. That is, their middle-class status derives from individuality and merit. And yet their social position is also secured because the popular group has not chosen or embraced them. It is the popular group's power to include and exclude that most bothers the girls and occupies so much of their time and attention, since such power arises out of unearned privilege and entitlement—the Acadia girls' particular "middle-class" pet peeve—and is often accompanied by hurtful and oppressive behavior.

In reaction to this exclusion, the girls defensively and proudly claim their outsider status. They laugh at the fickleness of the popular girls, who constantly bicker and fight:

Lydia: I wouldn't *want* to be in the popular group. You're constantly talked about, you're always, the friends are always like, "I don't like her anymore," and "Did you hear what she said about me?" It's like, "I'm gonna slap him the next time he says that." And it's just, it's all talk . . .

Kirstin: They're whiners.

Lydia: They're whiners.

Lyn: What bothers you so much about them? I mean, other than—

Lydia: I hate whiners.

Kirstin: They're conceited.

Jane: They treat us like we're nothing.

Kirstin: They're so conceited, they think—

Lydia: They're like the kings of the school . . .

Kirstin: They're so much awesomer than us. They're like—

Lydia: "You're stupid," or . . .

Kirstin: "Get away, you're a scrub. We're better." They don't say it, but they imply it so heavily it's disgusting.

The Acadia girls define themselves as more real and open, less snobby, and less class-conscious than the popular kids. Shopping at department stores like K-mart or Rich's, ferreting out deals at second-hand stores, and wearing hand-me-downs or homemade clothes, for example, signify their status as "regular" people. Dressed casually in jeans and over-sized t-shirts or sweaters, they joke about the popular clique's policing of clothes and behavior. "If you wear the same color Champion sweatshirt," Kirstin says with a smirk, "they're like, 'Take that off, I don't want to take mine off!' " The girls joke disdainfully about conformity and the "wannabes" who so shamelessly desire to be included in the "high" group, even as they struggle with the knowledge that there is no simple or clear solution to the popular kids' tyranny. "What I don't get," Lydia says, her expression now serious, "is if you're being made fun of because of the stuff you wear, then you wear the stuff they wear, and then you're still made fun of."

In turn, the girls create a cerebral line of defense, imagining various witty come-backs and practical jokes that would put these "kings of the school," particularly the boys, in their place, revealing them to be the "dumb," "mean," "obnoxious" "oafs" that the girls "know" they are. By contrast with the popular group, the Acadia girls claim their own creativity and difference. "We have the wit," Lydia exclaims condescendingly. "They have the stupidity!"

The constant attention the Acadia girls give to "those" kids who "think they are the higher point of life" speaks volumes about their ambivalence and the level of anxiety they feel about their own social status in their school. Even though they describe the hurtful and embarrassing things the popular kids do to them and allude to their propensity at times to protect their more vulnerable classmates—and as much as they resent the popular group's power and intimidation tactics—they are quick to distinguish themselves and their friends from "the lower life."

Valerie: What are your friends like? You've told us what they're not like. What are your friends like?

Jane: Mine aren't all wonderful at sports.

Kirstin: They have to be nice.

Jane: Interesting and smart.

Theresa: Interesting.

Jane: Oh, and they've got to be, well, they can't, well, they've got to be, they can't be scrubs or whatever.

Lyn: Can't be what?

Jane: The lower life, or, the unpopular people.

Lyn: But what was that word you used?

Jane: Nothing.

Kirstin: You said it! We were all thinking that but we didn't say it.

"Scrub," Lydia then explains, refers to the fact that "like your hands need to be scrubbed." Or, Kirstin adds, "like scrub my garbage dump." The term implies, twelve-year-old Jane says, that "you come from a garbage dump. Well, not from a garbage dump," she adds, revealing her reluctance to appear too mean. "Well, garbage dumps aren't always bad, but . . . You know, you have to come from really bad homes, whose father are, are—"

Elizabeth: Gone?
Jane: Yeah, whose fathers are all gone, and stuff.
Kirstin: Gone, and their mothers offer them pot, and stuff like that . . .
Lydia: No, their dads do; moms never do that.

And so while the Acadia girls question the social hierarchy of their school, they also attempt to explain it, and at times participate in it. They make commonly accepted associations between class and morality and between class and personal choice: kids from otherwise "good" families choose to align themselves with the "troublemakers"; unpopularity is justified by poverty rooted in families in which fathers leave and parents offer their kids drugs.

But the issue is more complicated than it appears on the surface. The Acadia girls actively struggle to connect their social experiences at school with the prevailing ideology and discourse about the middle class that they hear at home and on the nightly news, and the way they do so provides clues to the reproduction and regulation of their class positions. In one session Lydia makes connections between the "political stuff" they talked about in her Spanish class and her emerging rage about the "inconsiderate," "rude," and "mean" ways she and her classmates are treated by the popular boys in school. Her associations lead the girls into a conversation about the injustices of a tax and welfare system that "poops on" the middle class.

Lydia: [In Spanish class the other day] we get to the point of like, you know, if you defend yourself against somebody who attacks you, and you kill them in defense of yourself, you can get sent to jail. That's stupid. And then I got really mad, and I feel like I can't wait until tomorrow, until Keith talks to me, so I can really yell at him, you know?

Lyn: So what's the connection? You're talking about that in connection to your feelings about other people outside this group?

Lydia: Yeah, I mean, when you get talking about it, you really get
emotionally eruptured . . . You know, you just kind of want, you
can't wait to show, you know, what you've learned . . . You
really get all worked up . . . I'm being a lot more aggressive in
Social Studies. I have [all those guys] behind me . . . they just
talk and talk and talk . . . and they're so mean to Jacob. I mean,
they kicked—

Jane: And Peter.

Lydia: They pushed a chair over—

Elizabeth: And Wayne.

Lydia: On him, and the chair was like on top of Michael. And you
know how he gets all worked up . . . and it's really . . . I call that
a suspension . . . send them home. I mean, it's either suspension
or detention and detention is like the teachers are like being so
nice; it's like free time. And that's not, it's like jail. Jail, they have
like TV, they have like cable. *I'm* not even allowed to watch
TV . . .

Kirstin: I don't have cable.

Lydia: And they have like weight rooms and saunas, hot tubs. I
mean, they're living off our money. I mean . . . it takes us five
years to save up to build a kitchen. And they're just like, it's
sick, it's not even punishment. Punishment—my jail—would be
dirty . . . There'd be cells, you'd have a board [to sleep on]. I'd
give you a blanket and a pillow . . . And you'd get like very meager servings, but three meals a day. And you wouldn't have TV
and everything. You'd be sent to go and work, you know, like
on the chain gangs or whatever. Like that, I mean, that's punishment.

Lydia's initial frustration derives from the popular kids' oppressive
behavior and her inability to protect herself and her more vulnerable
male classmates from their abuse. Like those who kill in self-defense,
she may be the one to suffer should she retaliate. And even if the

boys are caught, their punishment, like that of those who languish in her image of comfortable jail cells, will be minor, not even close to what she feels they deserve. Here Lydia's attention suddenly shifts away from the unfair privileges accorded the popular students toward a judgment of the disadvantaged, as her associations fall in line with the prevailing rhetoric about the position of the American middle class. Once she has reproduced the social hierarchy in these terms, the bulk of the blame falls to those in the group below the girls.

Lyn: This conversation is interesting in the context of your feelings about these other people. I mean, it seems to me that it's placed right in the center of . . . these other feelings, like these guys in your class aren't getting their just punishment. Is that what you're saying?

Kirstin: They aren't. They get away with—

Lydia: It's really hurting the middle class. I mean, the rich people, oh, they don't even have to pay taxes, and the poor people, they're like, they get, they're on, what's it called . . .

Kirstin: Welfare.

Lydia: Welfare. And they're like, "Oh, this is great." I mean, "I don't even have to work or anything and I'm getting money."

Lyn: But it's complicated, Lydia—

Lydia: And the middle class, the middle class, we're getting pooped on, you know? It's just . . . [*throws her arms in the air*].

Jane: And you know what the poor people do? They, you get a certain amount of money for how many kids you have, and they take other people's kids, and they have their names, "This is blah, blah, blah." And the kids, they're all standing there crying, and supposedly shivering cold and hungry. Then when the people are gone, they, you know, straighten up and go home.

Lydia: They, like, make themselves be poor . . . A lot, I mean, some people just get pregnant, and have as . . . so they get more money.

Kirstin: A lot of them are very capable of getting jobs.

Lydia: 'Cause they're lazy. But some of them don't want to; they're lazy.

Speaking through the voices of conservative, white middle-class America, the girls move away from the reality of their experiences and their observations of the way their school is structured. By doing so, they obfuscate the ways in which the unearned advantages of the popular kids and the climate of privilege they create contribute to a tiered system that circumscribes the Acadia girls' own actions and possibilities and creates a group of "outcasts" or "spit-upons."

The girls actively struggle within this construction, however. As their conversation continues, they decide that "not all" poor people are the same, as Lydia admits; indeed, "half the people on welfare, they're really working hard and they're trying to get out of it." When Kirstin recalls her interaction with a girl who signed up for the free hot lunch at school because her "mom got a job and so they won't give her welfare money anymore, and now . . . [they're] really struggling," the pendulum swings dramatically in the other direction.

Kirstin: It's harder for them without [welfare], which is why people don't do it even when it's easier. Which isn't right. That means welfare's too much or jobs pay too little.

Lydia: Why doesn't it come out of the rich? Why doesn't it come out of the both of us?

Kirstin: I just don't think it's right for people to be getting, like, um, somebody that lives right here [in town] just sold their company and got $400 million . . . and I don't think it's fair. I mean, he's never going to use all his money. He has more than people are ever gonna need, no matter how many luxuries you have.

The Acadia girls are certainly trying out, with one another and with the women in the room, different voices and understandings from the adult world as a way to create their own meanings and intentions. But I would suggest that the girls choose this particular discourse because it explains their feelings of frustration and anxiety about their social location in their school. The girls struggle with what Paulo Friere calls an "existential duality"—they are caught between their contempt for the powerful group and their passionate attraction to them. In either case, looking to the "higher" kids for meaning, the girls risk being "submerged" in an "order" designed to serve the popular kids' interests, and thus they risk losing sight of their own collective and political power.[3] Within this order the girls fight for recognition against those "who have, like, power and think it's their thought," and who treat the "middle group" as though "we have no feelings." The anxiety that accompanies such dehumanization, and the risk that acting on behalf of those who are lower in the order may devalue one's own social currency, work to reify the hierarchy, casting the unpopular kids as either hapless victims or deserving troublemakers. In this manner the Acadia girls both struggle against and participate in the deeply classed culture of their school.

Policing the Borders

This struggle between rejection and desire, the propensity to define themselves against, and thus also in relation to, the popular kids, greatly affects the Acadia girls' constructions of themselves and their views of femininity. Who they are seems always in relation to who they are not, and they are *not*, they insist, "those" girls.

The lines the Acadia girls draw between good girls and bad girls reflect, to a large degree, familiar dichotomies that have long regulated white middle-class feminine behavior: nice girls are kind and caring, they listen, they don't hurt others, they don't get in trouble or cause scenes, they don't express anger or say what they want directly, they don't brag or call attention to themselves. Bad girls, by contrast, are sexual, express their desires, dress provocatively, speak too often and too loudly, and express their anger directly; they call attention to themselves, and thus are "out of control" and "obnoxious." The Acadia girls endorse these divisions through their dress and behavior, their talk of other girls, and their teasing of one another.

The Acadia girls are confused and outraged by the fact that the popular girls don't acknowledge or respect these boundaries, and that they not only get away with it, but appear to flourish. Such popular girls are not "bad" per se, at least not in ways people, particularly adults, seem to see or care much about, but from the Acadia girls' perspective they are often insensitive and mean, "whiny" and "conceited." While not necessarily sexually experienced, some dress in short shorts and tight tops and therefore call attention to themselves; they change their personalities when they are around boys; they react instead of act, always metaphorically testing the winds of popular opinion; they are shape-shifters, chameleons. The Acadia girls cannot understand how such clearly disingenuous people carrying on in apparently fraudulent relationships can curry so much favor and maintain their "high" position. They watch in amazement and dismay as these girls, who "talk about people behind their backs," who, if "they don't like you . . . [will] cast you out," command the attention of the teachers, other girls, and especially boys.

Lydia: Even the most obnoxious, ugliest, self-centered people in the popular group . . . always get to the top; they always get ahead of us, and I don't see why. Or like, they're always out with somebody. What do they see in those girls? I really don't get it.
Valerie: Those guys that they go out with, are they guys you would want to go out with?
Jane: Not really, but I suppose we're jealous anyway.

Drawing on a language laced with liberal feminism, the Acadia girls justify and police the boundaries that exist between themselves and these others. Their group covers a range of body types, and they reject the kind of girl who is always "tan, skinny, [and] gorgeous," acutely aware that attaining such an image is harmful physically. They connect such obsessions with looks to passivity and sexual objectification. Those other girls are nothing more than ornaments for boys, and they have no interest in things that "really" matter, such as academic achievement and competitions, drama, music, or art. Furthermore, the popular girls participate in their own objectification and subordination by dressing "prissy" or acting dumb "when they could be smart"; in this sense they are, as thirteen-year-old Robin suggests, "insults" to other girls. They are, unlike the Acadia girls, immature and silly. "I don't get this," Lydia says, shaking her head:

The popular girls, they always do this thing, and it's like this cat
    food commercial or something.
Jane: "Meow, meow, meow, meow, meow, meow, meow, meow."
Lydia: They always do it and I don't get it . . . [On our class trip],
    at a fancy dinner, they're sitting there . . . "Meow, meow, meow,
    meow" . . . and it's so stupid, and they're like playing patty
    cake over the table, and if one gets up to go to the bathroom,
    like this whole horde goes to the bathroom, you know? It's just
    pathetic.

The Acadia girls say that they could not act like the popular girls even if they wanted to. And yet their "catty" behavior speaks to their own brand of conformity. The exaggerated distinctions and devaluations inherent in their gossip, a thin cover for their anger over the attention these other, more popular girls receive, and also perhaps a sign of their anxiety around sexuality and relationships with boys, firm the boundaries around their own behavior. Positing this particular "other" clarifies the characteristics the girls ascribe to themselves by allowing them a measure of distance and resistance to certain conventionally feminine roles and expectations.

To the degree that the popular girls are known to perform such feminine roles, then, the Acadia girls resist them, labeling them damaging, unproductive, and mind-numbing. The popular girls become, to the Acadia girls, a certain narrow caricature of a girl, one who mirrors what boys want, someone who "is really shallow" and has "more cleavage."

Jane: A boy's image is pretty and, um—
Lydia: Pretty and that's all.
Kirstin: Basically he can't see below the surface. They don't even
    care about that.

Jane: They have to be pretty in jeans and be able to dance good, but—
Lyn: But nothing else?
Jane: Yeah. Well . . . [*smiles knowingly*]
Lydia: And she has to make money.
Jane: Yeah. She has to be rich.
Lydia: That's like shallow.

They are themselves, they insist, a different breed of girl altogether—smart, strong, interesting, and thoughtful. "We *are* girls," Kirstin says, her blue eyes focused on the camera, but Lydia interrupts, "We're deeper." "And we know our feelings," Jane adds. In opposition to the group conformity of the popular girls, Lydia defines herself and her friends as "individuals": "We're individuals who stick together. It's like a track team. You do individual events, but yet you score as a team."

In this way, through objectifying and mythologizing the popular girls, Lydia and the others claim space for their brand of white middle-class femininity—a particular combination of individualized identity development, a firm belief in capitalism and meritocracy, and a sort of feminine authenticity tied to deep feeling and responsiveness to others as well as to an awareness of the world around them.

Over the course of the year, however, the Acadia girls reveal the power and attraction of dominant cultural voices of "appropriate" femininity as they struggle increasingly to articulate their experiences of themselves as individuals and their relationship to "the team." Their desire to be the smartest, to be singled out for their accomplishments, seems ever in tension with the security and anonymity of the group—anonymity supported also by compliance with idealized notions of feminine behavior. The tension begins to take its toll on their relationships. Reflecting on times when they felt down on themselves, for example, Jane raises the issue of competition, particularly with her close friend Elizabeth:

Jane: Um, Well, sometimes Elizabeth gets a better grade on her test than me. And everyone in the class somehow finds it out, I don't know how. And then they say, "Oh, yeah, of course Elizabeth got a good grade on her test." And I may have gotten a 90 and Elizabeth got a 100, and they're saying all this stuff about Elizabeth. "Of course Elizabeth got a 100 on her test," and stuff like that.

Elizabeth: It's not my fault!

Jane: [I feel] jealous . . . Because she did do well. They're saying that she's a lot better than me.

Lydia: They always think there's competition between us . . . They always think that. And there's not. We're like best friends, right?

Jane: Well . . . not anymore.

Lydia's attempt to cover over Jane's jealousy, and Jane's half-serious response to that attempt, signal the tensions in the girls' relationships as they struggle to remain friends in an increasingly hierarchical, competitive school context. For Jane, who later says she would feel better if Elizabeth got a 90 too, because then she would have company, the issue is both competition (who is seen as the smartest) and relationship (being in it together). In Jane's construction, however, relationship, which seems necessary and important to these girls who feel excluded from the popular group, comes at the cost of highest achievement; it would, in fact, cost Elizabeth her 100. "Having company" in this sense means "dumbing down" in school.[4]

Revealing their anxiety around this tension, the girls tease one another and correct one another's minor mistakes, enjoying, in the safe context of play, the challenges of standing apart and above, "proving someone wrong." But as the months pass, the Acadia girls become more guarded and cautious with their ideas; their teasing becomes harsher, more pointed, as they claim their voices comparatively and competitively. Since it is not appropriate for "nice" girls to relish openly, much less acknowledge, success and high achievement, the girls save their angry feelings around these issues for the group. As they become comfortable expressing their thoughts and feelings in the sessions, the distinctions between what they will say publicly and what they will reveal privately become more apparent.

They expect both informal and institutional compliance with this boundary. As an angry Lydia says one day when the girls are complaining bitterly about teachers who pass papers back by row, thus allowing other students access to their grades: "You know, there *is* a state law that states, um, the Buckley Amendment, that your grades are only . . . unless you choose to, it's between you, your parents, and the teacher."

As the girls move out of psychological relationship with one another in their search for individual merit and the highest honors, their solidarity comes to depend on their loyalty to tacit rules of behavior, on staying within the lines that separate them from the popular girls. In turn, they find support in their common struggle for a livable, breathable space amid all the pressure they feel to be perfect in every way. "We all have that feeling [that] people think we're perfect," Lydia explains, "because we're all pretty smart here . . . and when we do something wrong, that's really hard on us."

Jane: They're like [*opens mouth in shock*].

Kirstin: I hate that!

Lydia: It's really hard on us because they think that that's like amazing that we—

Kirstin: I get a B on a paper, and someone sees it and they make a big thing out of it. Someone else got a D and who cares?

Lyn: How does that make you feel?

Lydia: Like awful.

Kirstin: Like pressured to get good grades . . . It's not fair to us; it's kind of a stereotype!

Trapped in "kind of a stereotype" and guarding their knowledge and success even from one another for the sake of their relationships, the Acadia girls feel that the "creative," "smarter," "deeper" aspects of themselves remain largely unseen and unappreciated. Their conversations about how others see them in relation to the popular girls are punctuated by anger and frustration. Because nice girls do not publicly criticize the unearned privileges and attentions of others, they watch in disbelief as others take center stage. How, given all the school rhetoric of meritocracy and individual achievement, they wonder, can "conformity" or who you are "going out with" be the basis for approval and attention? And yet, it appears that it is.

It is, surprisingly, quiet and unassuming Theresa—dressed in gym shorts and sneakers this day, her long brown hair pulled back in a ponytail—who leads the way out of this ideological and relational conundrum by challenging its basic premise: the fraudulence and the conformity of the popular girls. The ensuing arguments are both revealing and painful. When Theresa, who is on a sports team with some of the popular girls, objects to the Acadia group's categorical rejection of the popular clique, her protest begins a heated discussion that weaves in and out of several sessions:

Lyn: Do [the popular girls] get in trouble with their friends for being nice [to you]?
Kirstin: Yes.
Theresa: No.
Kirstin: Yes, they're like, "Don't talk to them."
Jane: They don't really talk to you in front of—
Theresa: No, they don't say that.
Jane: Unless you do them a lot of favors.
Kirstin: Yes they *do!* Deirdre was walking down the hall with a bunch of friends, with Cassie, and I dropped like a book or something, because I was carrying a whole bunch, like that, because I didn't want to be late for class and one of them fell off, and she picked it up for me, and I was like, "Thanks," and Cassie goes, "Don't talk to her."
Lydia: Cassie is really . . . it's like prejudice.
Theresa: Well . . . I'm not necessarily popular, but like almost all the girls on the team are . . . and they, they never say anything like, "Don't talk to her" or anything. They wouldn't do it.
Kirstin: Not to *you* . . . because you're like in close, like close to them, and they respect you for being good [at basketball].
Kirstin: [Cassie's] a snob.
Jane: I *know* Cassie. She was in my class all last year.

Theresa repeatedly confronts the other group members' tendency to overgeneralize in their criticisms and judgments of the popular girls, calling on her personal experiences in support of a more generous and complex reading. When Jane tries to explain the differences in how the Acadia group and the popular girls act and think, Theresa explodes.

Jane: We look to the future, and they think about, a period ahead of time, "Is my homework done for science?" We think about like, where we want to go for college, and—

Theresa: How do you know? How do you know? . . . Jane, how do you know what, how they think?

Lydia: What are you, devil's advocate or something?

Jane: From what I've seen . . .

Theresa: No, but you can't say that though.

Jane: I can.

Theresa: No, you can't.

Jane: I can!

Theresa: No, you can't!

Jane: I can say whatever I want!

Theresa: But your information is not true.

Jane: It's from what I've gathered.

Elizabeth: She inferred it.

Theresa: But you can't say that they—

Jane [*now shouting*]: We're talking about me, my personal opinion!

This argument is complicated and layered—it is, on one level, a struggle for the power to define truth and reality; on another, a determination to define for oneself the contours of acceptability and inclusion; on still another, a confrontation over the meaning of relationship. It is, above all, a threat to the group, which has, by constructing its identity in opposition to the popular group, found its collective strength in fighting a common foe. While Lydia and Jane want to continue to speak of the popular girls as a generalized other and to define their distance from them in almost metaphoric terms, Theresa pulls away, demanding that their impressions be accountable to her personal observations and experiences. Theresa's insistence on having this difficult conversation interrupts Jane and Lydia's desire for a collectivity that empowers them with clear distinctions and borders, grounding their emerging personal anxieties in a group reality. The sarcastic nature of their response to Theresa, and to Elizabeth, who defends Theresa after she has left the group early to go to practice, speaks to their sense of loss and betrayal. In typical fashion, Elizabeth chooses her words carefully.

Elizabeth: [Theresa] wasn't happy with Jane.

Lyn: Why?

Jane: Because I inferred something.

Lydia: Well, I mean, we're entitled to our opinion.

Elizabeth: But sometimes you kind of said "they" or "we," meaning all of us.

Lydia: Well, sometimes *you* said "we," and I don't think she agrees with the things you said. I mean, I didn't agree with everything you said, either.

Jane: Okay. I, I. Me—

Elizabeth: That's not the way you put it.

Jane: I can't tell the distinction between the two groups. *I* don't know.

Lydia [mocking]: I don't like them.

Jane [laughing at Lydia]: Shut-up [*Jane feeds Lydia candy and begins whispering to her*].

Lydia's allusion to the fact that she and the others have, in the past, readily suppressed their disagreements for the sake of the group suggests that the central issue, at least for her, is loyalty. The need for group loyalty is understandable in an environment in which the Acadia girls feel unheard and unrecognized and, at times, beleaguered. Theresa's resistance is threatening because it forces the girls to confront what their relationships are really all about. Lydia and Jane underscore what is at stake when they separate from Elizabeth in a manner symbolic of the abandonment they feel.

It is not surprising that this discussion, held quite late in the school year, heralds the beginning of a deep rift among the Acadia girls. Even though after this session the girls occasionally fall into old patterns and generalizations, Jane and Lydia—usually the most vocal and opinionated in the group—pull back into their relationship, often leaving the other girls' thoughts and feelings hanging without support. In this way the two girls protest the breaking of tacitly agreed upon ties that bound the girls together. Although on the surface the girls remain nice to one another, their sense of comfort and confidence in shared reality has disappeared.

In a variety of subtle and not-so-subtle ways the Acadia girls reveal the classed and gendered boundaries that give their lives structure but that also threaten to cut them off from one another and from other girls. They maintain clear-cut notions of appropriate femininity, carefully policed white middle-class definitions of success and individual achievement, and firmly held assumptions about the proper and the good—at least until these notions and assumptions are disrupted by their inherent contradictions and tensions or, more simply, by the complexities of lived experience and the demands of genuine relationship.

Unlike the Mansfield girls, then, these white middle-class seventh-graders identify both with dominant cultural ideals of femininity as selfless and with adult maturity as individualized success and autonomy. Jane wishes for Elizabeth to give up her high grades for the sake of their friendship; Jane and Lydia expect the others to hold back their strong feelings and thoughts for the sake of the group. And yet each girl struggles to be visible, to be the smartest and most individually accomplished in her class. The tensions between these two voices seem nearly unbearable by the end of the school year. Their group has reached a relational impasse, a crisis, to which there seems no good solution: "Either they will give up their voices to others, learning to think, feel, and say what others want them to think, feel, and say, or they will give up their relationship with others and learn to be self-sufficient, entire unto themselves."[5] Rather than reject the terms of this relational struggle, the girls defensively break into smaller factions, publicly maintaining their relationships while privately becoming increasingly distrustful and separate.

Holding in and Holding Back

Whereas the Mansfield girls often express longing and want, the Acadia girls are more likely to reveal linguistic signs of constraint: holding in strong feelings, modulating opinionated voices, restraining desires, expressing in their conversations a sense of being acted on or held in by social norms and expectations. In fact, these middle-class girls express signs of constraint about three times more often than the working-class girls. Their conversations are peppered with such phrases as "I had to," "they made us," "I had no choice," "I can't say what I want," "we have to go," "I'm afraid to do stuff," "you can't do anything about it."

Moreover, while the Mansfield girls, too, speak of feeling constrained, they do so under very different conditions, and they respond to others' expectations and attempts at control in ways radically different from the Acadia girls. In nearly all cases, for example, the Mansfield girls tie experiences or feelings of constraint to specific relationships and situations. They describe feeling pressured, controlled, and held in place most often by teachers who demand allegiance to unreasonable or unfair rules or structures, by boys who want sexual relationships they are not quite ready for, or by the pushes and pulls of those who are physically or sexually abusive. Feelings of constraint are nearly always braided with anger, outrage, and intense struggle. The working-class girls thus openly resist attempts at psychological, physical, or social control, wearing their refusal, their toughness, and their invulnerability to such pressures like badges of honor.

In contrast, the Acadia girls seem frozen in the headlights of social norms, expectations, and conventions of behavior. Although they struggle with particular others—their parents, teachers, or popular kids at school—they understand that their anger, public critique, and open resistance are unwelcome. Their battle is thus waged privately against and within culturally and racially circumscribed definitions of femininity that constrain their movement and expression, pushing them from public view.

These differences between the two groups of girls are underscored by the ways they speak, particularly in their use of the second-person plural pronoun, "you." Virtually absent in the Mansfield girls' expressions of constraint, speaking as they do in the "I" or "we" voice, "you" saturates the Acadia girls' conversations, indicating a general or shared knowledge and experience of social constraint. "You have to be dumb . . . You have to," Kirstin complains, alluding to the pressures she feels, not from any particular person, but from the rules of a social context within which she desires to fit. And, having expressed this urgency, she articulates her capitulation in distant, passive terms: "I find myself pretending I'm stupid." Over and over the Acadia girls speak to the power of dominant cultural expectations that threaten to hold them in and hold them back: "You don't speak up . . . You don't want to tattletale . . . you can't really . . . you're intimidated . . . You can't do anything . . . I'm like afraid . . . I'm afraid to do stuff . . . you don't know what to do."

Even as the girls distance themselves from the popular kids, they experience their power and describe the way it permeates the school like an invisible gas, affecting the emotional and psychological atmosphere and constraining their movement. "The people that are really popular," Kirstin complains, "you don't even dare walk in the hall with them, because if you touch them, even, they'll be like, 'Ahh, gross!'" The girls not only think twice about showing who they really are in school, but also feel the weight of the popular kids' judgments outside the classroom.

Lydia: For instance, at the dance, nobody was dancing, but you see our middle group, we're kind of, we want to be wild and we want to have fun and everything [*Kirstin pantomimes John Travolta's disco moves*], and so we want to get people dancing. But you want to move out to the middle and start dancing so everyone will catch on. They won't let you do that.

Kirstin: You can't go anywhere near the speakers, or they're like [*makes a face that signifies disgust*].
Lyn: What do you mean they won't let you?
Lydia: You go up there, and they're like, "Skid, get out of here."
Kirstin: You can't even walk near the speakers.

In response to such social control, the girls say, they "just walk away." In fact, they react with shock when, one day after a series of such stories, I suggest that they stand up to the popular kids: Theresa laughs; Elizabeth smiles at my ignorance; the others simply stare at me.

Jane: They'd say [*in a low voice, indicating ridicule*], "Skid. Sad skid."
Lydia: Their fist enters your . . . no——
Kirstin: Then they all gang up.
Lyn: There's a lot of you.
Lydia [under her breath]: That's true.

But the fear of judgment and "embarrassment," and perhaps even violence (though this seems unlikely), wins out and the girls quickly move on, trying to figure out when such divisions first began to tear their class apart, and wondering how it was that these popular kids came to be in the position they now occupy. "I don't get it," Lydia muses. "Why do we have to fit in with the popular kids? They're popular because they want to be popular, you know, they're popular but they don't have to be."

Kirstin: Insecure.
Lydia: Yeah . . . You know, if we don't think they're popular—
Jane: They're really jealous of all of us.
Lydia: Yeah, they're jealous.
Kirstin: They are. I'm sure they are. I know they are.
Lydia: If we don't think they're popular, then who's the popular group?
Lyn: Because someone has to invest them with power; someone has to invest them with the label "popular?"

Lydia: Yeah, because everybody labels them popular. If we didn't
   label them popular, then everybody wouldn't be—
Kirstin: They wouldn't be friends anymore. All their friends are
   gone.
Lydia: It would be hard for them to overpower us.

This moment of realization electrifies the group: the popular kids'
collective power depends on everyone, the Acadia group included,
buying into their charade. Publicly expose them and they fall apart.
But the feeling passes quickly as the girls raise the specter of authority; that is, of their teachers' participation in this drama. Regardless
of what they do, if the "pushy" popular boys and the "conceited"
popular girls still receive favorable responses from their teachers,
from a higher authority, the sham remains, the center holds.

These girls feel constrained by conventions of white middle-class
femininity that prescribe what being a "good" girl is all about. First
and foremost a good girl follows the rules, even when they are arbi-
trarily or unfairly applied, even when they clearly benefit the undeserving. One day Jane tells the group about a competitive game in
her language class in which the students, working in groups, "had to
do whatever [the teacher] said and you get two pieces of candy
instead of one credit." The rules entailed no talking or laughing.
When Aaron, a popular boy, deliberately ruined his group's chances
by laughing, and then talked back to the teacher, announcing, "I
don't care. I didn't want any [candy] anyway," Jane feels angry but
does nothing because there was "nothing I could do." "Standing up
to Aaron [is] where you get problems," Theresa agrees. But more
important, Jane says, it was the rule that "we couldn't talk, it's part
of the game" that held her back. For Jane and the others, playing by
the rules is an appropriate justification (or rationalization) for silence
or inaction. As good girls, the Acadia girls find it transgressive to
speak their justified anger directly and publicly. Their underground
critique and ridicule of the popular kids provide a measure of relief,
and occasionally move them to resist, but all too often these private

murmurings have the unintended effect of emphasizing their feelings of immobility and lack of control.

The Acadia girls relish the benefits of being "labeled" smart, good, and nice: they take pleasure in the attention and accolades of teachers, the admiration of other students, school prizes, and even the jealousy of some classmates. And yet they also feel trapped in their own goodness and perfection. The constraint they feel and the controlled performances they give take their toll at the end of the day, when they leave school for home and the privacy to burst out of their perfect-girl personas. As Lydia explains, "We don't speak out a lot in class and in school, and um, except between ourselves, you know. I mean at the end of the day I go home and I usually just yell, because I can't . . . we're always so quiet during the day and we never really crack a lot of jokes and laugh silly and, you know."

Subterranean Living

The Acadia girls' public presentation of themselves as "nice" girls thus threatens to bury more private desires, struggles for recognition, observations about the way things go, and strong or deeply felt emotions such as anger, sadness, and disappointment.

Conversations about their home lives, which seem on the surface unremarkable, at least compared with some of the Mansfield girls' stories of abuse and material struggle, revolve around feelings of invisibility. From their perspective, Jane, Lydia, and Kirstin, for example, have to contend with less-than-perfect, disruptive, and demanding siblings who claim their parents' emotional and psychological energy. Their own predictably good grades and good behavior make them backdrops to more pressing family concerns. These girls describe themselves as the reluctant peacemakers, the mediators of family disturbances, the care-takers, the ones expected to know better, to be no trouble. This shadow life continues in school, where teachers look over their raised hands to call on the less-interested but more disruptive boys in the back of the room.

Well aware of what is publicly acceptable, the Acadia girls move their strong feelings and unspeakable desires into those private spaces where they can be themselves, where they feel relatively certain that their strong feelings will not betray them, jeopardizing their movement into white middle-class womanhood. Sometimes, in the privacy of the group or with best friends, they feel they can talk about their desires and express their frustrations and their anger. These girls count on the loyalty of those they trust to protect their outlaw feelings, or they move such feelings far underground in diaries and journals. "I write in my diary," Kirstin says, "when I'm upset and it's like, and it seems like I can't talk to anyone."

The Acadia girls are particularly reluctant to talk about sexuality and intimate relationships, at least in this context. In group sessions they dance around the subject, make subtle, indirect allusions, and exchange knowing glances. When, during one session, I ask the girls directly about relationships and desire, there is a long pause. Finally, Kirstin begins by describing the ideal boy. He would be "cute, tall. No, not tall, short." Jane interrupts her, quipping that while she, herself, might be interested in a boy who "doesn't think of himself *all* the time . . . most of the boys in our school, all they do is think of themselves," except, of course, for those few, she adds, laughing, who "need to think *more* about themselves."

But here the conversation withers; Elizabeth looks down at her hands and Theresa slouches noticeably lower in her chair. After a moment or two Jane tries to explain, "They're not interesting. We don't understand them. They're lethal, stupid." Lydia, however, jumps in to pick up where Kirstin left off—"He'd be smart, and, um, I don't know, just a well-to-do person"—but stops short when the others react. "What are you laughing at?" she asks the others, picking up on their smirks and rolling eyes. "You know, and I guess you really don't know until one of them comes along," she continues, her voice now fading into silence. The discomfort builds as Kirstin begins teasing Theresa. "I think it's Theresa's turn now. Theresa, what's your ideal boy? Come on, Theresa, open up . . . We won't tell if it's Devon." Again silence. The girls begin shooting balled-up candy wrappers at one another until finally Lydia, who has tried in vain to talk through these distractions, gives up. "I think we're all embarrassed to talk about it," she observes. "I'm not," Jane retorts. "I think it's stupid to go out with people at this age." Speaking in the voice of a lecturing adult and shaking her finger, she adds, "'You're a little young for boys.'" Besides, she complains, shifting back to her own voice, "Boys are boring. I don't want to talk about them."

Lydia: I don't think we're really in the mood right now. You know?
Jane: If you call us tonight.
Lyn: Tell me why you don't want to talk about them?
Lydia: I think. I really do think we're shy about it.

Undoubtedly if I were a girlfriend and in the phone loop I would hear an earful about relationships and desire (and also, no doubt, about this day's group discussion). Indeed, the girls make numerous indirect references to their knowledge about sexuality, a subject in which they are clearly interested, although they refuse any open discussion of the issue. Talking about such feelings in the group context, in my presence—for Valerie is not here this day—obviously makes them uncomfortable. And yet when, at the beginning of another session, I react with surprise to Jane's t-shirt bearing the slogan "Co-ed naked bungi jumping: It's fun going down," she grins broadly, reads the shirt aloud, and assures me that she knows exactly what it means. During another session the girls laugh hysterically as they pass around an explicit diagram they have found in a *Reader's Digest* article entitled "Joe's Prostate."

When the girls do discuss dating and romantic relationships, a more serious tone emerges. They are not so much "shy" or "not in the mood" to talk about such relationships, they admit, as, in Jane's words, "tired . . . tired of feeling so left out and stuff." They struggle to understand what the boys see in the girls they date. Again it is the confusing issue of the popular girls, their fickleness and disingenuous relationships.

Lydia: I know, [the popular girls] always go out, they go out for like one day, and the next day it's like they have another boyfriend.

Jane: "I dumped him!"

Lydia: I know! It's like, "Oh, guess what, I've had forty-two boyfriends this month!" And it's like, what are you, keeping track? You know?

Lydia: Actually, boys won't ask us out because they, I think they feel that we'd want a long-term relationship. We might become too serious.

Jane: And they aren't ready for . . . for the responsibility of having us.

Lydia [laughs, looks at Theresa in shock, and puts her hand over her mouth]: Of course not!

Here again is the allusion, the laughter, the knowing glance. Unstated is the worry, just below the surface, that boys will not find them desirable if they are too serious, if they are not "airheads."

Knowledge of sexuality and expressions of desire rarely see the light of day. Like other unacceptable feelings and behaviors—pride, self-satisfaction, confidence, self-promotion, entitlement—they hold the potential for rejection and exclusion. Such expressions cannot be easily explained or integrated into white middle-class constructions of the feminine woman as pure, nurturing, self-effacing, and always nice and compliant, and the Acadia girls—smart, complex, and truly driven—know this.

But it is not only desire or strong feelings like anger that remain submerged; it is the astute political commentary on class and the critique of hurtful behavior and unfair school practices that the Acadia girls articulate so clearly to Valerie and in the privacy of the group. Their stellar public performances of sweet, bland, uncritical acceptance lead their teachers to look over them, and often lead educational researchers to believe they are passively taking in and accepting the lessons of gender bias they experience in school. Time and again the girls express their critique to one another and to Valerie and me; time and again they admit that they do not speak their critique publicly.

This split between public presentation and private experience in middle-class white adolescent girls has been noted repeatedly, as have the long-term psychological and political consequences.[6] When the girls take their voices out of public discourse, their questions, emerging perspectives, concerns, and fears are "left relatively unanalyzed, unchallenged, and in critical ways buried."[7] They lose the power of their collective critique and, in time, they risk losing touch with what they know to be true from experience; that is, they risk dissociating from their thoughts and feelings.[8]

It is perhaps not surprising, given the Acadia girls' struggles with dominant expectations and conventions of femininity, that their most fervent desire for the future is to be genuine, "to be myself," or that their scattered expressions of want and longing tend to focus on their desire to break from expectations, to be "wild" and "crazy." While this is a sign of their privilege—they need not worry about going to college or making a good living—it is also a signal of their intense desire to be free of the demands and constant pressures they feel, their wish to integrate the public and the private.

Anger, Class, and Femininity Revisited

As with the Mansfield girls, the Acadia girls' understanding and expressions of anger are deeply affected by the messages they receive from their families and from the community about appropriate femininity. Anger for these middle-class girls is, for the most part, a negative emotion that cuts off relationships; something that, as Elizabeth explains, "feels bad . . . I don't like it . . . I just don't feel good . . . it prevents me from saying things or doing things or being with people." "[Anger] feels like—it doesn't feel good or anything," thirteen-year-old Theresa agrees. "It feels like you're all tight kind of. You're not relaxed and you feel like if you open your mouth, you might cry, because you're annoyed so much."

Unlike the Mansfield girls, who describe feeling the powerful release of angry feelings rushing out, the Acadia girls talk of anger held back and held in. Although the Mansfield girls struggle to control their angry feelings with the close friends they rely on for support, they do not distinguish between private and public expressions of such feelings. For the Acadia girls, expressing anger is rarely, if ever, constructive, and anger is, most of all, to be kept out of public life, an emotion not to be shown in school, but to be expressed alone: "Have a conversation with yourself or with like God or something instead of with someone else," Theresa advises. "I just kind of say it, to myself, or just to no one."

Prohibited from speaking publicly, the Acadia girls move their anger underground or into their relationships in carefully camouflaged ways. "I don't get angry in front [of people]," Lydia says. "Well, yes I do, but I don't really show it. I just kinda get a little more hostile. And that's how I show anger. I get hostile." Instead of directly saying what they want, think, and feel, these girls become skilled in the art of subtle expression: impassive faces, "dirty looks," averted eyes, or a shift of the body carry their underground messages of anger or displeasure to others. "When I get angry," Elizabeth explains, "people can usually tell . . . If I'm mad at a particular person, if I don't speak to them, then they can usually tell that I'm angry at them. I just kind of give them dirty looks or something." "This one kid came up behind me," Jane tells the others one day, "and started hitting my backpack and acted like, he was being an idiot and stuff like that, and I turned around and stared at him. I *felt* like kicking him." "An icy stare," Elizabeth concurs. "I give them the evil eye," Lydia adds.

The girls count on one another to read their signs of anger, to know what it is they are "really" saying, to recognize from seemingly insignificant clues the range and intensity of their feelings. "I think you kind of want [your friends] to know what you feel," Elizabeth explains. "You don't want to have to tell them, because you're angry at them, so you should know why I'm angry with you." "Yeah," Jane interjects, "you should know *why* I'm angry, and you should know *when* I'm angry."

Unlike the Mansfield girls, who openly express their anger, in part because they feel it has to go somewhere, the middle-class girls choose silence, their general philosophy being that if you ignore it or express it indirectly it will eventually go away. Elizabeth's angry feelings remain unspoken, and, from her description, relational conflicts dissipate seemingly on their own, with little or no participation on her part:

> It just plays out . . . it's just really intense for like a little while and then it just kinda goes away after a while . . . I'm just kind of doing other things and thinking other things and it just kind of goes away . . . [Making up] just kind of happens; sometimes a person will initiate it but . . . it just kind of happens.

Although such a resolution to conflict may appear to be a sign of emotional maturity—that is, neither violent nor aggressive—Elizabeth is not actively present in her relationships during these moments. In fact, her language—a shift from "I'm mad" to "it . . . plays out . . . it . . . goes away . . . it just kind of happens" reveals her distance from her feelings and her disaffection from the power of her anger.

The risk in this scenario is that Elizabeth will move out of relationship with her anger, such that, over time, her strong feelings will not be recognizable or available to her. In fact, such dissociation has been identified as an effective way to defend against feeling angry.[9] At the very least the Acadia girls, because they do not bring their anger into the public world of relationships for debate and reasoned response, begin to struggle with the source, and thus the political value and legitimacy of their feelings. Disconnected from its source, anger becomes privatized and personalized. As Lydia puts it, "I think I don't show [anger] because I know that the cause of my anger is my fault . . . If I think back far enough . . . I'll find a reason why it's my fault. It's really complicated."

The Acadia girls are most likely to express their anger and outrage at the undeserving privilege and unearned attention of the popular kids in their class, as well as the mean and insensitive ways these kids treat others who have less power or status. Such strong feelings seem not only reasonable and justified, but critically important in a school that espouses meritocracy. It is particularly ironic, then, that Elizabeth does not express anger publicly because "it's not right." While she means to differentiate herself from those who are "mean" to others, she takes away any chance she and her friends might have to stop unjust and hurtful behavior. She and her friends also lose the chance to see the limits of their perceptions and objectifications of these others. Her statement underscores the power of white middle-class feminine conventions to remove girls from their strong feelings, jeopardizing their capacity to see clearly and name the external sources of their anger, and thus ultimately preventing them from engaging with and affecting the world in which they live.

And so, quite unlike the Mansfield girls, the Acadia girls remove their anger from public life, taking it into the underground to be expressed to those they most trust. The "feminist individualism" they voice, as well as the undercurrents of competition in their conversations, contribute to this privatization of strong feelings and opinions, undermining the psychological and political power of collective action.[10]

The Mansfield girls' expressions of desire and sexuality, their directness and toughness, in combination with their close and protective relationships, interrupt any simple notion of white femininity, just as their material desires invite a reconsideration of the complicated relationship between want and racial privilege. The Acadia girls' attraction to idealized notions of feminine perfection and their incorporation of white middle-class conceptions of self and success create a private tension and psychological struggle that also alerts us to the subtle regulation of girls' fantasies. Listening to these two groups of girls talk about themselves, acknowledging the different ways in which their lives are affected by social norms and material conditions, thus reveals the instability and mythologic nature of dominant notions of femininity.

five

Voice and Ventriloquation in Girls' Development

> Wash the white clothes on Monday and put them on the stone heap; wash the color clothes on Tuesday and put them on the clothesline to dry; don't walk barehead in the hot sun; cook pumpkin fritters in very hot sweet oil; soak your little cloths right after you take them off; when buying cotton to make yourself a nice blouse, be sure that it doesn't have gum on it, because that way it won't hold up well after a wash.
>
> JAMAICA KINCAID, "GIRL"

From the age of three or four, sociolinguists tell us, girls tend to shift their speech style depending on whether they are talking to boys or to other girls. According to Amy Sheldon, girls are more likely to use "double-voiced discourse" than are boys; that is, their conflict talk has "a dual orientation in which the speaker negotiates [her] own agenda while simultaneously orienting toward the viewpoint of [her] partner."[1] This capacity to be assertive in the context of relationship is a strength, but Sheldon also notes the value-laden language that others use to interpret gender differences in young girls' talk: "To say that boys are more forceful [that is, better] persuaders hides the important work that mitigation does to further self-assertion in the conflict process."[2] Girls' thoughts, feelings, and actions cannot be separated from their audience—from the relationships that sustain and support them, or from the patriarchal lens through which they are filtered.

Discourse about "appropriately" gendered behavior interlaces children's everyday experiences. Consider, for example, the following story of sexual harassment between poor and working-class six- and seven-year-olds in an all-white, rural primary school in Maine.[3] The principal, a woman of about thirty-five, described the scene to me:

> We had these girls go to a teacher after lunch-time and they were upset, visibly upset. And they said the boys were saying some words to them that were scaring them and they didn't like it . . . The boys started to say, "Well, you're my girlfriend. And I'm gonna marry you and . . . we're gonna have sex." And . . . [a] little girl . . . said, "Oh, I know you. You just want to tie us up and have sex with us." And the little boy went on and on and pretty soon two other boys joined in, until there were . . . four boys . . . and it got pretty aggressive and real loud and pretty soon there were lots of things coming out from all the boys: "Yeah, we're gonna have sex with you," and "Yeah, we're gonna rape you; we're gonna kill you." And "Yeah, 'cause you're our girlfriend." And then one boy said, "I'm gonna put an engagement ring on you 'cause that's what you do when you love someone, but I'm gonna NAIL it on 'til the blood comes out!" And another boy said, . . . "Well, I'm gonna . . . put an ax in your head 'til blood comes out your eyes."

Talking with the children after this incident, the principal became convinced that they did not fully understand what they were saying —did not know, for example, what the word "rape" meant—but were repeating things they had heard elsewhere and knew were powerful. The one little girl who spoke back to the boys said she had overheard junior high students reading the opening scenes from the Stephen King novel *Gerald's Game* on the school bus. The novel begins with a man tying his wife to their bed, enacting his sexual fantasy. The boys said they were repeating comments they had heard on afternoon TV magazine shows like *Hard Copy* and *Current Affair.*

But while they may not have fully understood the words or comprehended the overlay of violence on female-male sexual relationships, the boys and girls evidently understood the incident at the level of feeling. The boys felt powerful using hostile language they knew would strongly affect the girls; the girls, including the more assertive child, felt uncomfortable, frightened, and angry.

A few days after the incident I interviewed the children, and it was clear that the girls, in particular, were still trying to make sense of it. Seven-year-old Melissa struggled to comprehend how her friend Donald, someone "who be's, um, nice to me," would also call her names and even hit her. Her dilemma was solved when she suddenly remembered, with delight, her grandfather's assurance that "if boys chase you then that means that they love you." At the young age of seven, with the encouragement of a grandfather who cares for her and no doubt means well, Melissa has begun to channel her contradictory experiences with Donald into a culturally familiar, acceptable construction of heterosexual romance.

Here is the underside of the "double-voiced expressiveness" that Sheldon celebrates in young girls, an expressiveness born of the internalization of cultural voices steeped in gendered meanings and intentions. These six- and seven-year-olds, taking in voices and images from TV shows, a popular book, and older children—voices and images that are, in Melissa's case, partially supported or explained by a close family member—have re-told and re-enacted such constructions of relationship in their own lives.[4]

In Bakhtin's terms, these children are engaged in the very natural process of *ventriloquation*—a process, that is, "whereby one voice speaks *through* another voice or voice type."[5] Like the ventriloquist's dummy who speaks only the words of the ventriloquist, we speak only the words of others. But unlike the dummy, we struggle to appropriate these words and make them our own. Prior to this moment of appropriation, however, the word does not exist in a neutral and impersonal language (it is not, after all, out of a dictionary that a speaker gets his words!), but rather it exists in other people's mouths, in other people's contexts, serving other people's intentions: it is from there that one must take the word, and make it one's own. And not all words for just anyone submit easily to this appropriation, to this seizure and transformation into private property: many words stubbornly resist, others remain alien, sound foreign in the mouth of the one who appropriated them and who now speaks them; they cannot be assimilated into [her] context and fall out of it; it is as if they put themselves into quotation marks against the will of the speaker. Language is not a neutral medium that passes freely and easily into the private property of the speaker's intentions; it is populated—overpopulated—with the intentions of others. Expropriating it, forcing it to submit to one's own intentions and accents, is a difficult and complicated process.[6]

The words of others enter and become part of the inner dialogue that constitutes the psyche as a result of a difficult and complicated *developmental process* that Bakhtin calls "ideological becoming." "One's own discourse," Bakhtin argues, "is gradually and slowly wrought out of others' words that have been acknowledged and assimilated, and the boundaries between the two are at first scarcely perceptible." Others' words come, quite simply, from the different speaking voices that a child hears in the context of her various social relationships and social interactions—voices engaged in the ongoing dialogue that constitutes the culture in which she lives. A child hears (and interacts with) a multitude of voices: the voice of her mother (as in the case of Kincaid's "Girl"), her father, her grandparents, her teacher, her baby-sitter, her friends, characters and personalities on television, popular musicians, and so forth. Moreover, these voices, more often than not, represent competing points of view. Thus the process of ideological becoming results from an "intense *struggle* within us for hegemony of various available and ideological points of view, approaches, directions, and values."[7]

We hear this inner struggle with differing values and points of view when, during her interview at the end of the year, Jane, now thirteen, recalls how she came to her present views on abortion.

Lyn: Can you tell me about a time when what you were thinking and feeling was not what others were saying and doing?
Jane: Um, on the abortion issue. I think people should be able to have abortions. I think it's legal. But last year someone asked me that question and I said that I think that they should be legal and they looked at me like it was just the weirdest thing anyone had ever said and that I shouldn't think that. Then I decided it was wrong, so I've kind of tried to switch myself over to thinking, "Hey, you shouldn't kill people." But my reasoning was that people can do what they want. They might have to have an abortion because they're too young or . . . because they have diabetes or AIDS or something and they don't want their children to inherit that. And the world is already overpopulated, so I mean it's not very nice, but you don't know the person and their personality and they're not born. So that's what I thought. But every time on TV I saw that people were fighting against abortion and that's all I saw. And so that's what I believed, until I met a friend, Ariel. And she's really outgoing. She dyed her hair fuchsia. She's nice and she thinks the same on a lot of things that I do . . . And she did her Social Studies report . . . on abortion and she asked me what I thought and I said, "Well, I suppose that they shouldn't have them." And she said, "Do you really?" and I said, "Well, no." And she said, "That's what I think, too." And so, now I'm going to stick to my first opinion. I think that they should be able to.
Lyn: People should be able to have the choice?
Jane: Yeah, people should have the choice. Because her father told her—he's a child doctor; he makes sure they're not hurt or beaten by their parents, something like that . . . and he said— Ariel quoted him—and he said that women should have a right to choose what they want to do with their bodies. So I think

that's right, but for a while I thought that I wasn't right and I shouldn't be thinking that because people on TV were against it and all my friends were against it. So I thought I was wrong and I asked my parents what they thought and they thought there shouldn't be. So that pretty much clinched it until I found someone else that thought what I did.

The importance of struggling with another's discourse cannot be overestimated, argues Bakhtin, in understanding how and why a person ultimately comes to her own sense of "ideological consciousness":

One's own discourse and one's own voice, although born of another or dynamically stimulated by another, will sooner or later begin to liberate themselves from the authority of the other's discourse. This process is made more complex by the fact that a variety of alien voices enter into the struggle for influence within an individual's consciousness (just as they struggle with one another in surrounding social reality). All this creates fertile soil for experimentally objectifying another's discourse. A conversation with [another's] word that one has begun to resist may continue, but it takes on another character: it is questioned, it is put in a new situation in order to expose its weak sides, to get a feel for its boundaries.[8]

One also hears this struggle for liberation in the Acadia girls' conversations about people on welfare. We hear their dramatic shifts in voice and feeling as they try on different viewpoints—those of their parents, their teachers, or writers of articles they have read in newspapers and magazines—and we hear their momentary objectification of opposing discourses on the poor. The girls bring these varied perspectives into relationship with their own experiences in school with the popular kids, signaling their attempts to make these views more fully their own, to liberate them from the authority of others' discourse. Their dramatic shifts in opinion signify their experimentation and their struggle, and point to the creative potential of their conversations.

Girls' Development

What begins as boldness and an ability to express a plurality of feelings and thoughts in young girls seems to narrow over time as girls become increasingly pressured at the edge of adolescence to fall in line with the dominant (that is, white, middle-class, heterosexual) social construction of reality. At this edge, girls' childhood experiences strain against words and categories that "stubbornly resist" their appropriation. In other words, girls' experiences, strong feelings, and opinions come up against a relational impasse that constrains possibilities and shuts down their loud voices, a wall of "shoulds" in which approval is associated with their silence, love with selflessness, relationship with subordination and lack of conflict, and anger or strong feelings with danger and disruption.[9] Girls describe how they feel in words that "sound foreign" to them or "remain alien" to their experience but nevertheless exert enormous power, influence, and authority.

Essential to adopting ideals and images of conventional femininity is a process of voice-training whereby adults—parents, teachers, or therapists—invested in dominant cultural values reinforce images of female perfection by encouraging girls to modulate their voices, by admonishing them when they express strong feelings such as anger or when they speak openly or straightforwardly about what they see and hear around them.[10] Many girls move off or silence their voices as they learn that speaking up or speaking out leads to trouble. Others refuse to remain quiet, even though they know that there are consequences for their impertinence. In a qualitative study of forty-eight adolescents from diverse racial and ethnic backgrounds, for example, more than one-half of the girls completed the sentence stem "What gets me into trouble is _____," with phrases like "my mouth or my big mouth." So similar were their words in naming the source of their trouble, the researchers comment, that it was as if they were "repeating a mantra given them by a higher authority."[11]

In order to re-vision and re-voice themselves so that they will blend into cultural images or stories of white middle-class femininity girls are required to move away from the evidence of their senses and onto shifting ground. Ventriloquating conventionally desirable images of femininity, girls' voices become breathy, whispery, and higher pitched before puberty; that is, before there is actually any physiological basis for such changes.[12] They do so even as studies in social psychology find that higher-pitched voices are heard as less competent, less potent, and even less truthful than lower-pitched voices.[13]

"Voice is natural and also cultural," Carol Gilligan explains. "It is composed of breath and sound, words, rhythm, and language. A voice is a powerful psychological instrument and channel, connecting inner and outer worlds. Speaking and listening are a form of psychic breathing. This on-going relational exchange among people is mediated through language and culture, diversity and plurality."[14] Working with girls and women in acting workshops, Kristen Linklater and Normi Noel join Gilligan in exploring the complicated braiding of psychological, cultural, and physiological aspects of voice. Describing the difference between a voice that is "an open channel—connected physically with breath and sound, psychologically with feelings and thoughts, and culturally with a rich source of language— and a voice that is impeded or blocked," they note the connections between physiological changes in voice resonance at the edge of adolescence and social, cultural, and relational contexts that increasingly impede or constrict girls' voices at this developmental juncture.[15]

Moving into the dominant social construction of femininity demands that much of what girls know, feel, and think disappear, or at least that girls compromise what they know about themselves and the world through experience. In this struggle, which girls frequently describe as "coming up against a wall," words and experiences that held particular significance in their early lives come into tension with conventional definitions of femininity that, because they carry the force of the dominant culture, override girls' knowledge or, at least, enforce their public conformity.[16] Thus what has long been deemed a natural shift, an immutable developmental progression as girls adapt to cultural conventions, can be interpreted, from a more critical perspective, as an example of how power constrains and regulates discourse, knowledge, and desire.

Listening to girls thus raises profound questions about what happens when the words of others carry the force of the dominant culture. What is the effect of legitimized, privileged, or valorized discourses, of controlling categories or normative behaviors, on the development of persons who stand outside the dominant cultural frameworks of white, middle-class, heterosexual, and male? How do those on the margins retain voice, engage in genuine, mutual dialogue where they have the possibility of being heard, much less the opportunity to define and redefine the language and assumptions of the status quo?

Caught in the Act

The difficult transformation of public language into private consciousness is most apparent under conditions of struggle; that is, not only when, as Bakhtin suggests, words "stubbornly resist" appropriation, "remain alien," or "sound foreign in the mouth of the speaker," but also when persons actively resist external pressure to appropriate others' words, language, and forms of discourse.[17] Indeed, issues of power are central to a critical understanding of girls' development.

At early adolescence girls speak about, struggle with, and often resist the reconstruction of their experiences. The boundary line between girls' experiences and others' expectations is exposed to view for a brief time as girls negotiate the pressures they feel to re-voice and re-vision their reality. For a time they seem caught between contradictory realities, living the fragmented, homeless lives of double (or triple) agents. Thirteen-year-old Robin, a member of the Acadia group, illustrates the effect of this shift on her sense of self. Asked if there was a time when what she felt and thought was different from what others were saying and doing, Robin echoes other young resisters when she exclaims, "Oh, every day of my life!"[18] Aware of, but adamantly refusing to comply with, what others want, especially from "nice" girls, Robin speaks to the tension between herself and what others in her public school expect girls to be like. In her musings over the course of a two-hour interview she frequently voices her frustration and anger over the difficulty, sometimes the impossibility, of claiming herself against an authoritative discourse of white middle-class femininity spoken to her through many different channels and voices. Adult expectations and reprimands, the rejection of boys, and the distancing of other, more popular girls repeatedly remind her that she is off the trodden path.

Robin's direct voice and implacable nature poke through the glossy veneer of idealized femininity, irritating and confusing her classmates, especially the boys. "Most of my disagreements are with guys," she explains. "I don't know why they get so—they have very short patience with me, the way I dress, what kind of music I listen to, who I hang around with and what I like to do with my spare time." Signifying her refusal to impersonate conventionally feminine ideals by her dyed black hair, oversized plaid shirt, baggy jeans, and mismatched sneakers, Robin describes the frequent anger and verbal abuse she elicits from boys.

Last Friday a guy came up to me in the gym . . . and I happened to be dressed like I am now, and he asked why on earth I dressed like that. I said, "It's comfortable and I like it." He said, "Well . . . I suppose it doesn't matter anyway because you're ugly." And I was just like—I got really mad. I go, like, "Oh yeah, well I'd rather look like me than you." I said, "I'm so sorry I do not fit your image of the perfect woman." And I'm so glad I don't because his girlfriend [said in a high voice]: "Hee, hee, hee. He's so funny." I don't like that kind of girl. I think that's an insult to other girls and making them all look like they're like that. And we should all just turn into a total airhead . . . The first thing that came to mind was a picture of his girlfriend wearing really tight short shorts and "hee-hee-heeing," chewing bubble gum all the time. That bothers me . . . And that really sickens me to—you know, is that what guys are like? Are they that dumb?

Robin's questions are not rhetorical. She, like the other Acadia girls, really wants to know. Are things what they appear to be? Is there room for her—a smart, unconventional girl—somewhere in these relationships with boys? Robin distances herself not only from girls who appropriate and ventriloquate a largely male-constructed image and voice of femininity, but also from this "perfect woman's" counterpart, the "slut":

There was [a] guy that I just met recently [skateboarding] . . . I hadn't known him and . . . I found out he hated my guts. He thought I was a slut or something. I was like, "Why am I a slut?" I never made grotesque comments. I don't throw myself at guys. I don't dress promiscuously. I'm not what most people see as a slutty person. It's just, I was like, "Oh, that's great! What did I do?" Nothing.

Robin's own ideological becoming depends on her struggle with and against the complicated and contradictory voices of conventional femininity that she has heard over the years and that now, at early adolescence, confront her in ever pressing and narrow terms. To remain connected to herself, to claim her personhood, she must distance herself from certain kinds of girls and what they represent. As she sees and understands it, boys' versions of the perfect girl are mindless airheads—they chew bubble gum, speak in high voices, and giggle when they are with their boyfriends; they dress for boys' pleasure, not for their own comfort. Sluts, by contrast, transgress some imaginary line of propriety to make grotesque comments, dress promiscuously, and throw themselves at boys. Robin separates herself from these two kinds of girls in all the ways available to her—her interactions with boys, the social activities she chooses, the clothes she wears, what she reads, how she behaves in school, and by openly disparaging girls like "them." She is not who or what these other girls are; and yet what they are maps onto conventional notions of girls.

Robin's dismissal of these categories of girls, therefore, does not interrupt the classifications themselves. Rather, her rejection entails a kind of "ventriloquistic cross-dressing"—she is an adolescent girl speaking a patriarchal discourse about appropriate behavior for girls and women.[19] Speaking through masculinized voices about ideal femininity, she unwittingly contributes to the stability of narrow feminine ideals and categories; inadvertently she participates in the regulation of girls—and thus of her own—voices, desires, and behaviors. And yet, to move outside these categories—to be neither perfect girl nor slut; to be her complicated, sometimes contradictory and resistant self—means either to occupy a liminal space, misunderstood or rejected by those around her, or to be a "boy."

Robin's fervent desire to be understood "as a person who was skateboarding rather than as a girl skateboarder" is thus layered and complicated. Partly her struggle is about objectification, the refusal, as she puts it, to be "treated as a piece of meat" or to be accepted solely as an ornament or a sexual presence rather than as a human being who happens to be an athlete and a girl. Robin rejects feminine stereotypes that limit her potential. Her high-pitched imitation of the "hee, hee, heeing" girlfriend is a parody of that category of girl and hence an act of critical distance. And yet she struggles with the limits of a language steeped in the denigration of women. For thirteen-year-old Robin, the path toward self-definition is filled with contradictory voices, ideas, and images. Occasionally she finds herself pulling back, questioning her reading of reality, as she did when the boy she met skateboarding called her a slut.

> I was beginning to wonder at that point. I almost quit [skateboarding] because I was wondering, is this really worth it? Or is it worth having guys call me names like that? He just really treated me really bad. I was, I guess, reevaluating all my roles and what I was thinking and I couldn't really decide if these people were really out

to hurt me or they were intimidated by girls who might possibly do something better than them.

The immediate shift Robin makes from the boy's treatment of her to a reevaluation of herself serves to illustrate the dialogic nature of her self-construction and also the psychological impact of such judgments, backed as they are by cultural prescriptions. "I don't know," Robin responds repeatedly when I ask her how she would define herself in her own terms. She seems caught in the moment, caught in the act of interpretation.[20]

Robin's struggle to define herself "as a person" outside the constraints and regulations of conventional femininity is also complicated by a masculinized discourse of adolescence: adolescence, by definition, is a "masculine construct," observes Barbara Hudson, a drama populated by actors such as "the restless, searching teen; the Hamlet figure; the sower of wild oats and tester of growing powers." Hence, she suggests, "any attempts by girls to satisfy society's demands of them *qua* adolescence, are bound to involve them in displaying not only lack of maturity (since adolescence is dichotomized with maturity) but also lack of femininity."[21] Any simple efforts to move easily into the dominant culture thus falter as girls adjust for this incompatibility between femininity and the "normal" course of adolescence. Will girls be "good girls," "bad girls," or "the good kind of bad girl [who] plays by male rules of friendship, risk, danger, and initiative"; that is, will girls be one of the guys?[22]

For Robin this is a pertinent question, since it is not the other girls toward whom she directs her desire for understanding, but the boys. Listening closely to four adolescent girls' "interpretations of the discourses of adolescence, femininity and feminism," Fine and Macpherson heard the construction of similar desires:

Adolescence for these four young women was about the adventures of males and the constraints on females, so their version of feminism unselfconsciously rejected femininity, and embraced the benign version of masculinity that allowed them to be "one of the guys." They fantasized the safe place of adolescence to be among guys who overlooked their (female) gender out of respect for their (unfeminine) independence, intelligence, and integrity. For them, femininity meant the taming of adolescent passions, outrage, and intelligence. Feminism was a flight from "other girls" as unworthy and untrustworthy. Their version of feminism was about equal access to being men.[23]

For these adolescent girls, diverse with respect to race, culture, and class, "the desired Other is one of the guys"; the undesirable are "unworthy and untrustworthy" girls.[24]

Robin, who is younger than any one of these four adolescent girls, is not so settled on these options, although they are spread invitingly before her. She struggles with the possibilities open to her; her anger at the immaturity of boys and disillusionment with their treatment of her give her pause as she hangs back, uncertain who she wants to be with and be like. She is not, by definition, by appearance and self-expression, a "good" girl; she is not, by dress and action, a "bad" girl; and although her desire to be seen as "a *person* . . . rather than as a *girl*" would seem to subvert the possibility of gender solidarity by aligning her with "the good kind of bad girl," that is, with the boys, she is not altogether comfortable with this definition either. She and a small cadre of her close female friends seem to be making their own contradictory and fragmented way. And yet she repeatedly finds herself caught in untenable positions: by rejecting one narrow feminine characterization, she "run[s] the risk of being cast in another unacceptable role from which she must also extricate herself."[25]

In her exploration of girls' misogyny—of "girlfighting and girlfearing"—in a diverse sample of four hundred girls, Sharon Thompson notes how common it is for girls to define themselves against other girls:

Most teenage girls posit an "other girl" when they talk about social and sexual relations. Good girls treat other girls bad; bad girls derogate girls who have a different vice or more stigmatized identity: drugs instead of sex, lesbianism instead of promiscuity, bisexuality instead of lesbianism. Or, other girls are traitors to their gender—two-faces or backstabbers. You have to keep your eye on them all the time. Even those who embrace sexual freedom often take a righteous and divisive line. Their other girls are rigid prudes or teenage mothers.[26]

Thompson found, among a smaller but significant number of girls, a "story of splitting and attaching, distinguishing oneself from most 'other girls,' and simultaneously fixating the need for love on one particular boy or man." Such internal, psychological division, Thompson warns, has social and political implications. Among these girls there was almost no expression of female solidarity. Rather, it was not unusual to find an intense displaced anger, with girls "hating girls, instead of boys or men, for injuries inflicted by boys or men."[27]

Such "horizontal violence," Paulo Freire argues, is tied intimately to the divisiveness brought on by the internalization of the voices of those in dominant power positions.[28] What Thompson refers to as "girls' raging misogyny" is tied intimately to the transformation of publicly sanctioned discourse about girls and women into private consciousness.[29] Girls' ventriloquation of the dominant culture's denigration of femininity and female relationships serves to disconnect them from other girls. It works ultimately to divide them from themselves through self-hate and deprecation, thus threatening to secure their subordinate status within the prevailing social order. As I have argued, however, this process of ventriloquation is by no means simple or fluid—girls often valiantly struggle against such appropriation.

Class Accents

As the Mansfield and Acadia girls discuss themselves and their relationships, talk of other girls and women emerges frequently. These "others," revealed through the girls' gossip and put-downs, serve as a guide to ventriloquized voices of conventional femininity; that is, to patriarchal definitions of the feminine that the girls most fear or reject in themselves.[30]

There is a common belief, expressed repeatedly among the working-class girls, that "other" girls are, by nature, indirect and deceitful, that they talk behind people's backs and have a propensity for breaking confidences. Such girls are "two-faced" and untrustworthy, and make private conversations public out of revenge or to seek attention. Often the Mansfield girls complain, in voices full of anger and disgust, that these are the same girls who are "stuck on themselves," "who think they're the best," who want to be "the center of attention," and who "strut around" all "stuck-up," with "an attitude problem." Such girls will do anything for attention, including lying and stealing other girls' boyfriends, and are, therefore, deceitful and traitorous, perhaps two of the oldest character flaws associated with femininity.

Such associations and opinions instigate perhaps the most clear and striking examples of ventriloquized patriarchal voices: the ways in which the Mansfield girls appropriate sexist, misogynist, and homophobic language to tease or poke fun at one another and, more pointedly, to denigrate those girls, mothers, grandmothers, aunts, and women teachers who they feel have betrayed or hurt them in some way. "She was a bitch," Corrine says of a teacher who treated her badly the day before. Later in the same session she exclaims, "My mother's a cheap ho!"[31] "I called Dawn a 'ho,'" Rachel admits, explaining why she was in trouble with one of her teachers. She and her friend cannot "be together," with another girl, Susan laughingly explains, "not unless she's a lezzie." Like a Greek chorus, the girls shout derogatory comments about other girls and women. Terms like "hos, bitches, lezzies," accompanied by remarks like "Maybe it's PMS," "She's such a cow," or "What a bag," assault those others who the girls feel have let them down.

Such misogynic phrases seem funny to the girls; on the surface they are playful in a threatening sort of way, a linguistic sign of their insider status with the group. Sometimes they are a verbal test of toughness, a way to patrol the boundaries of group behavior or to ensure group loyalty—and also a way to resist middle-class feminine values. When asked why they say these things, they deny that such words mean anything significant. "That's just joking around," Amber protests when Diane asks her if girls' feelings are hurt when they are called "hos." The other girls interrupt one another in their eagerness to dismiss the significance of the word. "Hoe?" they shout in practiced voices. "It's a garden tool!" "It doesn't hurt me," Nina insists. "Everybody does that!" "We just fool around."

The Mansfield girls' put-downs of other girls and women also signal their momentary alignment with dominant views of women. That is, they speak about girls and women in language steeped in a patriarchal history of women's oppression. In this sense, their forms of expression forge an unexamined truce with the prevailing social order that polices the borders of appropriately gendered expression and ultimately situates girls and women, to the degree that they express such "feminine" qualities, in subordinate positions relative to boys and men.

Forswearing their connections to other girls and aligning or bonding with male views of femininity require these girls, if they are to be strong and willful and direct, to distance themselves from anything explicitly feminine. For them this means both vulnerability and bitchiness, but also homosexuality. By using terms like "fag" and "lezzie" to put down others, as they do often, the girls participate in a conventional sex/gender system that normalizes oppressive structures and categories.

Acting tough, talking trash, giving the camera the finger, pushing and pinching one another, and shouting "Shut the hell up!" or "He's a jerk-off!" or "She's a bitch!" invite Bakhtin's questions "Who precisely is speaking, and under what concrete circumstances?" Such actions and discourse self-protectively distance the girls from the traditionally feminine and align them with the observed behavior and discourse of boys and men they know. Talking about "really cool," "really funny" guys at a party, for example, the girls are quick to put down a girl who was, as Stacey explains, "playing hard to get. The bitch." When the boys begin to bet on whether this girl "would do it" with the boy she was with, some of the girls try to join in.

Stacey: Yeah, he goes . . . he said . . . he told her to "come on, I've got five bucks riding on this!"

Susan: No!

Stacey: No, he said that to her. 'Cause him and Charles had a bet.

Rachel: Yeah, they did. And I did too, but I didn't have enough money, so they wouldn't let me bet.

Stacey: Yeah, me neither. I only had eleven cents.

Diane: Well, who was betting who?

Stacey: Charles and Jon. Charles won.

Rachel: He's so nice. He's really cool.

In this instance the girls fully accept the boys' reading of the reluctant girl's refusal to have sex at the party—she is "a tease" and "a bitch"—and identify with their behavior by trying to join in on the joke. They further align themselves with these "cool" boys who were "sitting there swearing in the car," bragging about who "could kick the piss out of" whom, by insisting that they too, as Rachel explains, "swear all the time."

In other instances, the girls struggle to understand the sexual and physical abuse that they have experienced or witnessed, see-sawing between the evidence of their own senses and the perspectives of the abusers. Although fourteen-year-old Donna, who has been physically assaulted by her father, talks in one session about how she learned through counseling that "no one deserves to be hit" and describes her attempts to learn karate "to see if I could protect myself," in another session she explains why she refuses to believe her father's girlfriend when she complains of his abuse. Accepting her father's explanation that his girlfriend deserves what she gets because she lies and is too demanding, Donna tells the story:

He beats her . . . He put her in the hospital once, 'cause she tried saying that he raped her in the hospital bed when he was in there. And I doubt that. I even told her that. He wouldn't do that. He don't rape. He doesn't do that. Anyway, he said that, like when, [she] has long fingernails, you know, and she uses that, she claws him, 'cause when she asks dad something and dad doesn't answer back—he's mad or something—he like walks away and she runs after him and wants an answer from him. And dad, when he gets mad he just walks off, and he wants to deal with it on his own, and she runs after him and tries to get answers and so he got mad and hit her . . . She had a bruise right here (pointing to the side of her face), and a bruise on her forehead and he threw her . . . and she hit the top of the door thing and broke it, broke the door.

In spite of the fact that she herself has been the object of her father's irrational rages, Donna defends him against his girlfriend's charges of rape and ventriloquates his justification of the abuse he delivers. Her description of his girlfriend's battered face carries a subtle "you should see her" awe that serves to idealize her father, who inflicted these bruises with great force, and also to play down his girlfriend's injuries—not only did she ask for it, but she apparently can take it time and again. Unlike her own story of unprovoked abuse and failure to protect herself—the karate lessons, after all, didn't work: "I don't know, I just, my mind went blank every time he hit me anyway; I couldn't remember to use my karate."—this situation allows Donna the opportunity both to present her father as reasonable and his actions justifiable and to portray his girlfriend as vocal and violent; that is, although she is badly hurt, she is not a passive victim in this drama. She, in effect, is not Donna, and this situation is radically different from her own encounters with her father. This difference is important. Distanced from this situation and this woman, Donna is free to admire, to identify with, and to embody her father's power as she tells this story through his voice. Such identification depends on her separation from and denigration of the girlfriend as needy, demanding, and manipulating—that is, as pejoratively, conventionally, feminine.

Whereas the working-class girls sometimes distance themselves from other girls and women on the basis of relational treachery, vulnerability, and dependence, which they see as signs of feminine weakness, the Acadia girls speak in voices that reflect categorical divisions mapped onto white middle-class femininity, predominantly opposing good girls with bad. There is little space between these carefully constructed and policed categories for the Acadia girls to imagine themselves as complicated, whole, interesting young women. They are always in danger, it seems, of being misunderstood, their behaviors and motivations misinterpreted: in wanting to be noticed for their accomplishments they risk being seen as selfish or too self-invested; in expressing strong opinions they risk being viewed as bitches, or worse, as angry feminists.

Whereas the Mansfield girls appropriate misogynic language to ridicule one another and distance themselves from other girls and things feminine, the Acadia girls appropriate historically weighted conceptions of girls and women as superficial, false, and trite to distance themselves from other girls. In Robin's terms, such girls are "mindless airheads," always "hee, hee, heeing," or, as Lydia claims, they are "whiners" and "complainers" always expecting to be the center of attention, or they are deceitful backstabbers who constantly whisper and conspire against one another, especially when there is a possibility of advancing their social standing. Against these "feminine" qualities, the Acadia girls admire and identify with "masculine" characteristics such as independence and autonomy, rationality, creativity, intelligence, and cleverness. And yet they struggle a good deal with the fact that these qualities, when embodied by "nice" girls like themselves, have a different resonance, are less visible or recognizable, are invested with less power, and are more likely to be misread. Here they are caught in a bind. Good girls do not demand things, certainly not recognizability. And yet their longing to break out or to claim their space is palpable. "Boys," Jane explains, are "supposed to be more outgoing and they're supposed to be brighter . . . So far, I would like to be outgoing sometimes, because boys who are outgoing get their way . . . It might be nice," she adds, "to just . . . let it go."

The Acadia girls thus struggle a good deal with the contradictory relationship between the white middle-class feminine voices they take in and the radical individualism they admire and that seems to serve the boys so well. Speaking through conventionally masculine characteristics, they also, by association, denigrate opposing, feminine qualities as mindless, weak, and superficial. By distancing themselves from girls who, they say, are obsessed with appearances and their bodies, who are stupid, deceitful, and fake, the Acadia girls ventriloquate such a gendered polarity.

In this chapter I have considered what it means to ventriloquate and appropriate voices that deform, devalue, or subjugate oneself, or more basically deny whole aspects of one's experience. Ventriloquation can be "a powerful strategy of silencing, of speaking on behalf of another, of disrupting the boundaries of a propertied utterance," argues Elizabeth Harvey, and has long been used in patriarchal culture to mute or shape feminine speaking by calling into question the gender of the voice that speaks and the power (or lack of power) a given voice therefore possesses.[32] Women and girls who speak through patriarchal voices do so in part to appropriate the power these voices have in the world, and yet the voices they speak carry with them the attenuation of female power, both personal and political. Such ventriloquation of conventionally feminine voices thus unwittingly reflects and contributes to a larger cultural silencing of women.

But if girls at early adolescence are aware and struggle so, what keeps this definition of the proper in place and why is it so difficult to resist? Foucault asks and answers this question in his discussion of power:

> If power were never anything but repressive, if it never did anything but to say no, do you really think one would be brought to obey it? What makes power hold good, what makes it accepted, is simply the fact that it doesn't only weigh on us as a force that says no, but that it traverses and produces things, it induces pleasure, forms knowledge, produces discourse. It needs to be considered as a productive network which runs through the whole social body.[33]

Certainly the costs of refusing conventional femininity (the hostility, ostracism, and even violence) as well as the rewards of at least performing such femininity (acceptance, pleasure, a seamless move into the dominant culture, good grades, and promises of security and safety) entice girls, especially white middle-class girls, to embrace such notions of the ideal. In this sense one might ask whether such dominant constructions of femininity might best be construed as "a defense against the frightening possibility of stepping over the gender divide."[34] Do girls and women assert and reassert such idealized images out of suspicion and for fear that they are not true? Do the paranoia of the powerful and the anxiety of the powerless keep such truths in circulation? Or do girls use the construction of "proper" femininity as a protective cover for their power, as a way to safeguard "a different set of desires and organization of pleasure from those that can be articulated at the moment or are sanctioned" by such legitimized fictions?[35]

Girls at early adolescence have a heightened sense of their ill fit with the fictions and fantasies of idealized femininity. Here, at the edge of adolescence, girls seem most acutely conscious of the expectations to conform to ideal femininity and are most likely to express frustration with and resist demands placed on them. The contradictions girls live and breathe during this time arouse anxiety, anger, and outrage, and explain their preoccupation with interpretation, with hypocrisy and betrayal, with fraudulence in relationships. Their feelings of displacement and confusion are indications of this disease. Anger, in particular, is an indication of the pull of convention or the ever-tightening regulation of girls' thoughts and feelings.

For Bakhtin, words and language always come with certain meanings attached: "There are no neutral words and forms—words and forms that can belong to 'no one,' " he argues.

Language has been completely taken over, shot through with intentions and accents . . . All words have the "taste" of a profession, a genre, a tendency, a party, a particular work, a particular person, a generation, an age group, the day and hour. Each word tastes of the context and contexts in which it has lived its socially charged life.[36]

The language of the Mansfield and Acadia girls has the "taste" of their generation and age group, but also of their gender, their race, and their respective social classes. The people and opportunities they have experienced, as well as the voices they have taken in and speak through, give their language a distinct flavor. Given their different social locations, similar words and concepts such as femininity, relationship, anger, and aggression hold distinct meanings and intentions, and their struggles to define themselves draw from the orchestration or interplay of quite different voices and images. In the next chapter, I focus more closely on these different meanings and intentions, particularly as they inform girls' creative resistance to idealized femininity.

six

Resisting Femininity

It's too bad that I have to [bleach my hair and look good] to get my anger accepted. But then I'm part of an evolutionary process. I'm not the fully evolved end.

COURTNEY LOVE, LEAD SINGER, HOLE[1]

Most recent accounts of girls' development emphasize their capitulation to cultural ideals of white middle-class feminine behavior and appearance. Such portrayals are too simple and too pessimistic. They imply that girls inevitably fall victim to media representations of ultra-thin bodies, and that their voices are silenced by the sheer force of a monolithic sexist culture. They suggest that most girls give up and give in without a struggle, and that those who do not are somehow inherently different from other girls, possessing a unique resilience. And they imply by their broad, descriptive strokes that all girls have the same experience, encounter the same culture and the same pressures, and respond in the same ways.

We have already seen that such *simplicity* does not do justice to the gradual, complicated, and very difficult process of ideological becoming; the different ways girls struggle against voices that endorse silence over outspokenness, passivity over active resistance, a pleasing ignorance over knowledge of the complexity and difficulty of lived experience, and weakness over physical strength and aggressiveness. In arguing against such *pessimism* I now focus on the subtle and creative strategies of resistance that the Mansfield and Acadia girls employ in the face of pressures to not know and not speak—

the ways they play with, in, and around the boundaries of "appropriate" expression to disrupt the social construction of gender and
to invent spaces and possibilities for themselves. This focus on resistance does not deny the power of dominant cultural expectations of
femininity on girls' sense of themselves. On the contrary. But it does
give back to girls the power of their *response,* the deep feelings, the
frustration and anger, the cleverness, and the potential for a different
outcome that is rightfully theirs. Thus, while ventriloquation can be
a powerful tool for silencing, it can also be a process of creation,
holding within it the potential to contest conventional categories and
frameworks, offering up new discourse and language.

Early adolescence constitutes a critical period for possibility and
potential.[2] Girls' struggles with the pushes and pulls of often contradictory voices telling them who, as young women, they are or should
be, provide an opening in the life cycle where the incongruity
between the personal or experiential and the "externally authoritative" comes into focus and where the processes of ideological becoming are salient and pronounced.[3]

In their struggle with different conceptions of what it means to be
female, adolescent girls destabilize the categories of girl and woman,
revealing them to be what Judith Butler calls "structures of impersonation." They expose the fact that gender is "a kind of imitation
for which there is no original," a phantasmatic idealization of what
a woman is supposed to be in a given culture.[4] In their resistance to
increased attempts to regulate or train their voices and actions, girls
at this developmental juncture call attention in different ways to this
idealization, and to the demands and costs of female impersonation.
Their strong feelings and their questions are disruptive of the way
things "naturally" go, and so are anxiety-provoking for those who
like things the way they are.

Renegade Voices

The Acadia and Mansfield girls' struggles reveal the complex relationships between discourse and power, language and domination.

They also reveal what bell hooks calls the possibility of "outlawed tongues, renegade speech."[5] "Like desire," hooks claims, "language disrupts, refuses to be contained within boundaries. It speaks itself against our will, in words and thoughts that intrude, even violate the most private spaces of mind and body . . . Words impose themselves, take root in our memory against our will."[6] The Mansfield girls find strength in the renegade voices and outlawed tongues of those who refuse to be denigrated or made invisible by the authoritative language, dominant categories, and expectations of femininity. These working-class girls convey their parents' mistrust of and disrespect for any authority derived solely from material wealth or status, and reiterate their parents' stubborn refusal to be dismissed, as well as their predilection for expressing strong opinions directly and openly. For example, according to Susan, her courage to speak out and openly criticize the way the school is run and the values it espouses "comes from my parents. They always taught me if I had something to say, just say it."

Echoing their parents and other adults in their community, the Mansfield girls resist middle-class values and notions of femininity endorsed at their school. Speaking through their fathers and mothers, many of whom work more than one part-time job, the girls talk of the practical necessity of hard work and their willingness to do menial jobs and endure long hours of physical labor to achieve their dreams of having enough. Qualities fostered at home such as toughness, boldness, and straightforwardness often label them as difficult and disruptive girls at school, even while they connect them with one another, their families, and their community. Reprimands from teachers and administrators for such behavior, in turn, invite anger from their parents. Indeed, a few of the girls' mothers are well known at the Mansfield school for their support of their children's right to protect themselves physically or to fight for a just cause, and have been to the school a number of times in their daughters' defense. The girls openly admire their mothers for both their physical and their emotional toughness, qualities they themselves imitate.

Indeed, the girls' pride becomes most apparent when they speak of their mothers' belief in self-protection and the defense of those weaker or less powerful than they, and when they invoke their mothers' devotion to the family, their sense of humor, and their beliefs about what it means to be a woman. Other women, too—aunts, cousins, and friends—embody and give voice to the possibility for an economically successful, healthy, contented life against the dire predictions they read in many of their teachers' faces.

Over the course of the year, Diane Starr provides a language and course of action for the girls to resist unfair school practices. The girls take seriously Diane's bold commitment to them, a commitment which interrupts the prevailing discourse about these girls as difficult or "stupid," and which complicates also the girls' sometimes too simplistic descriptions of all teachers and all administrators as uncaring, unpredictable, and unjust. Channeling the girls' strong feelings and opinions into constructive avenues, Diane facilitates what becomes a formidable group of resisters over the course of the year.

Renegade voices from diverse sources thus take root in the Mansfield girls' minds and bodies. Their oversized t-shirts, baggy shorts, and the slang expressions they use, read negatively in one light, also loosely identify them with the boldness, resistance, and marginalization of black rappers they see on MTV, particularly their favorites, Salt 'n' Pepa. And too, these white adolescent girls play with and appropriate the sexualized audacity of Salt 'n' Pepa. Taken in and taken on by these white working-class girls, such voices, gestures, and ways of dressing become highly contradictory, heightening their resistance to white upper-middle-class feminine ideals of niceness and sexual purity, as well as their tension with the relentless expressions of material abundance relayed through television—particularly the MTV shows the girls watch, such as *The Real World, House of Style,* and the popular but short-lived *My So-Called Life.*[7] Such tensions among voices and viewpoints open the Mansfield girls to creative possibilities, alternative values, feelings, and thoughts, and also give voice to longings and desires that contrast sharply with their material realities.

The Mansfield girls occupy that liminal space between childhood and adulthood where intentions are questioned and meanings are indeterminate. In their struggle for personal truth and self-definition, they expose and wrestle with the contradictions, limitations, and hypocrisies in their lives. In their anger, expressed throughout the interviews and group sessions, they react stubbornly to the constraints that white middle-class femininity, indeed, the traditional category "girl" or "woman," places on them, and to the frustrations they experience as they search for words to speak what they know.

There is, in this struggle, the possibility of creative alternatives, the possibility that the languages they inherit and voice can be "possessed, taken, claimed as a space of resistance."[8] Within the comfort and intimacy of their group sessions, for example, such alternatives to the dominant discourse emerge in the way the Mansfield girls interrupt conventional meanings and definitions of femininity, or playfully reappropriate such words as "slut" or "ho," and also in the way they collectively question their middle-class women teachers' interpretations of their experiences and behaviors.

But these girls struggle to know and trust these openings when they are in the public arena of school, where their potentially creative moves, born of the interface of two disparate and sometimes contradictory realities, risk misunderstandings and confusion. Their distrust of their teachers and the lessons promoted in school sits uncomfortably beside their desire for adult love and approval and for the future successes that such lessons, well learned, promise. Against such contradiction the Mansfield girls publicly voice their anger and frustration, distancing their teachers from the intimate group space that is creatively their own.

The Acadia girls, too, occupy this liminal reality; they, too, struggle against the gendered boundaries pressing upon them. But unlike the Mansfield girls, they embrace their education as the medium for refusal and resistance. The ease with which they manipulate the conventions of language speaks to their comfort with, indeed their pleasure in, the privileged middle-class world of school they occupy. Experiencing the limits of "appropriate" speech and behavior, they create new, unofficial ways of expressing themselves. Robin, for example, introduces new words, as yet unpopulated with the intentions and meanings of the dominant culture, as a way to express her strong feelings and to carve out room for those pieces of her experience that are unfit for the public world of her classroom: "Teachers would be horrified by my opinions," she suggests. "They are very descriptive and colorful—even purple." "Purple," to Robin and her friends, means

> kind of really open. It's really flat out kind of sleazy. You know, not something too many people would like to hear . . . colorful in a way. I mean it definitely gets attention, but sometimes negative attention. A lot of times people don't want to hear it. It might offend somebody . . . I have a lot of fun with the guys that would say really nasty stuff, and I'll make some smart little retort . . . and it's like, "ROBIN O'BRIAN!" If you can talk like that, so can I!

Robin's "purple" language allows her to have "fun" with her passionate feelings and to interrupt notions of her as a nice, sweet, white middle-class girl. By using this language to shock the boys in particular, she disturbs the boundaries of "normal" gendered expression. In doing so, she claims a new space; her intent, it seems, is less to be like the boys than to be unlike the girl others imagine her to be.

Both groups of girls know the power of words to affect their teachers and their peers. But while the Mansfield girls appropriate socially unacceptable terms and endow them with their own meaning, the Acadia girls create new words. And while the Mansfield girls speak a "double-voiced discourse," simultaneously ensuring a level of intimacy and trust with their friends and keeping their teachers at a distance, they often do so loudly and directly. The Acadia girls, by contrast, tend to cultivate their creative language and shocking personas among themselves, in the active underground.

Although Robin does not bring her strong feelings or purple language into the public world of the school, her subterranean expressions hold a place for another identity, for another Robin. Anger, though not often seen above ground, is critical to such a disruption of the ideal, to such possession and reclamation. Throughout her interview, thirteen-year-old Robin keeps her anger focused. Anger is a justified emotion that she knows well: "I express [anger] in my writing and in my art and stuff like that. And in my general personality," she admits. "I mean I express a lot of anger at society and everything because a lot of this is—a lot of what makes me mad is a society that ideals the perfect woman. It really makes me mad."

For Robin and her classmates, white middle-class girls living in a postmodern world, "the picture . . . of what the good life for a woman consists in" is no longer a given that over-determines their life-course.[9] Although such indeterminacy creates situations where these girls find themselves moving between categories and, as Robin says, "re-evaluating all my roles and what I was thinking," their anger serves as a kind of touchstone, a sign that something is wrong or off in the relational surround.[10] While Robin is sometimes shaken by the intensity of others' reactions to her "difference," her anger moves her to question, to respond, and to judge others' attempts to define her in ever narrower terms.

As with the other Acadia girls, much of Robin's anger is directed at expectations that she will embody dominant white middle-class fictions about femininity; much of her resistance is against being regulated and constrained by these fictions. In these moments of struggle, Robin calls on other voices, "outlawed tongues" that have "taken root in her memory." The voice of her mother, who sometimes "thinks I'm too opinionated," but who nonetheless listens to and supports Robin, allows her daughter's "weirdness"—her dyed hair, unusual dress, "multiple personalities," and "imaginary friends" ("It helps with acting and everything," she explains); voices from the different cultures she traveled to when her mother was married to a military man; the voice of her anti-establishment uncle, who is "really, really funny," who "paints," and who defends her actions to her parents when she wanders too far off the beaten path.

Against the conformist voices of many of her classmates, the "wannabes" and the "posers," Robin hangs on the margins with her friends and listens to the "unusual music" of Prince, John Lennon,

and Kurt Cobain; against boys' desires that she be appropriately sub-
missive and attentive, she draws from "tough women" like Janice
Joplin and Courtney Love, who she claims is "a very strong person.
She's very talented, you know. She hasn't free-loaded off her [late]
husband's fame or anything; she's just a strong person." Against the
constraints of "nice and feminine" voices, she draws from the bolder
images on MTV and voices from magazines like *Skateboarder 90*,
where, she says, she picks up "good views of the world," views that
are "insightful" and "candid." She listens to the voices of friends
who, like her, claim their difference, and to the older actors in the
city theater group to which she belongs. She listens eagerly to the
outlaw voice of a woman teacher who is funny and eccentric, sometimes embarrassingly original, but "cool," who "doesn't lie to us. She
tells us the truth."

Like Robin, the other middle-class girls adapt to their own intentions a language constructed to serve the interests of more powerful
others. In their certainty of social place and simple ease of movement
they underscore their privilege, for such successful play and manip-
ulation necessitate an insider's understanding of the rules of the
game. Their creative resistance, too, hints at their astute observations
and understandings of the thin line between what is appropriate and
acceptable and what is out of bounds.

In some cases, as Robin illustrates, being a girl who speaks like a
boy itself creates new accents and possibilities, but more often these
girls delight in disturbing expectations and meanings: they look
words up in the dictionary then break down or reconfigure their
original meanings until, in their transformed context, they mean
nothing at all. During a conversation about the derogatory names
that popular boys call them, for example, Jane jumps up and grabs
the dictionary to look up the word "skid." The definition causes her
to shriek with laughter:

Theresa: Is it funny?
Jane: Kind of, in the way that they use it. It's a log or plank for
  supporting something above ground [*everyone laughs*] . . . Any

device that slows up or retards movement . . . or the act of skid-
ding, slide . . .
Lydia: We can tell them, "Oh, you mean a plank?"
Jane: "You're calling me a sad plank?"
Lydia: "You're calling me a sad sliding movement?"

Subverting language with language, outwitting the popular kids at
their own game, the Acadia girls signify their cultural and class privilege through their power to interpret more "appropriately" or
"correctly"—and also, then, to undermine—social conventions. Subverting power from the "inside," they are backed by their families,
friends, and at least some of their teachers. Their fluency in the meanings and terms of white middle-class experience allows them to
manipulate and ultimately reject the very language that would define
and contain them.

In this way the Acadia girls question and resist expectations of
what it means to be a girl. "I don't want to be just like anyone,"
Kirstin insists. "I want to be myself." She knows that this struggle
brings her into conflict with "people who have a hard time dealing
with changes," who "have a grudge against women having power
. . . because when they were young, women were lower and they've
just remembered that way."

Against different expectations and pressures and in quite different
ways, the Mansfield and Acadia girls create space in language and
culture for alternative versions of themselves. Experiences of struggle, ambiguity, and contradiction reveal the differing identities these
girls try on and sometimes embrace. Their ability to play and experiment allows for movement between categories, and their percep-
tiveness and anger, as well as their desire for personal space and self-
protection, motivates them to shift about, to experiment, to resist,
and at times to mirror what others desire and want from them. Whatever else these girls are, they are not easily indoctrinated with cultural
prescriptions. On the contrary, their responses to the pressures they
experience from different people give their lives the feel of creative,
active performance.

Female Impersonation

During a seemingly ordinary gathering one autumn afternoon, four white working-class girls illustrate the fictions of idealized femininity and also the failure of such fictions to define or contain them. After some pushing and much laughing, the girls excitedly arrange themselves in front of the video camera. "How would you describe the ideal girl?" Diane begins. The room is animated and the discussion moves at rapid-fire pace. Amber, a small, tough twelve-year-old, is the first to answer: "OK. The ideal girl is very pretty . . ." Stacey, also twelve, slim and herself conventionally pretty, immediately points to herself and interjects, "Me."

Amber: Talented—
Stacey [smiling, with a look of false modesty]: Me, again.
Amber: Smart, everybody likes her, everybody . . . [*Stacey shrugs her shoulders, throws up her hands, as if to say "Me, again."*] That's about it.
Diane: What do you mean by pretty?
Amber: Pretty, beautiful, good-looking. Long hair. I don't know. Pretty eyes. Nice figure [*Donna and Amber look at Stacey accusingly*].
Stacey: My idea of a perfect girl is somebody who's tall and pretty, and they have, like, perfect hair and perfect skin. They get good grades. Not afraid to make mistakes and stuff.
Diane: Does anyone know anyone like these perfect people? You guys know anybody like this?

At this question the girls look at one another. "No." "No." "No," they say in low voices. Diane continues, "Have you ever seen anybody like this?" The girls shake their heads; they have not. "Does this person exist?" Amber is certain she does "somewhere in the world"; maybe she is "not perfect, but close to perfect," she determines. The others, however, are not so sure, though they think they might like to become someone like this. "I already am," Stacey interjects again. "Just kidding."

Perhaps in response to this last comment, Amber continues.

Amber: I know someone who's really pretty, but her attitude is blown way out of proportion . . . is right out of it . . . Yeah, major attitude problem.

Stacey: Snobby.

Patti: Yeah, people who have attitudes . . . Nosy.

Diane: What do you mean, like stuck up?

Stacey: Yeah, two-faced.

Donna: They don't keep secrets . . .

Amber: She's accusing . . .

Donna [says aloud to everyone, but looks at Patti pointedly]: You can tell them anything and they give you good advice. You can trust them . . . I don't know.

Diane: So now we're getting a different picture of the perfect girl. Not so much looks.

Amber: Personality plays a big part of it.

Donna: You have to be able to trust them . . . A person that doesn't take over . . . in a group.

Stacey: Oh, yeah. They are trying to be the center of attention.

At this point Patti, at age eleven one of the youngest in the group, interrupts: "No one's actually perfect. I'd wanna be different than everybody else." But her comment is lost in a hum of debate, not about whether the girls want to be different from others, but about how they wish they could be different from who they are. Stacey begins in earnest: "I wish I was skinnier. A lot! I wish I could lose at least ten pounds." Amber concurs, "At least twelve or fifteen pounds!" To this fourteen-year-old Donna, tall and very thin, laments, "I only weigh 102." As the conversation turns inward and the girls murmur in low voices to one another about the ideal weight, Patti, the only one of the girls who is not small or thin, looks down. Sitting away from the other girls, she visibly pulls herself out of the conversation.

Diane: So what would be the ideal weight?

Donna: Eighty.

Stacey [in a definitive tone]: The ideal weight is 110.

Amber: One hundred and ten is NOT the ideal weight! I weigh 110! I should weigh at least 85.

Diane: Who says you should weigh 85?

Amber: I do! Look how short I am! I should *weigh* 85!

Stacey: I want to weigh between 105 and 110.

Donna: I would like to weigh 122.

Stacey: I think everyone wants to lose weight no matter what. Everybody wants to be better and lose weight.

Diane: No matter *what* your weight?

Stacey: Yeah. No matter what your weight.

Amber: Well, I'm always trying to be better. Taller. Skinnier.

Stacey: Well, I don't know, I could be . . . I could be happier.

Amber: If I was taller and skinnier.

Diane: You think being taller and skinnier would make you happier?

Amber: Oh, definitely.

As the girls continue to argue about how much they should weigh and how tall they should be, Donna pulls her right foot up on her chair seat to tie her shoe. This ordinary act has the unlikely effect of shifting both the tone and the substance of the conversation. It is as though Donna's movement signals something humorous in the exchange that has just taken place. What began as sincere and serious suddenly turns to a sort of theater of the absurd: "I want bigger feet," Amber says a bit too emphatically. "I want smaller feet!" Stacey exclaims. The girls laugh; Patti's face lights up as she rejoins the group. Diane decides to continue the new mood:

Diane: I want straight hair.

Stacey: I want curly hair.

Patti: I wish I had smaller feet.

Diane: Unfortunately, I gain a shoe size every time I get pregnant.

Stacey: Then I'm never going to get pregnant!

As the conversation turns to who has "big clown feet" and "shoes that look like hot dogs," the girls break from their orderly row of chairs. Amber jumps up and moves toward the camera. "I want to get closer. I want to get closer!" she exclaims, symbolizing, it seems, her desire to shatter the distance between her and the image she has projected. At this the entire group jumps in front of the camera, first putting their faces up close, then hopping on one foot, holding onto one another in order to keep their balance as they raise their feet toward the camera lens in a kind of clumsy chorus line.

Stacey: See my feet? They're all my feet!
Diane: Are they clown feet?
Stacey: Yes, these are my clown feet. Smell!

The girls shout to the camera, "These are mine! These are mine!" In the background Donna and Amber hug. In an exaggerated manner the girls then compare their heights. Standing back to back, they laugh and shout, "Who's taller?" "Am I taller? I hope not!" Amber pushes in front of everyone and says directly to the camera: "Ain't I short? I'm only 4′11."" The girls, laughing, compare themselves with one another and then with Diane, who has joined them in front of the camera. "What about me! What about me?" they shout, laughing uncontrollably. As the drama ends, Patti, who has taken Diane's place behind the camera, announces, "You are watching Channel Five News!"

Four different voices converge initially to create an image of the "perfect girl" recognizable to anyone who opens the pages of a teen fashion magazine: beautiful, tall, long hair, perfect skin, pretty eyes, nice figure. This girl must also be talented and get good grades; she is humble, modest, and liked by everybody, with a personality to match her looks. That these girls do not know or have not actually seen anyone like this does not dissuade them from expressing their desire to be like her. She is the standard against which others, quite literally, are measured, or so it would first appear—accusatory looks say that either you have come too close or you have swayed too far from her likeness. That dissonant voices are lost in the group construction of this image—Patti's wish to be different from the ideal, for example, and Donna's desire to weigh more rather than less—speaks to its potential to control their collective imagination.

And yet even as they speak, the limits and the absurdity of this ideal are communicated among the girls through their body movements and facial expressions. As they talk with great seriousness about trust and loyalty, about always being nice, about having a good attitude and not demanding attention, envy, competition, irritability, and signs of mistrust and betrayal seep into the spaces between them. Their bodies convey what is not directly addressed or acknowledged: the "psychic excess" that falls outside the narrow confines of such an ideal.[11]

Thus while the dialogue among Donna, Patti, Stacey, and Amber is ostensibly about their desire to imitate narrow conventions of white middle-class femininity, they simultaneously signify their inevitable failure and persistent refusal to do so. What falls outside the ideal, that which is and can never be fully expressed inside its boundaries, erupts within the intervals of the girls' gestures and interactions.[12] At the height of intense debate, an unremarkable, barely discernible act threatens to reveal what had seemed so true and possible and intensely important to be an illusion—indeed to be farcical and ridiculous.[13]

The girls' consistent failure to approximate the ideal thus provides an opening that threatens to reveal the perfect girl for who she is: a "phantasmic ideal" of feminine identity.[14] The potential of this threat to be disruptive or subversive depends on the girls' relationships—on their attention and responsiveness to one another in this key moment. Indeed, the association between Donna's tying her shoe and the girls' heightened mood ignites a dramatic shift in relationship. As the girls' concerns about beauty elevate to the level of parody, their collective voices gather momentum and their expressions toward one another change. Gone are the accusatory looks and the argumentative voices. Their wariness and defensive postures vanish as they jump from their seats, wrap their arms around each other, and move together. They are at once raucous, active, funny, loud, and loving—they are not, as it were, a "pretty" sight. Now the camera, rather than other girls or Diane, becomes the audience and witness to their performance; they are, in a sense, in this together, undivided, and from this group display comes their power to redirect and redefine the terms of the situation.

The significance of this collective, relational act cannot be overstated, since by definition the ideal girl is isolated in her perfection. By comparison, all other girls are deficient, and so she elicits the envy, competition, and disloyalty commonly associated with girls' and women's relationships. In their initial construction of this ideal, the girls too are separate: they are bodies in a row facing the camera, each concerned with comparing herself with the image. The fiction of the feminine ideal, in this sense, serves to divide girls psychically and socially, to disconnect them from themselves and from one another. Only when this fiction is disrupted and made ridiculous do the girls move together.

According to Judith Butler, the feminine ideal, constitutive of a compulsory sex/gender system, "is always in the process of imitating and approximating its own idealization of itself—and failing." Such "repetition," Butler argues, "is the way in which power works to construct the illusion of a seamless . . . identity." And yet, "it is this constant need for repetition that points to the very instability of the ideal, reveals it to be an imitation, an illusion, always at risk of coming undone—for what if it fails to repeat, or if the very exercise of repetition is redeployed for a very different performative purpose?"[15]

In one scene after another these working-class girls disrupt the repetition, and thus the controlling power, of the conventional feminine ideal. By elevating it to the level of parody or farce, or by dramatically shifting from identity to identity, they allude to the instability of the ideal itself, attenuating its power to regulate or contain them.

In another session, Corrine responds to Diane's request that she settle down by sitting with a flourish: dramatically crossing her legs, folding her hands in her lap, pursing her lips, and cocking her head. In the perfect parody of a proper lady, at once sincere and ridiculous, she looks wide-eyed into the camera, feigning rapt attention. In another session, when a boy pokes his head into the classroom, Susan, her face red with anger, yells, "Tommy, get out!" then turns to the camera, smiles, and says sweetly, "Thank you." Through such shifts in identity the Mansfield girls reveal to the camera—to Diane and to me—the girl they understand to be the feminine ideal: physically controlled and emotionally contained, compliant, innocent, cooperative, attentive, always nice and sweet and polite, positive, upbeat, and sincere.

These girls clearly choose when and for whom to perform this particular character. Stacey, for example, shifts from her usual self-assured voice to a tentative, uncertain waver as she reenacts a scene with her school counselor; Rachel reveals a sudden look of wide-eyed innocence when Diane confronts her about her swearing. During one session an intense conversation about anger and physical abuse hangs in the air when a teacher unexpectedly enters the classroom and asks to know what the girls are talking about. Almost simultaneously, the girls' facial expressions lighten, their voices rise, the cadence of their speech quickens, and without missing a collective beat, the conversation shifts, in well-rehearsed form, to a review of their earlier discussion of the "ideal girl." "I think the ideal girl is someone who gets all straight A's," Brianna begins. And the others follow suit: "And is a popular kid in school," and "gets a lot of boyfriends," and "never does anything wrong."

Although the perfect girl has made her appearance, in this last instance, on two levels—she is both character and subject-matter—the girls soon signal their animosity toward her. Since this particular teacher is one of their favorites, she is invited to join them in their resistance. In a few moments the girls, Diane, and their teacher are laughing, as together they make a farce of "her" presence: they wonder aloud if the ideal girl has "nose hairs," if she looks "like a Barbie doll," if she has "big boobs." Here again, the Mansfield girls reveal their psychic and social distance from the regulatory fictions of white middle-class femininity. Here, too, they reveal their desire to share this critical distance with women they trust.

These parodies, performances, and transformations into sweet, nice girls reveal the Mansfield girls' collective awareness of the expected feminine ideal and their understanding of the power of such an identity for the right audience—very often their teachers and other school authorities, as well as the camera, since they know I will be watching. Their sarcasm and animosity reflect their anxiety around this ideal and what their failure to meet it might suggest about them. At the same time, they reject the authority of the ideal by poking fun at those who most resemble her. Speaking in syrupy, sing-song falsetto voices, moving their bodies to imitate stiff, controlled postures, for example, they ventriloquate and perform their middle-class women teachers and administrators. "Be nice," Rachel sarcastically warns the other girls; "Respect the talker," Susan says in a "proper" tone, hands neatly folded in her lap. "Thank you for your honesty," Amber mimics in a high, sweet voice.

Perhaps in defense of the feelings of anger, confusion, and disappointment such voices arouse, these working-class girls also perform identities dramatically different from this conventional ideal. Resistant, oppositional voices of toughness and invulnerability disrupt the categories and fictions of white middle-class propriety promoted in their school. As they do with their teachers, the girls take great pleasure in shocking Diane and me with these voices and personas, with their language, gestures, and behavior. In one session, Rachel looks into the camera and gives the finger, stopping only when, laughing, she registers the surprise on Diane's face. In another, the girls hit and swear at one another, calling each other "ho's" and "bitches" until, uncomfortable, Diane intercedes:

Diane: So you guys can call each other mean names and everything, and you're still trusting friends?
Brianna: Yeah.
Nina: See, I just called her a "bitch" and she goes, "Fuck you."
Diane: And that's a friend?
Brianna [*hitting Nina on the leg*]: See, she's my friend.

Nina: Yeah. We just fool around [*Nina and Brianna exchange ever harder hits*].

Diane: So where's the turning point? When do you guys finally get fed up?

Nina: Until it hurts . . . But if it starts hurting, then I just punch her once and she starts crying.

Diane: And that's a friend?

Nina: Yep.

The girls' expressions of invulnerability, their raucous behavior, their swearing, and their tales of drinking and fighting seem at times to be performances for our benefit, a way to distance themselves from who they believe we are and what they think we might want, or perhaps to exaggerate who they think we expect they are. But perhaps more than anything else, the girls' heated arguments and debates among themselves reveal the parameters of the feminine ideal, not only what it requires of them and their relationships, but also their anxiety and rage at the ways it justifies unfairness and exclusion. Shifting in and out of their desire and disdain for perfection and idealized relationships, challenging one another at the level of experience, they bring into bold relief what such fictions promise and also what they demand: the level of not knowing or denial needed to operate as though the ideal were real and therefore possible.

Often it is Amber's voice of reality and experience that interrupts the other girls' collective attempts to envision idealized relationships. As the girls launch into a discussion of the ideal boy one day, Amber's refusal to play causes a disturbance. An ideal boy, the girls begin, is "good-looking" and has a "nice personality." He is "sweet, cute," and "has a nice body," and though he doesn't have to be rich, he "at least has to have some money to go out and get you a Happy Meal." Most important, however, a nice boy would not, as Nina explains, "pressure you" to do something "you don't want to do." There are murmurs of agreement among the girls.

But Amber, annoyed with these answers and their implication of feminine passivity, wants a more complicated discussion, one that includes the reality of her own desires and experience. In a barely audible voice from the back of the room she ventures a different view, but recoils at the way her desire sounds when dropped, untranslated, into the ongoing discussion: "Well, I like that. I like that."

Diane: Now wait . . . What Amber?
Amber: Nothin'.
Diane: You like a boy that pressures you?
Amber: No.
Diane: Does anybody agree with Nina on the boy that pressures you? Has anybody been pressured by a boy?
Amber: Well, it depends on what they pressure you on.
Diane: Well, pressure you on anything.
Donna: I have.
Amber: Well, if it's something not bad, that's all right.
Diane: What could a boy pressure you into that's not bad?
Amber: I don't know. I'm stupid.
Diane: No you're not.
Amber: I don't know.
Donna: I agree with Nina 100 percent.
Nina: It's not nice to be pressured. It makes you all nervous with the guy and stuff.
Donna: Because I've been pressured before and it's not fun.
Amber: Yeah, it is.

Amber cannot voice her desire or her experiences of sexuality in the terms of this discussion. Her attempts to articulate her experiences trip over the framework within which the other girls and Diane are working—conventionally gendered dichotomies of good and bad, pure and dirty, innocent and knowing, subordinate and dominant—a framework, she knows, that renders her confused, "stupid," and incoherent. And yet she defensively insists on interrupting the romance ideal by alluding to the reality and complexity of her relationships with boys, much to the increasing annoyance of the others. When the other girls all agree that a boy who pressures a girl must not respect her, Amber is not so sure: "Maybe," she says. "It depends." When the girls unanimously agree that they know when a boy is insincere, Amber disagrees. "No," she says, "you can't tell." When the girls divide over whether they would go back to a boy who cheated on them, Amber is more cautious. Again, she insists, "It depends on the situation."

Amber moves around the periphery of the group this day, disturbing the other girls, insisting on a complex reality that includes knowledge and fun, desire and danger, sometimes speaking forcefully and loudly and sometimes, in response to the others' romantic imaginings, sounding like that small voice in the back of your head that says in a tone of disbelief, "Oh, come on! You've got to be kidding!" However she responds, the girls cannot easily continue their fantasy in her presence; Amber relentlessly reminds them that they have left the real world of boys and relationships that she occupies and that they at least know about, even if they do not experience it themselves.

Diane: Why is it so hard to say no to these boys?
Donna: It's not hard for me, because I say no . . . I just say no. Because if you're not ready then . . . people say . . . "Wait until the perfect time; wait until you're ready," you know, "and it'll be the most romantinist thing [others laugh, Donna smiles, embarrassed, then laughs] that you've ever gone through."
Amber [snorts]: Romantinist thing?
Donna: I think you should wait until you're ready . . . because you're going to hate it if you're press——. Like if, you're gonna hate it if you do it now and not—
Susan [sarcastically]: Amber, What do you think?
Amber: I don't think shit. Shut up.
Diane: Do you get angry when a boy pressures you or do you feel bad when a boy pressures you?
Donna: I feel—
Amber: Normal.

Donna: Like it's my fault. I do . . . Because you say no, and they get mad at you.

Brianna: My favorite boy is someone that is sweet, cute . . . rich . . . romantic . . . that's all . . . and has a car.

Diane: What if a boy with all that pressures you . . . is he still an ideal boy?

Brianna: No.

Amber [in a low voice]: Yeah, he is.

In Amber's experience, "pressures" from boys are all in the course of a relationship, "normal" goings on that can be actively engaged, even fun and pleasurable. When the girls, arguing about the qualities of the ideal boy, finally agree that, above all, he has to be nice, Amber interrupts with another reality check, one informed by her own history of violent family relationships. "You can't really, if you first, when you first meet somebody," she explains, alluding to her experiences with boys and also, perhaps, to her mother's experience with her father, "you can't tell if they're the ideal person because most guys, when you first meet them, act really nice, but then as you go on they act like total jerks." Like her previous comments, this, too, is ignored. "Some people believe in love at first sight," Nina insists in response, and the conversation turns again to a boy's good looks and treatment of his girlfriend. For Amber, who thinks "looks are good," and yet who has also "liked ugly guys before," this conversation seems just too idealistically simple to be true. Her straightforward definition of a nice boy—someone who doesn't "cheat on you"—is lost in a host of romantic qualities discussed among the girls: boys who "are always saying you're pretty"; who "act nice to you"; who "make us feel good"; who "wear nice cologne"; and who "write you love letters." At this final comment, Amber cannot contain herself: "I hate love letters!" she exclaims. "I think they're stupid."

Throughout the year, in their group conversations and individual interviews, the Mansfield girls move in and out of their desire to be the kind of girl certain others seem to want—to have the clothes, the

money, and the relationships that promise what seem like uncondi-
tional approval and acceptance by those invested in the dominant
culture. They are acutely aware also of the expectations to perform
idealized notions of white middle-class femininity even as they experience the complexity of their lives—a complexity that assures themselves and others that they are, as it were, a bad fit within such a
narrow context.

In addition to affecting their feelings about themselves and their
relational desires, these expectations have particular implications for
their experience in school, where their persistent failure to fit this
fictional identity places them in tension with many of their teachers,
who operate as though the ideal were real and thus possible and
preferable. These girls often directly and openly express their frustration and anger to their teachers, but they also know well the
consequences of their outspokenness—a quality that, itself, places
them off the map of acceptability and thus out of relationship with
these teachers, even as it moves them closer to one another. Their
teachers' response to their strong feelings is both confusing and frustrating: "What can you do?" Susan asks. "If you do something, if
you say anything, then you get sent down to the office." As a result,
the girls learn to shift identities, swinging between defensive posturing and open refusal to engage what feels like the unreasonable
expectations and demands of their teachers, on the one hand, and
performing carefully constructed personas of idealized femininity on
the other.

The contradictions the Mansfield girls live during early adolescence bring to the surface a multitude of voices and visions that vie
for their allegiance. Their range of feelings and behaviors puts them
at odds with the expectations of middle-class teachers and other
adults invested in the feminine ideal, and thus underscores their displacement in school and white middle-class society. Cast against idealized notions of femininity, their strong voices sound off-key,
become unrecognizable, difficult to hear; their bold, self-protective
actions, necessary for their survival, become signs of failure or distress. Ironically, therefore, the very behavior that frees them from

stereotypic gender conventions may also label them, according to white middle-class notions of femininity, psychologically troubled, socially inferior, or marginal.

On one level the girls' shifts from local understandings of femininity to idealized notions of femininity, while garnering approval from authorities, negate the knowledge and relational strengths they have developed and thus attenuate their power. On another level, however, their resistance—the knowing looks, rolling eyes, irreverent gestures and movements, the group arguments and open disagreements, as well as the polyphonic nature of their speech and their subtly subversive shifts in voice—cement their closeness and give power to their collective refusal to be deluded into believing that the performance is real.

The Acadia girls, like their Mansfield counterparts, allude often to the absurdity of idealized femininity. They, too, interrupt the assumed reality of such fictions through performance and play, communicating their resistance, as well as their ambivalence and anxiety, through their interactions, gestures, and expressions. But for the Acadia girls, idealized femininity has long been made to seem plausible and possible; the uninterrupted repetition of the ideal has given "the illusion of seamless identity." Because, in fundamental ways, their parents, community, and teachers agree on the definition of feminine perfection and because the accouterments of this ideal are within their reach, the distinction between their experiences and the cultural ideal is more difficult to discern. Conventionally ideal girls, perfect girls, like them, look, speak and act in particular ways; they are white and well off, nice and kind, self-effacing, empathic, diligent, serious, generous, and compliant.

And yet, as we have seen, these white middle-class girls contest such feminine conventions. They stress in their group sessions and individual interviews that they are smart, creative, witty, athletic, and academically driven. In fact, the Acadia girls' most lively performances serve to disconnect them from those forms of femininity that traditionally have been used to dismiss girls and women. In effect they set up "straw girls" as a way to distinguish and clarify themselves. Creating a caricature of such femininity and embodying it with the "popular girls," they reject it, distancing themselves from its childish, vain, self-centered, hysterical, passive, fraudulent, deceitful, fickle qualities. In other words, as ventriloquistic cross-dressers, these twelve- and thirteen-year-old girls give voice to patriarchal views of idealized femininity, thus invoking and appropriating male power to reject and ridicule. They are not those girls who, according to Jane and Lydia's dramatic imitation, say "Hi!" in overly affected, shrill voices, shake the upper part of their bodies in excitement, and flip back their hair.

Lydia: "Oh my God, I got new shoes today! Oh!"
Jane: "Is my hair anywhere out of place? Ah!"

Such performances also underscore to Valerie and me, as they do to the others, that they are not girls who are stupid, who giggle, or who engage in childish behavior and backstabbing.

Jane [pretending to whisper conspiratorially]: "How come she likes him?" and "She said to me," and . . .
Lydia [in feigned angry voice]: "I'm gonna smack him across the face."
Kirstin: They always are in fights with each other. They're like, "Well, I don't like Mia today, she's being a jerk."
Jane: "But tomorrow I think I might, and the day after . . . My calendar is, um, Becky, Mia, Terry . . ."
Lydia: "On Fridays, we don't like Becky."

Unlike these giggly, unfocused "airheads," the Acadia girls describe themselves as serious, open, direct, and reasonable. Against this silly image, they insist, they are wise, grounded, strong, adventuresome, and smart, characteristics more often, in white middle-class culture at least, associated with boys and men. Indeed, when Lydia defines herself and her friends as girls who are into "horses and ice-climbing and bungi-jumping," she sets her jaw, widens her stance, and flexes her arm muscles at the camera.

As noted, the obvious problem with this strategy is that the girls clarify themselves against a narrow androcentric vision of femininity at the expense of other girls and women. When I attempt to raise this polarity between them and the popular girls, the Acadia girls do not seem to understand my point. When I use the phrase "ultrafeminine" to define what I hear them saying about the "other" girls, they laugh. "So what are we," Kirstin asks, "masculine?"

Kirstin's question is telling and her ambivalence palpable. As was the case in my interview with Robin, the girls insist that they are not girls but "people." Although they do not want to be boys, girlness they recognize as a hazard, and gender, they believe, has no place as a social or political consideration. And yet gender *is*, of course, a social and political consideration, and they are living proof. The terms of their struggle for self-definition and their need, in response to social expectations that threaten to appropriate or cover over their realities, to differentiate themselves from the traditionally feminine, underscore this fact.

Whereas the identities of the Mansfield girls shift dramatically, the Acadia girls seem at first resolutely and consistently "themselves" in their group sessions, partly because who they are here, in the underground, is quite different from who they say they are in the public world of the classroom. And yet, after reviewing the videotapes, it becomes clear that who they "really" are in these private sessions has shifted too, albeit gradually. They begin their sessions sitting in rows, looking seriously and intently at the camera, carefully gauging and monitoring their responses. Unlike the Mansfield girls, who shift and adjust within each session, depending on the audience and the question, the Acadia girls begin to relax only after several sessions. In time, as the girls become more comfortable and as they decide that the others in the room—girls and women—can be trusted, what becomes "real" shifts from nice and polite to bold, "bossy," "smart," "witty," and active.

It is soon clear, however, that few people want to know this lively girl; most, adults and peers alike, prefer not to hear what she has to say. And even this bold girl remains in control of her strong feelings and desires—except in moments of outrageous play when the girls shout at one another in mock anger or joke about boys. Although I am tempted to call this underground girl "more real," to believe she is closer to a true identity, this would be to deny who Valerie and I are to the girls and who the girls are to one another in this particular context. Trusted or not, we are still women who wield power in their lives in ways that matter a good deal to them.

The working-class girls shift identities to protect themselves psychologically and socially from classist and sexist judgments—and sometimes also as a way to claim aspects of themselves against such judgments. Idealized femininity offers the possibility of a middle-class life and the benefits that come with it; toughness offers protection and a satisfying impenetrability. For the Mansfield girls, then, idealized femininity functions, more consciously, as symbol, status, and performed role; their faces and bodies announce their awareness of their performances; their voices and actions signify their critical distance from middle-class norms and expectations even as they struggle to find ways to traverse this cultural gap, to be understood and to gain access to material advantages.

But while the working-class girls' performances both announce the regulatory power of conventional femininity and serve to loosen the hold of middle-class judgments and expectations, the middle-class girls maneuver within more subtle constraints, as likely to be held in place by security and approval as they are to struggle for authenticity and personal authority. They fight to create a space within a construction of femininity that, by definition, excises or buries the very qualities they say they like about themselves and one another. As with the working-class girls, notions of femininity are passed down from the women in their lives. As Theresa explains,

> In school I'm always quiet, but when I'm at home and with a friend, I'm not . . . I think [it's] because, well, my mother, she's always like taught us there's a time to be—like when I'm at home I can be myself, but at school I'm supposed to behave and stuff and that's probably why. I mean I know that I should just be

quiet—not quiet at school, but just be good, you know, and behave.

Theresa's mother, guiding her daughter into the culture, teaches her, not to dismiss herself and her feelings, but to recognize that "there's a time to be." A time to "be myself," Theresa interprets, and a time to "just be good . . . and behave." In Theresa's translation of her mother's advice, being herself in the public world of school means being bad. What might be intended as a simple lesson in civility has become, at early adolescence, a message infused with conventional expectations of white middle-class femininity. Certainly Theresa's interpretation is reasonable, since she knows and experiences the consequences of being too bold and saying too much.

Each of the Acadia girls describes herself as being very different at home or alone with her closest friends than she is in the public world of school. Indeed, the social boundaries between appropriate and inappropriate femininity are consistently and decisively drawn for them. For Theresa and her classmates, the costs of internalizing such a split between bad and good, cast as private experience and public performance, "really" me and what others want, are potentially high. Like other elite girls, they are "socialized out of using public talk to practice varied forms of womanhood," and thus are likely to "embody their resistance alone, through feminist individualism."[16] In so doing, they lose each other and the power of their collective critique. Indeed, the Acadia girls do speak of turning inward to their writings and diaries, which serve as a vital outlet for outlawed feelings like anger and desire. Such writing provides an opportunity for them to register their resistance to pressures to stay within the lines of white middle-class feminine behavior.

The Acadia girls' public performances of idealized femininity were belied by their intermittent outrageousness, cynicism, and laughter and their acknowledged expressions of an intense need to "let it out" or "let go" in the group or at home at the end of the school day. In these moments the girls would pause, as though to take a collective deep breath, before expressing their strong feelings to one another. And yet this intimacy waned over the course of the year, as the girls embraced notions of individual achievement. Their emerging "feminist individualism" threatened, through a climate of competition and distrust, to disconnect the girls from one another and thus take away an important forum for the expression of their thoughts and feelings.

"Where the notion of 'proper' operates, it is always and only improperly installed as the effect of a compulsory system," Butler argues.[17] Femaleness is voiced and mimed throughout girls' lives, but as girls move into the culture, the conventional gender/sex system and its intimate connection to idealized femininity become heightened, narrowed, and more controlled. Girls, to varying degrees conscious and unconscious of such control, react, either complying or resisting. How they respond to such attempts at socialization depends on where they are positioned vis-à-vis the dominant culture, as well as on the nature of their relationships with one another and with the adults in their lives.

According to Valerie Walkerdine, "We never quite fit the 'positions' provided for us in these regulatory practices. That failure is . . . both the point of pain and the point of struggle. It shows repeatedly that the imposition of fictional identities—or socialization—does not work."[18] As I listen to the Mansfield girls describe themselves as "stupid" and their personal and academic futures as "dim" and "black," I hear not only the pain of their failure to fit the positions provided for them, —but also their angry resistance to such predictions, their closeness to one another, and their distance from norms of white middle-class femininity. The voices of their parents and working-class community threaten to expose such norms and reveal the values that underlie them to be constructed, negotiated, agreed-upon fictions. Throughout the year, in session after session, their anxieties, struggles, and insights, born of a keen awareness of their difference from the ideal, reveal the limits of socialization. Their shifts in identity and changing performances disrupt any illusion of smooth continuity in identity formation and exemplify over and over again their power to authorize themselves in ways disruptive of the proper. These working-class girls are neither passive, unconscious characters, manipulated or duped by the larger social context, nor always active, always fully conscious or autonomous individuals.

Similarly, when I listen to the Acadia girls speak of their invisibility and hear them differentiate themselves within the prevailing ideology of white middle-class femininity, I am moved to question conventionally gendered "reality." With the pain and struggle, then, is also the possibility. Among and between these working- and middle-class girls, resistant, frustrated voices disrupt the regulatory fictions of idealized femininity, revisioning both who they are and who they might become.

seven

The Madgirl in the Classroom

The tension between theory and practice becomes a chasm of alienation when private sorrows are suffered silently, unredeemed by
collective reflection and response.

PETER LYMAN

Typical descriptions of girls in school classrooms, at least in recent
literature, are likely to conjure up images of cooperation, compliance, polite silence, or, perhaps, invisibility, hands raised or waving
patiently but rarely called upon by teachers who, while well armored
with good intentions, may be unaware of their own biases.[1] The
assumption seems to be that what you see of girls is what you get.

In ways both obvious and subtle, the girls in this study counter
such assumptions. Irrespective of class, these girls express a good
deal of anger, annoyance, and frustration with school, often focusing
on teachers who they feel ignore them or attend to unruly students,
usually boys, or who abuse their authority in the classroom. Sometimes they complain of school policies that leave them feeling unsafe
or uninformed; other times they speak to the sexism or stereotyping
that seems to pervade school grounds. The middle-class and working-class girls differ, however, in the intensity of their anger, the issues
that arouse the strongest feelings, and the manner in which they
express these feelings. Such differences have much to do with class-
related definitions and views of appropriate feminine behavior.

Acadia: Behind Closed Doors

The Acadia girls are in touch with their angry feelings. They make considered choices about whether or not to speak or act on their own behalf, often choosing silence because they have little evidence that speaking would change the situation, but ample evidence that doing so would "cause a scene" and invite trouble or unwanted attention. The patience and politeness that might lead one to imagine these middle-class girls as the educational counterparts to Virginia Woolf's "angel in the house" belie their frustration and annoyance.

"My English teacher . . . there's like two boys in the class that she really favors," twelve-year-old Elizabeth tells us, speaking in measured tones. "They're the ones that misbehave and act out and don't get their work done very much." Irritated by her teacher's "unfairness," Elizabeth sees no benefit to pointing out her observations. Although she admits that she and her friends usually talk only among themselves about such favoritism, she is quick to justify their silence: "It's happened so often that we don't really think about it anymore." Instead, she writes her angry feelings down in her notebook.

Kirstin complains that it is sometimes difficult "being smart."

> I hate [it]. There's a lot of times when I know answers and I want to say them [and don't] because I get dirty looks and people laugh and call me . . . it's just embarrassing . . . it's sometimes humiliating to be the only person raising her hand and you know other people know the answer . . . I guess . . . it's just cool to be dumb . . . But they're not. They're smart . . . It's like, "Well, why don't you raise your hand if you know the answer?" I don't understand the logic. Are they too lazy to lift their arm? [And then] some teachers just won't call on me . . . I'll be the only one raising my hand and . . . they'll call on everyone and then not call on me at all. Go on to the next question. Even if I have an answer to a question, all period, all week, they just won't.

In spite of her frustration, Kirstin plays down her strong feelings: "It doesn't really make me mad . . . I'm used to it . . . I don't really think about it that much." When she's angry, she explains, "I just try to ignore things and it just builds up inside me until I can't stand it anymore." Instead of expressing her anger, Kirstin reads fiction. Revealing the extent of her disconnection from others, she admits, "I don't really think about what—how I feel when I'm angry. I just know that I'm angry and usually I can blow it off by reading. Reading fiction helps a lot . . . [It helps] to know that other people have problems too and they get angry."

"Junior high," announces thirteen-year-old Robin in disgust, "is the virus that causes stupidity." "Teachers would be horrified by my opinions," she continues. "They are very descriptive and colorful—. even purple . . . I get really mad at people because they don't want to learn or because they're just dumb . . . I can't imagine anybody wanting to be stupid and not learn." And yet Robin, who gets "really mad," sometimes "furious," does not say much in class. "I used to do a lot of talking. I don't talk as much anymore in class . . . When it comes to class discussion I speak when I'm spoken to or if I really have something to say that needs to be said." Instead, Robin finds other outlets for her strong feelings—directing them at herself or incorporating them into her art: "I usually do something destructive like shave part of my head . . . or rip stuff or punch things, you know? . . . I express my anger in my writing and my art and stuff."

These girls speak candidly about who lurks behind the quiet, well-behaved, middle-class "angel" in the classroom: a girl who is frequently irritated, frustrated, and angry, and almost always measured and polite about it, at least in public. Given the opportunity in the privacy of their interviews and focus groups to talk about themselves, however, the girls candidly express their strong feelings and—against perceptions of adolescent girls as a passive, amorphous group—boast about their unique qualities and individual abilities, saying such things as "I'm very good at math"; "I'm being myself . . . I'm different"; "I like stuff my own way and I'm bossy"; "I'm trying to go ahead in everything"; "I play hockey . . . I'm pretty good"; "I've never been a follower . . . it's not in my personality"; "I'm creative."

But even though the Acadia girls agree that it is important to express their feelings and to say what they think, they are also well aware that girls who do so are perceived as "loud and obnoxious" and are not well liked. Such awareness leads them to mitigate, question, and even at times disconnect from their feelings. Anger begins to seem like too strong a word. As Jane explains, "I don't think I get angry . . . I just get very, very, very annoyed . . . I'm never angry at anybody. I'm just annoyed and I dislike them."

The Acadia girls also know that there are consequences for expressing their strong feelings publicly, and they know that they are judged by different standards than their male counterparts. "In school it's definitely not as acceptable [for girls to get angry as it is for boys]," Kirstin complains:

Like boys get away with so much. It's just that we're good all the time. If we do something moderately bad, like Theresa got in big trouble for calling a teacher by their first name. She just was so frustrated. She must have, you know, raised her hand saying so and so, so many times, saying, "Hey, listen to me," and it got [the teacher's] attention . . . [She] was like, "Excuse me. You have no right to call me by my first name." [Theresa] was just like—she didn't say it because she was—I could tell she was [saying to herself], "You have no right to ignore me every day. Do you remember I'm in your class?"

Theresa, usually a model student, "got in big trouble" for her inappropriate address, while the boys, Kirstin explains, "get away with so much, [like] swearing, being really rude to teachers, fighting." "You know," she contends, "teachers let a lot of things slide [with boys]. They're like that all the time. If we did anything half that bad, they'd be all over us." But in what begins to sound like the refrain from a Greek chorus, she adds, "It doesn't really make me mad though. I'm just used to it."

The Acadia girls also know that the boys are judged differently because they are perceived differently. "Like Devon," Jane explains,

We had a student-teacher once, and [Devon's] in my class, and she was just a science class student-teacher, and he's pretty outgoing and he made her laugh and stuff like that and he also got detention. But she sent a card back to us and he was the one she mentioned and remembered . . . out of all the seventh-graders she teaches. So they remember the boys a lot better, because they're louder . . .

Elizabeth: Of all the classes she teaches!

Jane: I know, all sixth period!

It becomes apparent to these girls that if you're a boy and "if you're outgoing and outspoken, and you have enough money," if you're "loud" and "have the right clothes," you've got it made.

Although boys are supposed to be "brighter," Jane explains, they "don't have to get good grades." Girls, by contrast, find themselves in a dilemma. "Girls are all expected to be smart, all of us," Jane says at one point, and then at another, "Well, girls shouldn't talk at all [in class] and shouldn't be smart." "Yeah," Kirstin agrees, "you have to be dumb." "Girls are too opinionated," Lydia adds sarcastically. What appears at first to be a contradiction is, rather, an accurate reading of the social scene that these middle-class girls confront daily. Girls are supposed to *be* smart and *appear* dumb. The point is not whether you are smart, but whether you are in tune with the social cues and willing to hide your capabilities in public, something these girls refuse to do.

Jane: If you're really really smart then . . . it's not that bad, but you
    have to be pretty smart . . . But not too much.

Lyn: What happens if you show too much?

Jane: I, I don't know . . . Elizabeth gets picked on.

Kirstin: If you're smart and people know it, then, "See ya!"
    Because like Sandy is really smart, but she never raises her hand
    that much, because she knows people will know she's smart.
    And I can't do that. I can't *stand* to sit and not raise my hand
    and watch people get the wrong answer, and go . . . I explode,
    and so I raise my hand.

Because she is smart and cannot hold herself back, Kirstin explains, she has to deal both with getting picked on and, more difficult for her, with people who "just use you for the answers," who copy from her in class, something that makes her "really mad." "I really hate it! Because people have copied off my paper for a test forever. I'm so used to it. I mean, they always do. I mean," she adds, incredulous, "some people ask me to please not put my hand there because I'm blocking the answers!"

And yet despite their awareness of different standards, expectations, and treatment, these white middle-class girls generally espouse a strong belief in meritocracy and the American Dream. By and large they trust their teachers and other authorities to be fair, to judge them on their merits; they firmly believe that hard work and perseverance, in school and in society, will eventually yield a happy and prosperous life. And so perhaps it is not surprising that their most intense feelings of anger center on the frequent times when this ideology is disrupted or violated, when others receive credit or favoritism or special privileges for unearned work, either because they are popular or wealthy, or simply because they demand attention and credit.

Not surprisingly, the girls are most annoyed by the special favors and attention lavished on the "popular" kids in the school. In story after story, they illustrate the privileges these students receive simply for being who they are. Kirstin tells how a "really conceited, cocky" boy who "thinks he's everything in the world . . . was kicked off the [school] trip" for swearing and hitting a teacher, but ended up being able to go anyway:

He had done something very wrong . . . And the night before the trip . . . he decided he really wanted to go. And the thing that really upset me was he got to go because his parents called and threatened to sue [the teacher] for not letting him go. Really. You know, and they're very rich and so he's so used to getting his way. I mean he even gets on the sports teams even though he's not very good . . . [And] he really didn't get any other punishment at all . . . And it's really unfair and a lot of times they get an advantage over us for something that we really deserve.

"It's ridiculous," Robin says. "My parents say if you earn your punishment, you better serve it."

Recalling another situation where a student nearly received a scholarship over a smarter and more needy classmate because he protested loudly and arrogantly that he deserved it most, Kirstin comments bitterly: "Yah, you're right, you [deserve it]. You never pay attention. You just think it's all a big game."

The irony, of course, is that it is, to a degree, a "big game," and though the girls are learning the social codes and rules well enough —the manners of speech and behavior and dress that will assure them a place in upper-middle-class society—they have yet to appreciate the socially constructed nature of the rules and who they are meant to benefit most. The girls constantly struggle with a tension between what they are told, and indeed practice religiously, and what they see and hear in the public world of their school.

The girls are especially angered by teachers who give special attention to boys simply because they "act civil and normal." If they "act like everyone else for the rest of the week and turn in their homework," Kristin complains, "they get 'Student of the Week,' when, when other people have to like try and do extra credit and stuff." "Yeah, I know," Lydia interrupts. "We like work our butts off every single time and we don't get squat!" As Elizabeth observes, "They're getting special treatment because they're behaving badly or not doing what they're supposed to do . . . or doing half the work." "I mean," Kirstin continues, "a lot of times their definition of good is like not even normal. And just, you know, they still mouth off. And the teacher gives them second chances [*said in an overly nice voice*]: 'Shhh, Eric, you better raise your hand or you won't get Student of the Week!' "

Whether or not the stories the Acadia girls tell are fully accurate, they reveal their perceptions of school and justify their anger and frustration at their teachers' favoritism:

Kirstin: And now Mrs. Cronin is going to change David's chaperon. I know she, I know she's going to relent to that because she wants him to go [on the school trip] and she'll be like, "Oh, OK David. I guess you can be with me."

Jane: If *I* wanted a different chaperon—

Kirstin: Mrs. Cronin would be like, "That's nice. You don't get your initial $50.00 back."

Jane: She's like [*said primly*], "Yeah, well, we'll refund the money that you've already given me except the $50.00 in the beginning. And we do have a few people lined up that want to go."

Valerie: So she wouldn't relent?

Kirstin: But she didn't say that to David. She's like, "Oh c'mon David. Please come. Please."

Jane: "We'll change your chaperon."

The girls are incredulous when teachers dole out unearned privileges to popular or favorite students, but they resist any suggestion that such transgressions undermine the school's ideology of meritocracy and just rewards. Jane, for example, complains about a teacher who "really favored this student . . . let [him] get away with a lot of things," and then tells a story of deceit and betrayal:

[She] said that he won a scholarship [to go on a class trip], but [that it] had only been available after everyone had signed up and he had gotten it because he was like the only contestant. And there was a girl that had wanted it too, and she said, "Why couldn't girls enter it?" and [the teacher] said, "Because this grandfather had a little boy and the little boy died and before he gave the scholarship to someone it had to be a boy."

Lyn: Was that true?

Jane: No, of course it wasn't true. And she paid it herself. She paid it herself because she really favored this student, and it was really unfair.

Although Jane chalks up this teacher's behavior to "her personality," this narrative suggests another, more troubling theme in the girls' stories of students "who are kind of getting a free ride." In every case the teachers in their stories of unfair treatment are women, and the favored students are boys. What makes such treatment most disturbing to the girls are the irreverent bantering and informal camaraderie that accompany it, compared with the more formal, unresponsive voices their teachers use with them. The boys "talk back," publicly challenge their women teachers, and engage in verbal play with them. Underlying such public performances are messages about power relations, particularly about women's desire for male approval, and also about women's relationships with other women. A sense of betrayal, more than infractions of school ideology, may explain the intensity of the girls' confusion and anger.

The fact that most of those who "act out" and get special favors are the more popular boys does not immediately occur to Elizabeth, though upon reflection she knows this to be true. Nonetheless, she concludes that she and her friends, not the teachers, are to blame for their being "overlooked":

> Sometimes it's because I think she doesn't hear us because we're not very loud . . . It's happened so often that we don't really think about it anymore . . . how it's kind of unfair and how the people who misbehave get all the attention . . . One of my friends is very quiet and I'm not as quiet as she is, so she sometimes gets overlooked. But the boys . . . they don't even raise their hands. They just call out if they think it's right or something. If they get it wrong she'll like kind of lead them to the right answer. She'll like, "Oh, no, maybe it's . . . No, I think that . . . Maybe, it's . . ."

There have been times, Elizabeth admits, when she has spoken out in this class, but she has been "told not to talk that loudly." She concedes that in those situations she probably was being a bit disruptive and deserved to be told to quiet down.

Whereas Jane, Elizabeth, and Kirstin are likely to attribute such favoritism to individual teachers' personalities and to share the blame for their invisibility, Lydia is more critical, more likely to delineate the structural outlines of privilege in her school and how it "typically" benefits those at the top. But though she comes close, she, too, falls short of condemning the classism and sexism she witnesses at school:

Lydia: Like, one time like in class the teacher, we were trying to get this project, it was a yearbook, and you had to sign up for stuff really quick before it would be all full. Well, the teacher, she was of course wanted by kids, and I was right in front of her, and I was asking her, and she didn't seem to listen to me, but when one of the people from the popular group asked her to put down a subject, she immediately wrote down his name. And it's, I thought it was rather unfair . . . I was right in front of her . . . it was kind of hard to . . .

Lyn: Do you think that's typical?

Lydia: Yeah. I don't see why they get better treatment . . .

Lyn: Why do you think it's like that?

Lydia: Because not everybody saw it my way or they wouldn't be . . . They're always the best dressed, and they have the most money and they're always dressed up so people tend to label them the popular ones.

Lyn: Do you think teachers do too?

Lydia: Yeah, they really do. Like we went on this school trip, and all the really fun chaperons and everything, they all picked them . . . and a lot of people and myself think that [the sign-up sheets] were rigged because all of the like popular, awesome people got all the awesome chaperons. Because they think they're the crazy ones, but actually we're, we're actually a lot more crazier than them; they think they're crazy but the things that they do are like stupid crazy. We're more crazy in the sense of mature. Like we, we're crazy like high school students . . . but they're more like fifth-graders.

For Lydia the difference in treatment, while typical, ultimately comes down to a more general problem of perception grounded in a failure of relationship. If only the teachers *really* knew us, she implies, they would prefer to be with us. The teachers, Lydia believes, are simply taken in by the surface of things. Embedded in Lydia's explanation is her desire to expose the popular kids for who they really are and to redefine popularity so that it would be judged on more genuine terms. Thus while Lydia challenges her teachers' perceptions, she does not, perhaps cannot yet, see the connections between such perceptions and classism on a more systemic level. Rather, she reveals her very deep belief in the ideology of meritocracy. In fact, she believes that she and her friends ought to have the attention and the social standing that the popular kids now enjoy so undeservingly.

Thus there is no explanation in the Acadia girls' ideology of meritocracy for their observations that popular kids and, more often, boys, generally get more attention in class and more breaks, for their longing for the freedom boys enjoy to express strong feelings in public, or for their own personal experiences of invisibility in the classroom. Although the girls collectively know that these differences exist, the white middle-class culture of individualism into which they have been invited threatens to particularize and personalize their stories, so that they blame themselves for not being or doing enough, individual boys for talking and taking too much, and certain misguided teachers for encouraging them to do so.

And yet their strong feelings continually reemerge, indicating that something is wrong, that the issue is not yet resolved. Infuriated with the way things go in school, they also sound genuinely confused about the discrepancy between the ideal and the real. Theresa, for example, struggles openly with the invisibility she experiences when she is her usual good-girl self in class.

Theresa: In a lot of classes, the teacher just seems like to ignore me. I don't know why but they—maybe because I don't speak out loud enough, but usually, I'm like trying to tell them something and they just kind of ignore me, so I just say, "Fine!" and go on.

Lyn: How do you know they ignore you?

Theresa: Because I'm like talking to them and they don't see me. I'll like ask a question and then they just like don't seem to hear me and they just like keep on talking to the person and like if they're talking—well, they just like don't answer my question. And they just talk to someone else.

This invisibility is something Theresa experiences "all the time": "I'm always ignored by everyone!" she insists. While she explains her teachers' behavior in individualistic terms—"They might just have their minds on something else," or "They don't really care"—and while she is adamant, when I ask her directly, that her invisibility has nothing to do with her gender, the construction of her response to my question suggests that she experiences the problem somewhat differently:

No. I think it's because these teachers, they won't listen to everyone, they just kind of . . . See, these boys—sometimes they have their hands up and everything but they never . . . They always say raise your hand but then when you raise your hand they never call on you. So you end up—you have to yell out and then you get in trouble.

Theresa, like the other Acadia girls, knows on some level that being "always ignored by everyone" has something to do with being a girl. The girls repeatedly either resist knowing or explain away their knowledge that gender pervades classroom interactions, even as they define the problem in gendered terms. "No," Theresa assures me, it's not about being a girl, but in the next breath she begins, "See, these boys . . ." A subtle shift in pronoun from the first-person "I" to the second-person "you" then underscores her awareness that her experience is shared by other girls. The problem for Theresa and her friends is thus not that they are girls, but that they are not boys.

That the Acadia girls' expressions of strong feelings and self-promotion are discouraged in public dialogue seems also, to them, unconnected to their success or failure to be recognized. Jane takes pride in her ability not to show her feelings—"I hide my feelings a

lot better than my sister does. I'm an actress"—even as she struggles
to be seen and known for her abilities. Calling attention to herself
sounds too selfish, and yet she admits, "I'm trying to get good grades
too and be recognized." Frustrated that she works "twice as hard"
as others who get more attention, and that even her girlfriends don't
notice how capable and smart she is, Jane sees no way to be recognized without being judged or ostracized. "I get better grades than
[they do] in science and math . . . I can act better and write better
than [they] can . . . I don't get anywhere in anything . . . I never get
anywhere in anything . . . It's frustrating," she admits. "I just can't
get anywhere . . . they'd think I'm bragging and I don't." When her
friends vote for another girl for an orchestra award, Jane feels immo-
bilized. She can't speak up and say, "I deserve this," because "I don't
know, it would probably . . . I'm more liked . . . more well liked,"
and to do so might risk her reputation as someone who is "flexible,"
who "can take teasing," and who can "just laugh" things off. "I could
still say something, but I don't know if I want to. I mean I never gave
them a reason to believe that I'm good . . . I just don't do anything
either way . . . and then I think, well maybe they're right and I just
try to see it from their point of view . . . That might be what they
want me to see . . . I have about twenty pages of writing [about this
in my notebook]."

Even as they feel unrecognized in their classrooms these girls ventriloquate and embody white middle-class femininity in ways that
ensure their acceptability and yet blend them into the amorphous
backdrop of "nice girls," existing just out of their teachers' conscious
awareness. They seem caught in the uneasy tension between their
descriptions of themselves as "bossy" and "smart" and expectations
that they should wait patiently for things to happen, holding in their
feelings and thoughts. Frustrated, they judge other girls for acting in
ways they themselves secretly covet—that is, for being "outspoken,"
saying what they feel and want directly and publicly.

Because they are pressed to stay out of the limelight, and tacitly
agree among themselves to keep their "real" feelings secret and their
accomplishments private, any girl who breaks out and commands

the public stage or works her way to the few token spots reserved at the top for the best female students risks eliciting feelings of anger and betrayal. Jane, who admits, "I like trying to be the best," pays the consequences. After she won a school contest, she explains, "[My friend] . . . wouldn't talk to me for two days. She was so mad at me and it wasn't my fault." All good students, the Acadia girls wish to succeed, to do well academically, and to be acknowledged for their excellence; unfortunately, their desires are in constant tension, not only with pressures to appear appropriately nonassertive, but also with their need to be in relationship, to stay together as a group, which often demands that they carefully downplay their achievements to their friends. Such group reliance offers them protection against mistreatment by those with more social and material power, and yet goes against the competitive spirit at the heart of their ideological leanings.

It is abundantly clear that the Acadia girls are neither passive recipients of nor victims to the ideology of white middle-class femininity. In their case, simply put, what you see is *not* what you get. Amid pressures not to speak too loudly or passionately or demand too much space or appear too smart, these girls find creative ways to express their feelings. In the face of bullying and denigration by the popular kids, for example, they rally to exhibit a collective condescension, manifest in a quick and clever wit and the creative use of language designed to confuse their perpetrators, or simply to make them look stupid or silly. Talking about a time when she wanted to say something but did not, Lydia comments:

> That happens a lot. I mean, the eighth-graders . . . and a lot of times they come up to you and a lot of times I have the right thing to say but then I don't say it and later, I'm like Oh . . . and I don't. But like now, it's like I'm so sick of it that I'm starting to revolt . . . and I'm starting to . . . A lot of times they just come and say something . . . and I speak in a different language.
> *Lyn:* You speak in a different language?

Lydia: Yeah. They're like [*makes a confused face*], and then they'll leave me alone, because they know how to respond to certain things, but when I'm a seventh-grader and they're an eighth-grader and I'm speaking strangely they want to leave me alone because I guess they figure I could . . . they don't understand and I say something and they say, "What'd you say to me?" It's so funny.

"I have other concerns more important," Elizabeth claims, explaining why she cannot be bothered with a boy who has been "annoying" her. The others agree with her. The boys who harass them, they have decided, are "childish," "stupid," "dumb," "bored," and "have no life." In response the girls show little patience. "Do you have a problem with keeping things to yourself?" Lydia recalls asking a boy when he hit her in the back with some balled-up paper. To another boy "who bothered me in the hall," Lydia is condescending: "I was already in the hall looking at music, and he came up and he was staring right over my shoulder," and he said [*in a voice meant to sound dumb*], 'What's that?' I go, 'It's called music' . . . and then I walked off." "Once at lunch," she continues, "these boys were trying to take over our table, and Jane said, 'Go find your own table,' but they didn't."

Jane: I said more but that was the basic . . .
Lydia: They said they didn't hear her, and so . . .
Jane: They heard me, but they chose to ignore me because they didn't think a puny little seventh-grade girl could actually talk like that to [*feigning awe*] an eighth-grade boy.
Lydia: Then they said the same to us. And it's like [*in a baby voice*], "The same to you." And then they left, and they started scowling like little children.
Jane: They bothered us for about half the lunch period, and finally Mr. Robbins saw them, came over, and told them to go find their own table. And ever since then they've been bothering us.

The Acadia girls quickly decipher and ridicule the cryptic phrases thrown at them by the popular boys, though if they pick up a sexualized edge to the boys' teasing, they do not share it with us. In response to the derogatory phrase "sad skid," they retort, "Sorry, I'd like you to answer me in English." When Theresa reports the newest insult in school, the girls laugh and joke about it and the other "stupid" phrases the popular boys use.

Theresa: Well, they have another like thing they say now. They call you—they say, "Smell good?"
Elizabeth: "Smell good?"
Theresa: Yeah. Jeff says it all the time. "Smell good?"
Lydia: "Yes, thank you. Thank you. I know, I smell wonderful, don't I?" . . . Also, you have to be able to say, "The rooster crows at midnight."
Kirstin: And go, "Skid in the hammock!"
Jane [laughing]: Yeah, you have to say, "Skid in the hammock" and—
Kirstin: I don't even know what that means—
Lydia: A board or log in the hammock . . .
Kirstin: It doesn't even make sense . . . They say the dumbest things. They call people guacamole stains [*lots of laughter*].

The girls poke fun at the boys' "childish" retorts and their appropriation of what they consider the baser forms of culture. If you said anything to them, Jane explains, "they'd just laugh, like go 'huh, huh,' doing that stupid laugh, like Beavis and Butthead. When the fire drill happened, they said, 'Cool, fire, huh, huh, huh.' "[2] Elizabeth agrees: "My whole French class was going, 'huh, huh.' So annoying. Stupid." But Lydia is outraged at what she considers the boys' disregard for more serious matters:

Lydia: Every time a person goes, "Beavis and Butthead are cool," I'm like, "No, they aren't cool. Do you want Beavis and Butthead for culture?" I think that's stupid. Have you heard what happened? I mean people are killing other people because of

Beavis and Butthead. Somebody burned down their house because of them, and their baby sister was inside, she was only two years old. She died, and you think that's funny? . . . And also they laugh about the Holocaust. I don't think that was very funny . . . I don't think it's funny when some child was under their bed, and they see their parents murdered in front of them. I don't think that's very funny, and I really, I *hate* it when they do that.

Valerie: Do you ever say anything?

Lydia: No, I haven't and I should. I mean, sometimes I say, "I don't think that's funny."

Whereas the girls reject the popular boys for being insensitive and rude, they distance themselves from the popular girls by underscoring their intellectual inferiority and silliness. "Hold you head high and stick out your tongue!" Lydia exclaims, in defense of her group against these girls. "They're making themselves the higher point of life when you know they aren't . . . It's like dumb to be smart. Stupid!"

The girls know that the popular kids' command of public space—in terms of both movement and language—gives them an advantage in school, and they openly resent it. "They're popular because they have like power," Lydia explains. "And last year they went around making everybody feel horrible. They ruin stuff that they don't like, and that's other people's property and they make kids cry."

This psychological terrorism infuriates the girls, as they witness and experience its power to control people's behavior. "They use embarrassment," Kirstin explains, and the girls give a multitude of examples: making fun of an exchange student's clothes, accusing a shy boy of reading dirty magazines, teasing and blaming someone for things he didn't do until he is in tears; calling an overweight girl who is "really nice" mean names and saying "I love you" or writing on the board "someone likes Katie." The girls struggle in these situations because, as Lydia confesses, "It's so hard. I mean, it's hard to stick up for people because you don't want to turn into how that person is being treated, so you have to be careful what you say." "A lot of times it does turn on you," Kirstin agrees. "It happens to me all the time."

The Acadia girls feel constrained by the power they and others have invested in the popular kids. "They feel like they can order people around," Jane says angrily. "And they can't," Lydia adds. "I'm not gonna stand for that." Whereas publicly Lydia and the others "just walk away" when the popular kids take over, in their underground groups they develop resistance strategies. Armed with their wit, and also with sarcasm, humor, and condescension, the Acadia girls counter the popular boys and girls' intimidation tactics. Feeling pressure to cheat from kids who are either "really popular" or can "get to the popular people," who either "have a lot of power" or are "real bullies," the girls devise creative responses:

Jane: What I do when people want the answer from me is, I say, "Well, what do you think?" And they give me an answer and then look at me like, "Is that right?" And I say, "Yeah," even if it's wrong.

Lydia: Chills them out.

Jane: Yeah. Chills them down a little.

Kirstin: Well, I tell people wrong answers all the time. I told Mitch and Dan that Caroline and the Captain [characters in a book the class was reading] were married.

Elizabeth: And they believed you?

Kirstin: Yeah, they were like, "Cool." And so I flipped to this one section in the book and I like found one sentence that said something like, "I bet they did it," or something, and I go, "See, look here [*the others are laughing*]," and they didn't even read it, they were like, "Cool."

The girls also explain that consciously speaking and performing stereotypically feminine voices and behaviors make it more difficult for the boys to respond. In a scene she plays out dramatically before the group, Lydia reveals this as a strategy for countering an annoying boy's behavior in class:

Lydia: Dylan, he sits behind me in Mr. Ballard's class. He had his feet underneath my chair, 'cause I was sitting right on the edge. And he was picking it up and it was bothering me. I didn't say anything, but what I did—he had his toes under there, and I stood up a little, and he was tipping it and everything. I came back down, and he wasn't quick enough, and I sat down really hard on his feet. He goes [*in pained, startled voice*], "Why did you sit down on my feet?" and I go [*in innocent, sweet voice*], "Why were they under there?" He was . . . quiet.

Lydia's theory about such boys is that "they want to get you mad. I think they enjoy making people mad." In response to their teasing and flirting, she performs a kind of controlled, naive femininity. But she is hardly sweet or innocent; she knows this is a psychological battle and she is determined to win. "If you don't get mad," she explains, if "you give back responses without getting angry or changing your facial expression, and they can see that . . . that means you've conquered them, and they haven't conquered you."

Outside of class, in the hallways, the Acadia girls are likely to respond more aggressively to boys who bother them. They get more mad and annoyed than uncomfortable, they say, and are therefore unlikely to remain passive or unresponsive. In fact, they quickly pick up on and use to their advantage words they know have power.

Elizabeth: They usually bother me in the morning, because I have a band locker . . . They'll like, stand in front of you, or—
Jane: Put their bags in front of your locker—
Elizabeth: Or take their hands and put them in front of your face, or . . . stupid stuff like that.
Lydia: To bother you.
Jane [smiling]: Yeah. Sexual harassment.
Lydia: Yeah. You should do that.

Jane: Yeah. Because they know I come to my locker every morning, and I always find at least five bags piled up there, and I like kick them away. And none of them have yet said, "Don't kick my bag away," but if they do, I'll know what to say.

While the girls joke about reporting the boys for sexual harassment, in fact they are not always sure how to interpret the boys' behavior. Even when they feel they should report an incident, they are uncertain whether the school's policy would be enforced.

Robin: A lot [of boys] make really slime-like remarks. Like, "Why do you wear those baggy clothes? If you've got it, flaunt it." And it's much more graphic than that usually. It's really—it annoys me because I don't think I should have to put up with that . . . and it's really annoying that they can sit there and do stuff like that or . . . The school just this year had a sexual harassment thing, so then you know, anything that's done that makes you feel uncomfortable, you should go to the office and the person can get suspended. But I mean, the teachers, even if they see it, they pretend that they don't. I hate that.

Lyn: You haven't had anybody use that policy and have it go anywhere?

Robin: It doesn't go anywhere! I mean I made comments in the office once . . . I mean it's certainly annoying. You walk down the hall and all of a sudden part of your anatomy is in somebody else's hand. It's just like, "Do you mind!" It's very annoying.

Pushed too far, however, the Acadia girls will fight back. "I like to keep away from violence," Lydia explains, "but once in a while you have to do it. I mean, it's not necessary but you can't control it."

Like in gym the other day, we had a substitute, and we were doing . . . it was mostly girls against boys, that's the way she set it up . . . and the boys were like keeping the ball out of our hands . . . and they were making sexist remarks and stuff like that . . . and so I got so angry at this one kid . . . so I started

hitting on *him*. It was funny, but . . . and finally he just dropped
the ball . . . He just kind of stayed away from me . . . but he's so
unfair . . . he'd throw the ball really hard from the back . . . and
so we'd do that, we'd throw it right at him . . .

Lyn: Did you say anything?

Lydia: I like went to sit down because I love gym, I mean, it's the
only activity I really love, because it's so active . . . and that's the
first time I ever sat down because of somebody else and . . . so
he goes, "What are you guys doing sitting down?" And I just
said, "You should be taken out and stripped naked." And he just
kind of walked away.

Such moments are rare. As angry as they are with the boys' behavior in school, the Acadia girls would rather distinguish themselves
from these boys than behave in kind. In a conversation about the
popular boys' sense of entitlement in the classroom, Valerie pushes
the girls to imagine being as demanding and insistent as the boys are.

Valerie: But why don't you get mad? Why don't you come right up
and say, "I'm not sitting there today!" Because if Kirstin was
bothering David . . . don't you think he would come right up to
me and say [*in an angry voice*], "I'm not sitting in that group
anymore because she's bugging me and she's talking and she's
cheating?" Why don't you guys do that?

Kirstin: I've tattled enough. I mean, it doesn't get you anywhere.

Jane: Don't you have enough problems as it is?

Valerie: But you feel like, why do you feel like you can't . . .

Kirstin: Because . . . people like that, they just have a name like,
they just have a name like that and they get away with those
things. I mean, teachers don't give them detention.

Valerie: But what if, what if Jacob [a popular boy] jumped up and
said, "I'm not sitting in this group because they're bugging me."
Why don't you?

Elizabeth: Well, because it doesn't seem as important as other
things like, getting on with the lesson, and then you know—

Kirstin: Making sure you get a silent reading book so you—

Elizabeth: Not stopping up, stopping the class . . . the whole class,
and trying to learn instead of interrupting.
Valerie: Mmhmm. But they'll do it.
Jane: We're not them.

This conversation underscores the entanglement of visible and invisible threads that bind the Acadia girls' expressions of anger and resistance. The weight of expectations—including their perceptions of what Valerie might want them to say—the pain of exclusion, the knowledge of class status and also of male power and privilege, and the awareness of how their actions affect others all point to the complicated nature of white middle-class femininity. The lines between civility—respect for their teacher and their classmates—and a feminine selflessness that would obliterate their anger are nearly indiscernible as the girls rationalize their refusal to speak out. In the context of their persistent struggles to be heard and taken seriously, such a refusal seems particularly problematic. There is, it seems to these adolescent girls, no way to be both good and visible, responsive and successful, caring and outspoken.

Listening to the Acadia girls' struggles with the contradictory voices they have taken in, as well as with the gendered polarities of the dominant culture, one can appreciate their creative strategies for expressing their anger and resistance. Their convoluted pathway to success and visibility is a reminder that, particularly with these girls, things are seldom what they appear to be. The concern, however, is that the performances these girls give will become, in time, persuasive even to the girls themselves; that the role of feminine perfection, silence, and selflessness will become their guiding ideology.

It is important that these seventh-grade girls remain in touch with their strong feelings. Researchers report that emotional expressiveness relates positively to some measures of well-being, whereas ambivalence about such expression relates to several indexes of psychological distress.[3] And while a number of studies connect suppressed anger to depression, others find that depression scores relate directly to the degree to which women endorse "care as self-sacrifice."[4] Anger, in the case of the Acadia girls, would appear to be not only a justified response to the sexism and classism they experience in school, but also a necessary protection against depression and other signs of psychological trouble.

Mansfield: Just Say It

As noted, the Mansfield girls do not share the Acadia girls' relationship with or trust in authorities, their belief in the American Dream, or their definitions of femininity.

"People don't listen because they don't like us," eleven-year-old Cheyenne says, her expression solemn as she addresses her group. "I don't like teachers so much . . . If I'm talking to a teacher, I'll tell them what I think." Some days, Cheyenne confesses, she finds ways to get out of class: if "I'm in a bad mood and I'm really frustrated . . . I bug the crap out of someone."

> Some days I'll just want to get in trouble so I don't have to be in classes . . . [I'll] take their papers and throw 'em on the floor or just tell the teacher that I don't, keep telling her that I don't understand this and I don't understand that. So she'll just say, "If you don't want to do it, then go down to the office," and I'll just leave . . . If I'm in a bad mood and I'm really frustrated and I just don't want to be near no one else, I'll get sent down to the office.

"You want to know something that really makes me mad?" asks thirteen-year-old Rachel. "When teachers think that they can do and say anything they want to us and they don't care how it makes us feel, but we have to be so careful what we say to them. It's really stupid." Rachel feels her anger intensely. Sometimes she talks back to teachers when she feels treated unfairly, but she holds in her anger and violent impulses toward her classmates: "I feel like [hitting people] a lot. I don't. I haven't yet."

Donna, fourteen, conveys her frustration with a teacher who hollers and points her finger at students:

Well, she aggravates me and she like says stuff, when she talks to me she like, I don't know, hollers and stuff. And one day she was hollering at me and I hollered right back at her . . . I've done it before, but she said if I did it again I'd get suspended . . . I told her I didn't like how she treats kids and stuff, and how she treats me, and I don't think she should holler at you. I think she should just talk. I told her that I just don't like how she points her finger and hollers at you and stuff . . . She sent me down to the office.

Thirteen-year-old Susan is known for speaking her mind: "I don't like people annoying me that much . . . and I don't like people talking behind my back about me," she admits during her interview, looking me straight in the eye. "I don't think there was a time," she assures me, when she wanted to say something but didn't.

Unlike the middle-class girls, the Mansfield girls do not hide their strong feelings from public view. Anger is not only more visible but frequently more intense, sustained, and sometimes physical than it is with the Acadia girls. In large part, these differences in behavior and expression hinge on their resistance to teachers and other authority figures in the school. Rather than trust teachers to be fair, these girls are angered and confused by what they perceive to be unpredictable and inconsistent treatment on the part of those in positions of power, particularly their women teachers. "What really makes me mad," Corrine complains, "is when teachers tell you to do something and then you do it and they say, and they go and tell you, 'Oh, why'd you do that?' and I'll say, 'Well, you told me to,' and they'll say, 'No, I didn't tell you to do that.' " "Like one day," Dana continues,

I was drawing on a poster thing and I was using [Miss Thomas's] little marker and she said I could use it. The next day she was in a bad mood and I go, "Can I use that marker again?" And she said [*in a mean voice*]: "What? You used that marker? I told you not to!" And she said I could use it the day before . . . She changes . . . And with Mrs. Evans you never know.

"Mrs. Nugent came in and started hollering at me," Donna complains. "I don't know why." "All the teachers are different," Patti adds. "Each day, I think they are different each day." "I don't like Miss Damon that much because she can get really moody," Cheyenne agrees. "You'll tell her something the week before and she'll forget and then you can say that and all of a sudden . . ."

It is not so much the teachers' anger that the girls resent, as the fact that they cannot always determine what they have done to cause such a response; there seem to be patterns of interacting and rules of communication inaccessible to them. The minute the girls think they have figured out what their teachers want, the rules change. Because, from the girls' point of view, their teachers are so unpredictable, the girls' attempts at reading their moods inevitably fail. The result is often explosive. "Um, Mrs. MacDonald, I get in trouble with her a lot," Rachel explains:

> Because like you can—everybody takes advantage of her because she puts up with so much and then once you push her too far, and she just stops putting up with it and you're in big trouble. Everybody thinks that they can do whatever they want in there because she don't do anything about it usually.
>
> *Lyn:* Is it unpredictable or can you tell when she's going to start to clamp down on things?
> *Rachel:* Well, sometimes you can, but then you don't think it's . . . I mean it's just like . . . she usually lets you go for a really long time and then sometimes you just start and she tells you to leave the room. She's known for it. She sends you down to the office or something.
> *Lyn:* How can you tell?
> *Rachel:* She'll tell you. She'll say, "One more time and you're down in the office." And you're like, "Already?" and like, "You usually put up with it longer than that."

What sounds like a conventional feminine response to anger—"putting up with it" until she is "pushed too far," then exploding in frustration—amuses the girls even though they don't quite understand it and don't know ahead of time how long things will be allowed to continue without consequence. The fact that "everybody takes advantage" of Mrs. MacDonald's tolerance, and tries, often without success, to predict her breaking point, signifies the distance the girls feel from their teacher and what she is about in the classroom. The girls and their teachers struggle to communicate, with limited success, across cultural realities firmly grounded in social class.

It seems odd that the girls would feel so distant from their teachers, given the long-standing relationship between the school and the Mansfield community, and given the relaxed, open structure of the school. In fact, a few of the women teachers grew up in the surrounding area and are considered community members. But such a personal history of enculturation would not necessarily ensure their connection to the girls or, for that matter, protect them from deep ambivalence about their role in the girls' lives. Although they are long-time Mainers and some have working-class backgrounds, they are also college graduates, students of teacher-training programs that are unlikely to address issues of class or critically examine dominant cultural norms and values. Indeed, in contrast with urban students, who may feel that their teachers cannot relate to them in part because they do not live in their communities, the Mansfield girls seem to feel betrayed that their teachers, many of whom *do* live in their community, either do not listen or cannot understand them.

Indeed, the Mansfield girls generally feel that their teachers cannot be counted on to respond, to care, or to understand what is *really* going on in the classroom; from the girls' point of view their teachers' moods are unreadable. Even the teachers she likes are confusing to Rachel:

> Well, Mrs. Harvey, she's fun, she like does fun stuff. And I learn a lot with her, but then she's easily not in a good mood. Like if somebody in one class gets her mad then the next class, when we come in, she's all mad still and it's like her mood changes easily.

And she gets really mad when she gets mad . . . We're always saying, "Mrs. Harvey is in a bad mood" when we hear her hollering.

With a few exceptions, the Mansfield girls feel that their teachers
do not take the time to listen or understand them. "I don't talk to
the teachers about [my opinions]," Susan explains, "because I don't
think they would listen to somebody that disagrees, and some of the
students do and [the teachers] just say that they disagree and they
don't find out our feelings about it." "It's like they're too busy to
listen when we need to know something," Rachel explains,

> and we have to follow 'em all around to get something, to know
> something. The teachers [are] always hollering at us, [about]
> everything. Like when they tell us to go do something, we'll think,
> why can't they do it theirselves? They're sending us everywhere.
> And I don't know—they're just hollering about everything. They
> can't like *tell* us, because they just always have to holler.

Unlike the Acadia girls, the Mansfield girls seem not to know what
their teachers want from them. They feel ignored and dismissed, even
when they think they are playing by the teachers' rules. Group sessions are repeatedly punctuated with their frustration and outrage.

Susan: I think that it's mean when teachers, like Miss Davis . . .
> yells at you because you want to ask her a question. And then
> she says, "In a minute, when I get done working." So when
> somebody else goes and asks her, she just goes and helps them
> and then . . . it just pisses me off.
Diane: So she's not listening to you when you ask for help. Well,
> why? Why aren't these people listening?
Amber: 'Cause they're bitches . . .
Susan: 'Cause they're ignorant . . .
Brianna: Like, um, Donna and I walked up to Miss Davis and she
> was like playing with a map or something. And she goes, "Go sit
> down! Go sit down!" And we sat down, and she said, "Go sit
> down and raise your hands." So we raised our hands, and we
> didn't get, I didn't get spoken to until the end of class, the end of

the day about what I wanted to talk about . . . And she was just ignoring me.

Diane: Why don't these people listen?

Stacey: Because they're ignorant.

The girls' complaints about their teachers hold a place for the power of their interpretations and the reality of their experiences. Collectively insisting on their teachers' ignorance and rudeness confirms the legitimacy of their requests and their manner of communicating in the classroom. And yet the intensity with which the girls express themselves speaks to the sense of both longing and loss they experience in relation to their women teachers. Their teachers, the girls say over and over, are "ignorant"—that is, they do not know anything about them—and yet many of the angry stories about their teachers are examples of possibility turned to disappointment, the possibility of being known and understood, the disappointment of lost relationships and shared knowledge. "When we're doing a subject like on friendship or feelings or something," twelve-year-old Brianna explains, "she'll like try to help you as much as she can. But then the next week, she'll just start [ignoring you] all over again." Others are stories of what the girls describe as their teachers' overreaction to ordinary behavior, resulting from their lack of awareness of who the girls are and indicating their lack of respect for their feelings.

Rachel: Today I was talking with James in [Mrs. Nugent's] room and he had [some things of mine] and he was passing them back to me and [Mrs. Nugent] told me to get out because she don't want . . . any of us in her room. She was really rude about things. She says, "Get out. I don't want any of you guys in my room." I go, "Yeah, just a second. Look, he's just passing them." And I was just holding out my hand ready for him to give them to me but he was being stupid, just holding them there, and she hollered, "Get out!" I go, "Will you wait a minute. I'm getting out!" . . . I was surprised she didn't come out and start yelling at me—but I just walked out.

Just as the girls cannot read their teachers, it would seem that the teachers cannot read the girls. From the girls' perspective, their women teachers allow no space for their ways of communicating and interacting. As a result the girls feel cut off, literally and figuratively pushed out of the classroom. In response to such situations, the Mansfield girls feel compelled to defend angrily their versions of reality and their behavior. For Rachel, "just being able to say what you want to say to a teacher, telling them what you feel," is something worth fighting for. "I'd get sent down to the office for it if I ever told Mrs. Damon what I thought about what she was saying to me," she adds. To others, watching teachers treat students "unfairly" or act as though "they don't care" is cause for resistance and reaction.

One day eleven-year-old Cheyenne shares with the group what she feels is a teacher's unfair treatment of her best friend, Donna. Her version of the story underscores a number of complaints the girls have with their teachers that surface and resurface over the course of the year; they complain about moodiness, overreaction, unpredictable behavior, and abuse of power:

Cheyenne: Yesterday, Miss Davis came in from recess and was really mad and nobody knew why. And she goes to [Donna], she goes, "Take off your coat." And she wouldn't take off her coat . . . Because she didn't feel comfortable taking it off; and she said, "Go out in the hall," and then half an hour later she went out in the hall with Donna and before she did that she was walking around and everybody would ask her for something and she'd start screaming at 'em.

Diane: Did she say why?

Patti: Maybe she had PMS!

Cheyenne: Wait! No. Anyways, they were out in the hall and she asked Donna why she wouldn't take off her coat and she goes, "Because I don't feel comfortable taking it off."

Donna: No, I said, "I didn't want to."

Cheyenne: Oh, because she didn't want to. And she goes, "I want
you to write me" . . . two pages on why she wouldn't take off
her coat.

Donna: No, two pages why she should let me wear my jacket.

Rachel: Oh, because she always . . . wears *her* jacket. [*some of the
girls start to talk*] Listen! She's like, at the end of last year, she
goes, "OK, when it's wintertime I'm going to have my window
open and you guys are going to have to live with it." So, okay,
we're wearing our coats. *She* can wear her coat when she's cold,
but we can't, we get in trouble for it.

Cheyenne: And then after that she says, "Go down to the office. I
don't want your kind here."

Diane: To you?

Cheyenne: No, to Donna because she wouldn't take off her coat.
And it's not fair because she can keep her coat on whenever she
wants—

Rachel: She thinks she can say whatever she wants.

Donna: I wrote a two-page letter and I told her . . . that if I didn't
want to take off my coat that I didn't have to and that she
shouldn't make me do anything that I didn't want to do . . . and
that she said that I'm going through a stage where I don't like
my body.

Diane: That's what she said?

Susan [*laughing, squeals in a high feminine voice*]: "I don't like my
body!"

Cheyenne: I don't like it when teachers say something and they
don't know what's going on though, and they say something
mean to you. They butt in and say, "Well, I know what's wrong
with you," and think they know what is going on.

Miss Davis's insistence on a rule that seems to the girls both arbitrary and unreasonable outrages them. This particular incident,
revisited a number of times over the course of the year, is emblematic
of what appears to be off or wrong between the girls and their

women teachers. Whether or not Cheyenne is quoting Miss Davis accurately, the girls generally feel that their teachers "don't want [their] kind here." In fact, it would seem, at least from this and other incidents the girls recount, that their teachers do not fully understand who "their kind" are. Miss Davis's explanation for Donna's resistance—that she is going through a stage where she does not like her body—echoes the voluminous literature on white middle-class girls' struggles with body image. But these white working-class girls are stunned and incredulous when they hear about the remark. Susan pokes fun at the very idea that this would be Donna's primary reason for resisting Miss Davis's no-coats rule. Cheyenne calls the teacher's comment "mean" and is angered by her presumptuousness. Donna, who refuses to write the letter Miss Davis asks for—flatly choosing to defend her actions rather than to submit to what appears to be a supercilious demand for explanation—concludes that Miss Davis "just wants something to bitch about." The girls' frustration and animosity toward their teachers center on the fact that, as twelve-year-old Stacey says at a later point, "teachers think they know what you are talking about."

When the coat problem resurfaces a number of sessions later, Diane encourages the girls to take their complaints before the school council. As they consider this possibility, the girls identify more clearly what most angers them about their teacher—it is not simply Miss Davis's unreasonable demands, but the way she uses her power to intrude on their lives, to presume that she has the requisite knowledge and intimacy to name their most private experiences:

Stacey: Miss Davis and her coats. What's her problem about coats?

Donna: I like to wear my coat . . .

Rachel: So why's it her business?

Donna: She wears *her* coat!

Diane: So, is this something you can bring up in student council . . . that you should be allowed to wear your coats if you want to?

Amber: Yeah!

Diane: Which one of you is going to bring it up at student council?

Donna: I will . . .

Rachel: It's not gonna work. I promise it won't. Miss Davis will explain, and it will all work out the way she wants it to.

Diane: What will Miss Davis say?

Rachel: What she says goes. No, she'll say, "There is no need to. Maybe it's not a school rule, but there will be no need to wear your coat. You can dress warm."

Diane: Well, could one of you say, "I have a personal need to wear my coat?"

Rachel: And she'll say, "What [is it]?" She thinks she has a right to.

Amber: Say it's personal.

Stacey: Then she'd take you aside and say, "You can talk to me," and just bitch you out . . . She has no right to do that.

Diane: Bring it up at student council then.

Stacey: Then she'll make us write a two-page paper on why we shouldn't—

Amber [who has been trying to speak]: "Shut the hell up!"

Sarah: Say, "No, we don't have to."

Amber: I know why she thinks we want to wear our coats. Because she thinks it's because we're afraid of our bodies, cause we're developing.

Donna: Yes, that's what she told me.

Rachel: I don't see why she should even have to know . . . If it's not a school rule, she shouldn't be able to say anything.

Sarah: She thinks she's so powerful, God, I'm so sick of it!

Amber: Before I leave this school I'm going to tell her off.

Donna: She thinks she can solve all the problems by telling us what to do and doesn't even know half the things she thinks she does.

Amber: I think she's going senile. She's losing her brain.

Rachel: I think she thinks that she knows everything, and that whatever she says is the whole thing . . . We're sick of her hollering.

Donna: It really ticks people off.

Diane: There has to be some way that this can get talked about with her . . . The coats you guys can work out, I think, because there's no rule that says you can't wear your coats.

Rachel: So next time she tells us to take our coats off, "just say no."

Stacey: I'm just going to say, "Is there a rule, is there a school rule that we cannot wear our coats?" And if there's a problem, I'll say, "Well . . ." and I'll let Donna take it from there [*laughs*].

The girls feel the weight of their teacher's "right" to their personal lives and the impossibility of publicly laying claim to their own interpretation of the situation. While Donna's desire to wear her coat might have something to do with her changing body, more likely it has to do with the obvious—the fact that Miss Davis keeps the window open in cold weather. Regardless of the real reason, the incident becomes something of a leitmotif for the girls, an example of their general resistance to their teachers' intrusiveness, a resistance Donna shows again later when another teacher catches her slouching in her chair: "She told me to sit up, and I go, 'No,' and she told me again and I said, 'No, I don't want to,' and she said go to the office." Whatever moves fourteen-year-old Donna to fold her arms stubbornly over her zipped coat remains unspoken in the face of Miss Davis's misinterpretation—and the girls' insistent belief that, no matter what they do, "it will all work out the way [Miss Davis] wants it."

Repeatedly, the girls point to a stalemate with their teachers—a failure of relationship grounded in an inability to read and accurately respond to each other's thoughts, feelings, and actions—that results all too often in frustration and anger and perceived hostility on both sides. At times during their group sessions anger fills the room. In frustration, Susan says of a teacher: "I'd just like to take her head and rip it off!" Amber shouts of yet another teacher: "I hate her! . . . I hate teachers!" "Teachers always make me mad," Rachel comments:

[They] yell too much, get so mad . . . I think that teachers should learn to control themselves and they ought to have more patience if they're going to be teachers . . . I hate it. They shouldn't be able to [yell at someone] in front of the whole class or anything. They shouldn't be able to yell at you and stuff . . . that totally embarrasses you . . . they should talk to you later or something.

Teachers, Cheyenne says, have a "massive attitude." It begins to seem to the girls, as Susan puts it, like "everything we do is wrong."

Indeed, as the girls talk about their teachers during these moments, there seems to be no common ground. The girls cannot understand why their teachers are so upset with them and so out of touch with their lives. And yet from what the girls say and do not say about their behavior in school—about pushing teachers to the limit, angry outbursts, acting out or getting in trouble so they don't have to be in classes—one can imagine how this communication gap feels from the other side. The girls' anger, however, points not only to their disappointment and loss, but also to their full engagement with this school drama and their desire for something to change.

The image of the cooperative, quiet female student was not constructed from the expressions and experiences of these girls, nor were the categories that so often define conventionally feminine behavior —selflessness, polite passivity, and discomfort with anger and conflict. The Mansfield girls frequently get in trouble not only for swearing "wicked loud" and for rough-housing, but also for being their plain-spoken, unsubtle selves—that is, for not personifying the white middle-class norms and ideals of femininity so valued in school and society.

Thus it is perhaps not surprising that though the girls have strong feelings and are likely to express themselves openly, they pretty much agree that their desires have little effect on the way things go. Should they say what they think, Sarah explains, "the teachers will jump down our throats . . . [they] don't listen to what we say." "What makes me angry?" Stacey asks. "If things aren't fair or if nobody will listen or if you can't, you don't feel as if you can say anything at school or if you don't think it would do any good." If she did persist, she continues, "I don't think [things] would really change," since what she tells her teachers "goes in one ear and right out the other."

In spite of their strong feelings, or perhaps, in part, because of them, the Mansfield girls find it difficult to participate in academic classroom discussions. Even though Amber expresses her frustration and anger with teachers and thinks "you should speak your mind and let everybody know how you feel," she doesn't actually talk much or participate in class: "I don't usually talk in the classroom . . . 'cause I just don't want . . . I just don't feel right . . . I don't like talking in front of a big group. I don't like being the center of attention." The other girls struggle in similar ways. "I don't like . . . I won't really say much [in class]," Cheyenne confesses, "because I think that I'll say something and the kids will like say, 'Oh, she's stupid to say that,' and all that stuff . . . I've seen them do that to other people . . . just whoever they don't like." Rachel, too, is sure she is not very smart and that she will always carry the burden of this fact. "I'm kind of stupid, basically," she laments in her group session one day. "I just don't think I'm good enough" to go to college or get a "good enough" job. As a result, school for Rachel seems futile, just a constant reminder of her deficiencies.

The anger, frustration, and hostility these girls express in school seem as much about their fear, alienation, and anxiety about their potential to succeed in and beyond school, as it is about an active or conscious resistance to authorities or to upper-middle-class ideals of femininity.[5] The way they are used to speaking at home does not serve them well in the middle-class culture of their school, where a different set of codes and rules applies. School, in a vague sense, just "doesn't feel right" to the girls, but they cannot always articulate exactly why. While their teachers are explicit about their power, their demands and punishments seem arbitrary and irrational. Without explicit explanation about what manner of behavior and speech they expect and why—that is, without an introduction into the "culture of power"—these girls experience themselves as stupid and their teachers as unreasonable, "unfair," and unresponsive.[6]

Against the backdrop of seemingly unpredictable and unreasonable authorities, relationships with their friends take precedence for these girls. Because they count on one another to listen, such relationships are the focus of a great deal of energy. In sessions the girls relentlessly tease and verbally spar with one another. As is the case with other white working-class girls, such ritual teasing, particularly about romantic and sexual behavior, is not only playful but collaborative—a way to support one another and to distance themselves from dominant cultural notions of feminine behavior.[7] The ritual teasing that takes place in the context of school, then, is understandable.

The Mansfield girls are comfortable turning their strong feelings outward. They express their disgust at the way the boys in their class behave and the differences in the way boys and girls are treated in the school. Sarah explains the nature of their conversations over the course of the year and the emerging group awareness of this as an issue:

> Well, we started talking about it, about how the guys are being so macho . . . like they have to do everything and do stuff first and have privileges more than girls. And the girls, you know, they just don't care. But they're starting to now. They're starting to get sick of the guys always wanting to be the best in everything and to them it means just everything, but we just kind of have fun and it feels good, and the guys have to win, but we just did it for fun.

For Rachel, the problem is "the way [boys] act . . . They're always loud and they're always talking so the teachers are always yelling at them and we'll have to listen to it." She finds it particularly disturbing that the boys get away with saying and doing "sickening" and "disgusting things."

Rachel: Like in one of the speeches Kevin wrote at graduation, they talk about sticks, and all that stuff and you know, like it sounds good if you're not thinking of it the way they are, but then all of a sudden they're laughing, because they . . .

Lyn: They're not talking about sticks. They're talking about something else.

Rachel: Yeah. And they always do it the same in all the classes because the teachers just think—they know that the teachers don't know what they're talking about.

Like the Acadia girls, the Mansfield girls notice that the boys are judged according to different standards; but unlike the Acadia girls, they acknowledge that these differences are gender based. The boys, Stacey notes, are usually "a lot louder" than the girls,

> and they usually try to be not as involved and they're usually the ones that get in trouble . . . I think they're allowed more time to do things. Say something needed to be typed and on a certain day and they didn't have it done. So, they will argue with the teacher and the girls don't really argue with them so they get more time to do it . . . They're, they're really pushy. But I don't think that's the only reason. I guess the girls are expected to have it done mostly.

And that, twelve-year-old Corrine adds, "is just the way it is."

Although Corrine, echoing the Acadia girls, sees this difference in treatment as almost inevitable—"it doesn't bother me, I guess, that much . . . it always happens, I guess, so it's just like life"—the Mansfield girls in general are more likely to fight the image of female subordination and to compete with the boys for time and space. When their teachers assume that the boys are "tougher," the girls react:

> *Sarah:* Like if it's something like moving or stacking chairs, they'll say . . . they'll pick a bunch of guys to go out and do it. They never ask us and I think . . . we can stack chairs too. Because the boys think they're so macho. They think the guys are tougher than us or something . . . I think there are some guys that are tough but then there are some that aren't and I get sick of it, about the guys thinking they're so tough and the teachers thinking they're so tough.

Rather than wait around to be asked to stack chairs, Sarah, twelve, explains, "we just go and do it . . . We try to compete with them harder, trying harder and doing better than we were before, to try to knock the guys down and win over them."

This resistance extends to the school playground as well. "Boys don't think girls can play basketball as good," Susan says, explaining why the boys feel entitled to the basketball court and constantly encroach on the girls' time. "I think that they should just change their attitude about it." Susan and her friends became so fed up with the boys' behavior that, with Diane's encouragement, they took their complaints to the school governing board. As a result, "the teachers decided that the girls will have the court one day and the boys will have it the next day." Although, as Susan points out, "it didn't work out" in the long run "because like the boys kept on coming on our court while it was our time," and because, Amber thinks, "the girls didn't push hard enough . . . and then it like died out," the girls, in typical fashion, continue on occasion to demand their full playing time.

Although these girls feel anger and often openly express it, they say that they are told time and again by their women teachers that anger is not an appropriate emotion to express in school. Since the teachers and administrators did respond to the girls' anger about unfair treatment at school, that is, about the basketball court, it seems that the girls are talking about the teachers' response to feelings that are more private. As Donna, who, with the encouragement of her mother and a therapist, has struggled for some time to express her anger about her father's physical abuse, explains:

I think [expressing anger] is a relief because when my dad and mom were married, I never expressed my feelings at all. I just, I don't know, because my dad used to beat up on me, so I like wouldn't say anything, you know, and I had to go to counseling and stuff, and then it just came. And my mom thinks I still have a lot of anger because of my dad and stuff.

Donna knows her anger is sometimes out of control at school—"I take it out on people and I know it's not right, but they say something and it just comes out"—but she doesn't know how to be in school with these feelings or how to be herself without them.

> I either try to talk to [the counselor] when she's here or when she's not here I, um, if I can't talk to her, I just sit there and do nothin', and I won't talk. I just sit there . . . A lot of people think, Miss Davis says [school's] not the proper place to express it, like your family problems at school because, you know . . . [she] says we should take it out in recess, but I don't know, then I might beat up somebody.

These working-class girls, who do not reify the separate spheres of public and private in the way the middle-class girls do, and who tend to see school in terms of "embattled relationships," find it difficult to understand such boundaries placed around the expression of feelings.[8] When Donna says school is not the proper place to express anger she means, in effect, the "family problems" that give rise to her feelings. Given the significant role she has played as mediator in her family and the value she places on caring for others—especially her mother—much of who she is and what she values is thus rendered inappropriate or invisible in school.

Rachel talks about how she deals with her anger in school in ways that suggest that the intensity of her feelings are, in part, a response to the regulation of her voice. She tells what happened when a teacher, in a bad mood, "sent me [down] to the office for going to the stupid bathroom."

> But I didn't go down. I didn't go down. She said I had to go see [the principal]. I didn't. And today I wasn't going to, but Mrs. Nugent went and told Mrs. Higgins that I wasn't cooperating and going down . . . When I came back up, it was even worse.

Diane: So how did you handle your anger over this situation?
Rachel: I just sat there and I wanted to punch something.
Diane: And you didn't do anything, you just held it all in?
Rachel: I couldn't! Well, what I wanted to do I'd get suspended for
 . . . Well, I always go in the kitchen and talk to people.

In this way the Mansfield girls struggle, with few structured or safe places to sort through their anger and express their rage; in a very fundamental way, they feel alienated from school and abandoned by their teachers. Donna feels caught between the messages she receives from home, that it's good to let her anger out, and those she receives from school, that expressing anger in public is inappropriate. Getting the message, she says she holds her feelings in, until a classmate or teacher pushes too far. Like one day, she explains, "I told Mrs. Evans that she was a fucking liar and I had to stay down to the office from 9:30 until 12:30 . . . I thought it was good for me to sit in the office because I knew if I went back upstairs that real trouble would have started and I would have gotten suspended." Rachel, knowing the consequences of expressing her strong feelings in school, holds her anger in and seeks out the familiar faces of the women who work in the cafeteria; they seem to understand her and care for her.

I am not suggesting that any and all forms of anger should be tolerated in school—certainly the girls' yelling and swearing make both teaching and learning difficult, if not impossible. Rather, I wish to highlight what appear to be radically different communicative styles and a clash of cultures, and suggest that the Mansfield girls' intense anger toward many of their teachers is, in part, about their emerging awareness of the difference between who they are and what their teachers want them to be. That their teachers "holler" at the girls so much, even as they demand their public compliance with middle-class conventions of speech and behavior, intensifies the girls' confusion and anger and contributes to their sense of betrayal. At best school becomes a place where these girls negotiate the intersection of cultural and class values; at worse, it represents a disingenuous imposition of "appropriate" femininity and middle-class views

that serve to denigrate their experiences and contribute to their growing distrust of authorities.

In many ways, these adolescent girls, both working- and middle-
class, interrupt our often unexamined notions of idealized femininity.
Neither group of girls represents the conventional ideal, and each
enters the culture struggling against the demands and costs of female
impersonation. Although the Acadia girls appear to capitulate to or
appropriate white middle-class ideals of feminine behavior, beneath
the surface they are frustrated and angry with the lack of recognition
and the invisibility such conventions demand. The angel in the classroom has her counterpoint in the "madgirl." Like the madwoman in
the attic of Victorian literature, she is rebellious, subversive, sometimes outrageous; she knows that her thoughts and feelings, especially strong feelings like anger, place her in danger of being called
pathological or monstrous.[9] As with the madwoman, the girls' strong
feelings are pushed out of view, cut off, figuratively locked away in
the cultural attic, or perhaps more accurately, buried in the basement.
The Acadia girls do say what they know, what they feel and want,
if only in the privacy of their interviews and focus groups. They are
aware at times that they are performing or impersonating idealized
femininity—that who they present themselves to be is not who they
feel they really are.

The Acadia girls' adoption of the American Dream and its radical
individualism, in conjunction with their discomfort with anger and
the direct expression of what they want and need, contributes to
intense underground competition, undermining what began as a collective, potentially powerful political resistance. Moving out of touch
with one another, they have little corroboration for their feelings and
express doubt about their perceptions. More important, they lose the
power of their shared feelings and common circumstances, a loss that
prevents them from seeing or reacting to the larger cultural picture
and their place in it.

By contrast, the Mansfield girls, because of their angry distrust of

authority, learn from one another and, in spite of often difficult interactions, stay in much closer relationship with one another. Their
resistance, with their capacity to be outspoken and publicly angry,
gives them a shared vision of a hostile world and, with this vision,
the power to organize. A number of times during the year the girls
supported one another through trying incidents, and in two cases—
the coat incident and the basketball court battle—with Diane Starr's
encouragement, were so vocal as a group that they were able to affect
school policy.

Unlike the middle-class girls, then, the Mansfield girls live their
"madness" in full view of their teachers, administrators, and classmates. And yet, their distrust of authorities, the confusing, often contradictory messages they receive about appropriate behavior, and
their justified belief that they will not be heard or taken seriously also
prevent them from developing genuine relationships with their
women teachers. Notwithstanding the girls' hostility and frustration,
there are numerous signs that their teachers do care and are trying
to listen. It was the school, for example, that notified the authorities
about Donna's abuse, and it was a responsive teacher who raised
concerns for Corrine's physical and emotional well-being; school policies *were* changed in response to the girls' complaints, and even
though Miss Davis may have misinterpreted Donna's refusal to take
off her coat, she seemed to try to engage Donna in a dialogue she
thought was important for her student. The problem, in fact, seems
not to be that the teachers do not care, but that unexamined class
and cultural divides prevent shared understanding between the girls
and their women teachers.

For both the Acadia and the Mansfield girls, anger is a source of
knowledge and motivation. It points to the heightened regulation of
their thoughts, feelings, and actions, and it announces their resistance. Although the politics of their anger is at times only barely
discernible to others, much less to themselves, the disruptiveness of
their response contests a construction of reality that denigrates, mar-
ginalizes, or buries their experiences. These girls, in their passion and
struggle, hold the potential for deepening our understanding of ide-

alized femininity by clarifying the damage it causes and alluding to the social and psychological forces holding it in place. Should we pay close attention to their anger, as well as to the discomfort it arouses in us, we may well find ourselves participating in a different kind of conversation, open to other meanings and new pathways.

eight

Educating the Resistance

They don't just sell you a dream in school, they pin you down with truth.

VALERIE WALKERDINE[1]

In a place where truth mattered, no one would betray her, and so her courage grew, and with it, her determination.

JEANETTE WINTERSON[2]

In her autobiographical novel, *Oranges Are Not the Only Fruit*, Jeanette Winterson describes a central struggle of her coming of age and coming into relationship with herself as a girl: how to stay in touch with what she knew to be true from her experience in the face of pressure to not know and not speak. In a chapter appropriately entitled "Exodus," nine-year-old Jeanette feels acutely the conflictive pull of an evangelical home life filled with good and evil, comedy and tragedy, and a different but equally absolute reality of girlhood and femininity promoted in school.

Struggling to do her "very best to be good and fit in," trying with all her energy to make herself "as ordinary as possible," Jeanette nonetheless upsets her teachers and her classmates with her observations, direct questions, and predilection for speaking personal truths. When finally, after many mishaps and missteps, she insists on embroidering a message from Jeremiah on her sampler in sewing class (rejecting the nicely suggested "To Mother with Love" or the popular "Suffer the Little Children" for the more dramatic and, to

Jeanette, perfectly suitable "The Summer Is Ended and We Are Not Yet Saved"), the confrontation with her teacher, Mrs. Virtue, is perhaps inevitable. From Jeanette's perspective her sampler—designed as a gift for an elderly religious friend, Elsie Norris—was "a masterpiece of its kind," complete with "a sort of artist's impression of the terrified damned." Elsie loved it and Jeanette decided to enter it in the school "Prizegiving contest":

> "Here's mine Mrs. Virtue," I said, placing it on the desk.
> "Yes," she said, meaning No.
> "I will enter it, if that's what you want, but to be frank I don't think it's the sort of thing the judges will be hoping for."
> "What do you mean," I demanded, "it's got everything, adventure, pathos, mystery . . . ."
> She interrupted.
> "I mean, your use of color is limited, you don't exploit the potential of the thread; take Shelley's Village Scene for instance, notice the variety of colors."
> "She's used four colors, I've used three."
> Mrs. Virtue frowned.
> "And besides, no one else has used black."
> Mrs. Virtue sat down.
> "And I've used mythical counter-relief," I insisted, pointing to the terrified damned.
> Mrs. Virtue laid her head on her hands.
> "What are you talking about? If you mean that messy blotch in the corner. . . ."
> I was furious. . . .
> "Just because you can't tell what it is, doesn't mean it's not what it is."
> I picked up Shelley's Village Scene.
> "That doesn't look like a sheep, it's all white and fluffy."
> "Go back to your desk, Jeanette."
> "But . . ."
> "GO BACK TO YOUR DESK!"[3]

As a result of this exchange, Jeanette reached a conclusion. Mrs. Virtue, it seemed,

> suffered from a problem of vision. She recognized things according to expectation and environment . . . I knew that my sampler was absolutely right in Elsie Norris's front room, but absolutely wrong in Mrs. Virtue's sewing class. Mrs. Virtue should either have had the imagination to commend me for my effort in context, or the far-sightedness to realize that there is a debate going on as to whether something has an absolute as well as a relative value; given that, she should have given me the benefit of the doubt.[4]

Clearly it was not only her sampler that was out of place in Mrs. Virtue's class, but Jeanette herself. This precocious girl who passionately describes what she sees and hears and who fights for her vision of art is disturbing to her teachers and frightening to the other girls. But just as the signs and symbols, discourse and actions of her religious working-class background are out of context in her classroom, so will her lesbianism soon be at odds with her religion. Jeanette's life is an ongoing struggle with the contradictions between and within world-views that each claim absolutism and promise absolution. Each demands all while severing some part of what Jeanette feels is essential: her desires, her directness, and her unusual angle of vision. Here in Mrs. Virtue's classroom Jeanette begins her long battle over the interpretation of truth and reality.

Jeanette's struggles not only illustrate the multitude of voices and identities children take in and take on during the process of their ideological becoming, but also bring into bold relief the subtle and not-so-subtle regulation of their voices by those in positions of authority. Her experiences illustrate, too, how girls respond and resist when they come to realize that their observations and experiences are rendered unrecognizable in patriarchal institutions, particularly schools. Most important, perhaps, Jeanette's story illustrates adult women's often unwitting participation in this regulatory process and their frequent inability to see and hear what girls' struggles and refusals are about.

Each year I teach *Oranges Are Not the Only Fruit* in a course on girls' development and education, and each year my students grapple with the complexity of Jeanette's journey through childhood and adolescence: her struggle against the powerful weight of religious judgment and dominant cultural norms of femininity and compulsory heterosexuality, the costs of betrayal after betrayal in the name of love and justice, the courageous fight for personal integrity, and finally, the contradictions, ambiguities, and unresolved feelings of an examined life. Jeanette's story interrupts my students' tendency, year after year, to respond primarily to the *losses* girls sustain and to underappreciate the possibility, even under the most oppressive of conditions, for creative refusal and resistance. This tendency intersects with the prevailing cultural discourse about girls' development, a fairly simplistic discourse of capitulation that has become so accepted that complicated and uneven stories of courage like Jeanette's sound so unusual as to be implausible.

Over the last few years I have talked with a number of junior high and high school girls about their experiences in light of such discourse. Our conversations lead me to worry that the current rhetoric of low self-esteem and accommodation has become a self-fulfilling prophecy. Some girls simply announce their loss of self-esteem to me, whereas others wonder aloud if and when this loss will happen to them. Still others impertinently ask, "Who exactly is Ophelia?" and "Where are the others?" by which I believe they mean, Where are the heroic girls and their stories of resistance and refusal?

What makes popular constructions of girls' development so disturbing, besides their simplicity, is the lack of alternative stories of possibility and successful struggle. Although the Acadia and Mansfield girls are clearly not meant to be representative of all girls their age, on the most basic level their conversations over the period of a year underscore that development is indeed complicated, that losses in voice and self-esteem are by no means simple or inevitable, and, when they occur, are certainly not passively accepted. Listening for different voices and the relationships among them—illustrates both the complex nature of the psyche and its relationship to culture, and suggests how and why certain voices are picked up, highlighted, and legitimized over other voices. Listening carefully to the girls also reveals that, though they may resist in direct or creative ways, such resistance does not always translate into higher self-esteem or effective change; indeed, under particular circumstances, it can be self-defeating and counterproductive.[5]

Adolescence, Michelle Fine and Pat Macpherson explain, "is a time in which young women must negotiate their multiple selves, through struggles of heterosexuality and critiques of gender, race, and class arrangements."[6] The Mansfield and Acadia girls reveal the degree to which the complicated terms of this negotiation itself are deeply classed and cultured. Although they live scarcely an hour away from each other, these two groups of girls are worlds apart in their experiences, in the voices and messages they take in from their families and local communities about appropriate femininity, in their expressions of their thoughts and feelings, in their perceptions of themselves, and in their understanding of their relationships with one another.

Class, Gender, and Race

Class has a particularly deep effect on the girls' feelings about themselves. The Mansfield girls' experiences and future imaginings are filtered through the reality of their material situations. Their expressions of longing and desire give rise not only to anxiety, self-doubt, and self-deprecation, but also to anger, frustration, defensiveness, hope, and determined resistance. Even as they long for riches and success, they anticipate lives of hard work, supported by friends and family members; they expect, against their most fervent hopes, that they will always be concerned about having enough. Of course, such realities affect the relationships they seek and the kind of people they imagine themselves to be: outspoken, direct, strong, loving, invulnerable to pain and hurt, ready to defend themselves and their loved ones against unfairness and cruelty.

Viewed through the lens of idealized femininity, such emerging subjectivities are disruptive, if not incomprehensible. In her recent book *Daddy's Girl,* Valerie Walkerdine argues that "the little working-class girl presents, especially to education, an image which threatens the safety of the discourse of the innocent and natural child. She is too precocious, too sexual . . . she is deeply threatening to a civilizing process understood in terms of the production and achievement of natural rationality, nurturant femininity."[7] In her description of a young working-class girl in relationship with her father, Walkerdine explores such a girl threat in the making: "She is his baby, but also his tomboy, his fighter. Such a combination of baby girl and fighter [does] not go down well at school and Joanne's strategies are noticeably unsuccessful with her teacher."[8] The Mansfield girls, like Joanne, are "noticeably unsuccessful" with their teachers. Their propensity to fight verbally, and physically when necessary, to speak the unspeakable, to be nurturing and also tough and self-protecting, threatens to disrupt the boundaries of appropriate femininity proselytized—though not always modeled—in their school.

And yet the Mansfield girls insist on bringing their loud, direct selves to school. In doing so, they engage in a daily public struggle with their teachers over the interpretation of reality and the contours of legitimate knowledge. Their refusal to be contained reveals, as it does in Wendy Luttrell's study of white working-class women, an implicit critique of schooling that ignores "the exigencies of poor and working-class families" by rewarding " 'good girl' behavior and traditional middle-class femininity" and denying "the reality and legitimacy of working-class femininity, an image of women as hardworking, responsible caregivers."[9] Because they tend to speak their mind, they unwittingly disrupt tacit boundaries between public and private speech; their laughter, playfulness, and anger disturb the "bourgeois class biases" that determine proper behavior and that shape and inform "pedagogical process (as well as social etiquette) in the classroom."[10] Their physical aggressiveness contests the well-mannered "good girl" most teachers imagine and hope to meet each day in school.

The struggle between the Mansfield girls and their women teachers is complex. Certainly the teachers seem unpredictable and irrational in part because these girls come to school with different conceptions of the relationship between gender, knowledge, and power, and because the signs and codes of the culture of power have never been clearly stated or explained to them.[11] The girls are often at odds with the school culture, and they are, at various moments, angry, sad, defensive, confused, entertained, and energized by this fact. Since there is little opportunity to express their anger, frustration, and hurt in ways that will be heard and understood, they protect themselves and engage their teachers by playing into this miscommunication—searching out those issues or behaviors that "get to" their teachers, taking bets on when a teacher will have "had enough," or simply, as eleven-year-old Cheyenne puts it, "bugging the crap out of them."

But there is more to the Mansfield girls' resistance. Cheyenne points to a deeper struggle when she observes that "people don't listen because they don't like us." The girls know that their presence in the school is disruptive. Their teachers' reactions—their anger, over-attention to rules, excessive interest in the way the girls speak and present themselves—reinforce the girls' sense of being different and hence inadequate. In response, the girls defensively profess their hatred of their teachers.

Although from the teachers' point of view the girls' anger, in some cases born out of or exacerbated by the terrible hurt of family stress and violence, must feel hostile and threatening, what these girls long for and seem unable to attain is a genuine closeness with their women teachers. They speak fondly of those rare occasions when they feel "closer" to a teacher, when "it feels more like she's a person," when "she really cares about us," or when teachers "know how I'm feeling."

The girls thus make a clear distinction between such care and the intrusiveness and false assumptions about which they complain so often. When teachers approach them with preconceived notions of what young girls should be, the girls are reminded that they are not what their teachers value and expect. Such voice-overs are reminders, too, that their teachers, who don't "really know" them, nonetheless have the power to interpret their lives and the meaning of their actions. This power is most visible and disturbing to the girls when they experience the contradictions between the way their teachers treat them and the way they themselves are expected to speak and behave. These experiences and reminders create barriers to the possibility of genuine relationship. What makes the working-class girls' interactions with their teachers so compelling is thus not only their angry refusal to be contained by dominant constructions of femininity, but also their vulnerability in the face of such barriers to relationship.

For the most part, the Mansfield girls' wishes fall on defensive, or perhaps frustrated, ears. What these girls believe are their attempts to be heard and understood, to be respected and taken seriously, many of their teachers seem to experience as deliberate disruption, lack of attention and effort, and impulsive, childish behavior. Without someone to assist them in negotiating this gap, these girls are disqualified both from relationships with their teachers and from the culture of their school—a culture supported even by those women teachers with working-class roots. As a result, the girls and their teachers unwittingly contribute to perceptions of the girls as rebellious or "stupid" and therefore marginal students, and risk that they will remain outside the system, disconnected, and therefore ineffective.[12]

Although in a very different way, the Acadia girls, too, struggle with the contradictory voices telling them what it means to be a good girl. Their material privilege invites expectations and fantasies of success constructed in the familiar, accessible terms of white middle-class America: voices of unfettered entitlement and radical individualism press them to go forth, to embrace competition, and to leave others behind. But acceptance, protection, and security, they also understand, are assured for those girls who attain and maintain the dominant feminine ideal—for those who do not call attention to themselves or make waves. Their teachers' preference for the popular girls and boys complicates this picture, by reinforcing the importance of wealth, appearance, and physical beauty, as well as the power of emotional relationships between teachers and their favorite students. While they say that they refuse to be the kind of girls who are the "teacher's pets"—preoccupied with appearance, feigning compliance and dependence, presenting false selves to fit in with the popular group or to please their teachers—the Acadia girls long for the attention, recognition, and power the popular girls gain by such facades.[13]

Deciphering and negotiating such contradictory constructions of femininity and possibility are difficult. The Acadia girls play it safe, holding back their strong feelings and opinions. In so doing, ironically, they bury the very qualities that would move them to act on their own behalf and prove them to be unique, creative, deep, and special—that is, the very qualities that they insist they "really" have, the qualities they will, in fact, need in order to be taken seriously.

The Acadia girls are thus more likely than the Mansfield girls to move their feelings and thoughts out of the public arena of school and into the active underground.[14] They hone the fine art of indirect speech, cultivate public smiles, and practice signs of rapt attention —their bodies bent forward in anticipation, their eyes wide-open, heads nodding, even while, behind the scenes and between the lines, they make faces of disgust or surreptitiously kick a bothersome boy.[15] They express their anger and resistance toward unfair school practices and social conventions quietly and creatively—providing wrong answers to the popular kids, developing witty but obtuse come-backs to sexist remarks, reappropriating derogatory terms, and speaking condescendingly or in carefully encoded language—and then they attend our group sessions filled with frustration or return home, where they say they can be themselves.

And yet, in spite of the middle-class girls' resistance to the regulation of their strong feelings and expressions, they and their teachers share a common understanding and language. Educated their entire lives in the "cultural capital" of idealized femininity and white middle-class values, they understand the rules and codes of the culture of power.[16] They share an "oral style" with their teachers. They know well, for example, what their teachers' indirect questions or suggestions imply; they understand that "veiled commands are commands nonetheless."[17] And they know well, as bell hooks explains, that "silence and obedience to authority" are "most rewarded"; that "loudness, anger, emotional outbursts, and even something as seemingly innocent as unrestrained laughter" are "deemed unacceptable, vulgar disruptions of classroom social order," are, indeed, "associated with being a member of the lower classes."[18] In school they participate in the policing of too loud, inappropriately direct voices, of less-than-subtle demeanors and actions, even as they react negatively to the demands such constraints place on them and the invisibility they ensure.

Thus, over the course of a year, the Mansfield and Acadia girls reveal how class is reproduced in their developing subjectivities and imaginations. For the middle-class girls it is evident in their preoccupation with where they fit within the social hierarchy of their school, their underground collectivity, which turns to more competitive isolation over the course of the school year, their disdain for other girls and emerging distrust in one another, and their belief in meritocracy over the reality of their experiences. For the Mansfield girls, class is evident in their miscommunication with, and eventual distrust in, their teachers and other school authorities, in their refusal to map onto the gendered polarities of middle-class culture, and in their intense struggle, against the negative identities offered to them, to imagine their futures, to believe in their capabilities, and to remain connected to their community. And yet, neither group of girls had ever had explicit conversations about class-related issues in their schools. Indeed, according to bell hooks , "nowhere is there a more intense silence about the reality of class differences than in educational settings."[19]

The struggles of the Acadia and Mansfield girls highlight not only the importance of class for understanding their emerging subjectivities, but also the intimate, layered relationships among class, femininity, culture, and race. Listening to these middle- and working-class girls, it becomes impossible, for example, to conflate whiteness with material privilege, or white femininity with indirectness and passivity or a desire to please others. Through their conversations and performances these girls disrupt such a monolith and, often unwittingly, specify the particular "locations, discourses, and material relations to which the term 'whiteness' applies."[20] As a result, they vividly remind us of how little we talk about the various cultural configurations and class identities of white girls.

More specifically, the working-class girls, in their difference from the mainstream, point to a construction of whiteness derived from their particular cultural identity, material disadvantage, and racial privilege. The voices of these girls carry the self-protective anger and moral defiance of a group living off the map of material wealth and privilege. Yet theirs is a position backed by the privileged history of the white race in the United States. Perhaps because the benefits of this privilege are out of their reach, the working-class girls and their families feel and express a sense of anxiety and frustration. Such anxiety and frustration may contribute to the family violence and abuse some of the girls describe, as well as to their willingness, at times, to protect and understand their abusers.

The middle-class girls reveal a childhood and adolescence in which race and class privilege are givens. Even their anxieties about their class position underscore this fact, since they reflect not self-examination or cultural critique, but a need to justify the prevailing concerns of the middle class in the United States: that no one is listening to their needs, that they are taken advantage of, squeezed out by the poor on the one side and the rich on the other. Not surprisingly, then, color and poverty are conflated and encoded in the Acadia girls' discourse, most obviously in their descriptions of the poor as lazy, deceitful, and fertile. This is so even though, in their experience, the poor are white. As with the white women Ruth Frankenberg interviewed, racism emerges not as "an ideology or political orientation chosen or rejected at will," but "as a system of material relationships with a set of ideas linked to and embedded in those material relations."[21] As seventh-graders, these girls have begun the active process of negotiating their identities, speaking in and through the voices most familiar and, for the moment, most persuasive to them.

"Subjectivity," Valerie Walkerdine claims, "is produced at the intersection of a number of, often competing, discourses and practices, all of which position and designate the subject."[22] We can best understand this construction of subjectivity in times of struggle. The girls in this study, balanced on the precipice of full-blown adolescence, reveal the difficult transformations of public language into private consciousness through their struggles to come to terms with the tensions between local and dominant notions of femininity, between their experiences and the unattainable ideal.

Resisting Education

The Acadia and Mansfield girls are creative in their identity struggles and their search for guiding ideologies. They play with language and forms of dress; they reappropriate different femininities and sometimes masculinities; and they shift identities depending on the situation and their audience. Their voices and body movements signal their play and reveal the possibilities open to them. While the form of this "shape-shifting" reflects their particular racial, cultural, and classed experiences, their struggle itself is, in large part, a response to the increasingly intense social efforts to control girls who are becoming women. Their reactions, their anger in particular, are the result of efforts to bring them in line with expectations about how "good" girls should look and sound and act.

Feminist writings about powerful learning experiences underscore the importance of expressing passionate emotions such as anger. Emotions "keep us aware or alert" in the classroom, bell hooks argues.[23] Strong feelings, allowed into the public world of the classroom, invite dissent, genuine excitement, and full engagement in the learning process. Encouraging the expression of reasoned anger prepares a place for social and political critique and serious consideration of the culture of power.

Indeed, Belenky, Clinchy, Goldberger, and Tarule find that the capacity to stay in touch with experience that is at the root of constructive anger is critical to girls' and young women's intellectual development. It is vital to their move away from an unquestioned reliance on external, usually male, authorities for knowledge and toward the authoring of their lives.[24] So, too, is anger vital to young women's capacity to critique oppressive and constraining educational practices. Tracing "interactive phases" of both personal and curricular change, Peggy McIntosh argues that anger is "absolutely vital" to one's ability to articulate a coherent world-view.[25] Anger marks the moment when white girls and women, gays and lesbians, people of color, and the poor and working class realize their absence in the curriculum and their invisibility in society; it motivates refusal "to see ourselves only as a problem," or to participate in a system in which we are encouraged to "unwittingly . . . overlook, reject, exploit, disregard, or be at war with most people of the world."[26] It is an embodied revelation that is inherently disruptive and conflictual.

And yet there is no guarantee that such strong feelings will be transformative, or even that they ought to be unconditionally supported. What is important is that we recognize the *potential* power of anger if and when it is heard, understood, and engaged in dialogue. Wherever there is a possibility for genuine relationship girls, particularly at early adolescence, are more likely to offer their often astute and critical observations of the social and political world. Moreover, they are more able to know and articulate the costs to themselves and to society of appropriating idealized notions of femininity. Without this opportunity, we risk girls' disconnection from themselves and from their learning, and their subsequent uncritical participation in the current state of "civilization."

Although schools defend their claims to neutrality, both the Mansfield and the Acadia girls reveal the hegemony of white middleclass values and goals. Echoing Foucault's analysis of the power of knowledge/discourse, Elizabeth Debold underscores how "the ideal —the dreamed for, the wish—can overwhelm reality, shadowing it and making it seem shabby. Within the eternal space between real and ideal, we are subjected most painfully and resist most hopefully."[27] The Acadia girls' impersonations of female perfection and the Mansfield girls' performances of toughness point to dominant cultural ideals of femininity and the ways such ideals intersect the lines of class and culture to create very different feelings, possibilities, and opportunities. Toughness and invulnerability, like perfection, threaten to separate girls from one another and pull them away from the reality of their experiences. And yet, in the space between ideal and real there are moments of creative struggle and hope.

One of my most vivid memories of school is of an encounter with a strict fifth-grade teacher. He was seated at his desk; I was standing by his side. He was an unusually tall, lanky man, and so to work with me, even sitting, he had to fold in on himself. As he huddled over my paper, I uttered an off-hand, irreverent come-back to a comment he made, something uncharacteristic of me in its impertinence. I don't actually recall what I said, but I vividly remember his reaction. He sat up straight and looked down at me, surprise registered on his face for what seemed, to me, like an eternity. I held my breath; which way would he go? Suddenly, startling me and the others around us, he laughed out loud. To this day I can feel the relief that flooded my body. He was, thereafter, special to me; he had chosen something real in me over the ideal. I was not "shabby" in my working-class reality, but interesting, clever.

Such relatively unremarkable events can have a powerful effect on girls' lives. Fleeting moments of genuine connection and understanding, "dangerous memories" of knowing and acting and speaking, can become the seeds of self-respect, the roots of an education for liberation.[28] Women recall such small events and also more significant "moments of rebellion" as turning points in their educations.[29] The moment of hesitation suggests the choice available to every teacher. Such moments remind us that every act in relation to girls, even one so minor, either supports a political resistance to dominant gender conventions and cultural oppressions or fosters a psychological resistance—capitulation to those conventions that contribute to resentment and the regeneration of not knowing. And such moments call on us to ponder what prevents those of us who teach and work with girls from hearing their irreverent voices as potentially courageous rather than as disturbing or simply annoying.

The working-class girls in this study say they want teachers who try to understand what they are really saying. They long for teachers who can see beneath the surface and read their intentions, know their real feelings. "I like teachers," Cheyenne says, who, "if I want to say somethin' to 'em, that they know I'm angry and I say something bad to 'em about what I feel, they won't like take me down to the office because they like, know how I'm feeling and they know that I won't . . . just say it because I want to say it. I'll say it 'cause I'm mad."

These girls want teachers who not only "really listen" but are not put off by the intensity of their feelings; who are able to stay with them and help them explore the reasons behind their actions. Informality seems to be the rule in the classrooms of the teachers the girls enjoy. After her classroom became less structured, twelve-year-old Amber announced: "I like this [class] now better, because I used to hate school. I like it now . . . I used to hate to come. I used to fake sick. I hated school. I like it now, though." Such informality invites the possibility of relationship, a possibility Sarah, also twelve, experiences when a teacher opens her classroom to cooperative learning:

> Since we've had this new program, I've gotten to learn like a lot more about the teacher and we've gotten closer. Like we can talk to the teacher a lot better than we could before. She's not so much like a machine like just sitting up there talking to us and teaching us. She's actually helping us once in a while, you know . . . I like it a lot better . . . it feels more like she's a person, she really cares about us, how we feel and what our best ways to learn are.

Such progressive approaches seem to offer opportunities for "connected knowing" unavailable in more conventional classrooms, and this invites the girls to bring more of what matters to them to their learning.[30] Connected knowing, according to Belenky and her colleagues, is "characterized by a stance of belief," as opposed to doubt, and involves "entering into the place of the other person or the idea that one is trying to know."[31] As an affirmation of the subjective reality of the other, a "swinging boldly into the mind of another," it requires careful listening and moves one toward a collaborative search for understanding that leads to insight and the construction of knowledge.[32] The Mansfield girls feel the strain of the miscommunication and misinterpretation they typically experience with their teachers and jump at those special moments when affirmative humor and informality promise relief. Indeed, they say repeatedly that they want a teacher who "ain't so serious about everything," someone who "would make [class] fun," someone who uses humor to break up "all that tension."

Not unlike the Mansfield girls, the Acadia girls say they want teachers who let them "talk openly," something Theresa admits that she doesn't "dare to do . . . [because] some teachers will get really mad at you." Reflecting their particular concerns about authenticity, these girls want a teacher who is "always herself." Such favorite teachers, the girls agree, "know a lot about life and stuff."

Being themselves pretty much guarantees that cherished teachers will be irreverent, a little "off," and therefore somewhat disruptive. This describes Robin's "cool" teacher, who is demanding when it comes to disciplining her students, but who is also "really funny" and does outlandish things in her class to engage her students, including organizing games of "Truth or Dare." But what is most important to Robin about this teacher is that "you can talk to her. She's like a second guidance counselor." She is someone, Robin insists, who "doesn't lie to us. She tells us the truth."

Robin points to perhaps the most important quality that both the Acadia and the Mansfield girls look for in their teachers. Favorite teachers are loyal not only to themselves—holding to high standards, in touch with their own thoughts and feelings, passionate about their work—but also to the students in their charge, always looking for ways to bring out the girls' unique qualities. For the Mansfield girls, loyalty takes the form of "listening" and "being there," just as Diane Starr is there for them—not turned off by their anger, but ready, always, to help them transform their strong feelings into knowledge and action. For the Acadia girls, loyalty means not acting as though truth does not matter by pretending not to know what is really going on—whether it is special favors for the popular kids, unearned attention for the boys, or hurtful and harassing behavior.

When and how girls forge genuine relationships with their teachers or express their anger at fraudulence and betrayal depends on teachers' and other school authorities' listening and taking the girls' strong feelings seriously. For girls at the edge of adolescence, the responsiveness of their teachers, and their ability, in one teacher's words, to help their students "turn anger into knowledge," are crucial.[33]

But experiencing girls' anger and outrage is not easy, particularly for women teachers who may struggle, themselves, with the acceptance and expression of their own strong feelings and their relationship to the dominant culture. Judy Dorney's narrative account of the personal and professional transformations of a group of white women teachers reveals the powerful changes that can occur in the classroom when such women do the hard work of coming to terms with their own feelings around anger and conflict.[34] When Dorney asks "what an education which takes seriously the voices and knowledge of girls and women would look like," a teacher responds "that such a classroom would not be 'very nice' at all," by which she means, in the encoded language of the white upper classes, not a quiet, passive, authoritarian place, but one that invites debate and passionate response.[35]

The girls in this study, like so many girls, are hungry for such relationships and sites of radical possibility. The Mansfield girls, in particular, offer us examples of the many women in their lives who provide safe spaces for their feelings and thoughts—aunts, older sisters, family friends, mothers. These women know them, love them, and teach them. Such meaningful relationships, echoed in the urban girls she interviewed, cause Amy Sullivan to critique the traditional role of mentor, a "helping model . . . which often assumes deficiencies in the adolescent" and locates knowledge and power in the adult, and to offer, instead, the role of "muse" and the possibility of "evocative relationships."[36] Such relationships, Sullivan explains, are "distinguished by girls' ability to speak freely; by women's ability to listen to, understand, and validate girls' feelings and experience; and by women's willingness to share their own experience as well."[37]

Women's openness to talking candidly about their own experiences, in particular, is vital. "For women to join with girls," Jill Taylor, Carol Gilligan, and Amy Sullivan write, "means connecting with passion—a word whose Latin root means suffering—the desire, love, hope, anger, and pain that both girls and women feel. And these feelings, strong and closely held, are sometimes the feelings women do not want to risk with each other or fully experience themselves."[38] Entrusted with the nurturance and education of girls, women teachers are "engaged in a kind of socio-cultural balancing" of themselves, their students, and their communities—struggling with the conflicts and contradictions among their roles and identities as women, mentors, and socializers, and as transmitters of patriarchal culture.[39]

The Mansfield girls, in particular, allude to this socio-cultural balancing in their descriptions of their women teachers. While their teachers' concerns with control and discipline and the girls' occasional performances of idealized femininity indicate what their teachers value, the pervasive "hollering" and "yelling" point to their ambivalence, to the anxiety the girls evoke in them, and also perhaps to the intensity of their fears for the girls' futures. Raging with "tongues of fire" at their students, these white women teachers, particularly those with working-class roots, may see themselves as preparing the girls in their charge for the harsh reality that lies ahead.[40]

Janie Ward points to the demoralizing effects of such "bold, unreserved, 'in your face' truth-telling," and contrasts it with "resistance-building truth-telling" in the service of "liberation." Such resistance for liberation not only "replaces negative critique with positive recognition," but also provides girls with the tools necessary to think critically about themselves, the world, and their place in it.[41] Before the teachers can prepare them, however, they must understand the relational crises and systemic oppressions that girls face and "validate the identities that their students have taken on as part of growing up."[42] And before they can validate the girls' identities, they must first confront the "cross currents of desires and values and of traditions and loyalties" that define the realities of their own lives and that, unexplored, seep into their work with girls.[43] Otherwise they risk becoming a source of "the hidden injuries of class."[44]

Connections between girls and women are complicated and difficult, particularly across class and cultural lines. Such relationships, as Lisa Delpit explains, demand "a very special kind of listening, listening that requires not only open eyes and ears, but also hearts and minds":

> We do not really see through our eyes or hear through our ears, but through our beliefs. To put our beliefs on hold is to cease to exist as ourselves for a moment—and that is not easy. It is painful as well, because it means turning yourself inside out, giving up your own sense of who you are, and being willing to see yourself in the unflattering light of another's angry gaze. It is not easy, but it is the only way to learn what it might feel like to be someone else and the only way to start the dialogue.[45]

Through such a relational stance, girls perceive connection and the commitment of adults in ways that open up possibilities for creating identities and making life choices that allow them to hold their hearts and minds together.

Clearly, class differences inform the girls' expectations of their women teachers. Whereas the middle-class girls want a teacher who will hold to her beliefs and convictions, the working-class girls are looking for someone who can put her beliefs on hold and thus create space, through humor, play, and fun, for new understandings and possibilities. Both groups of girls thus desire their teachers' loyalty and, conversely, have a sharp eye for betrayal. "By betrayal," Jeanette, who began this chapter, explains, "I mean promising to be on your side, then being on someone else's."[46]

Evocative relationships, in which girls' questions and women's ambivalences are brought to the surface, provide the scaffolding for public critique and political resistance. Such relationships are central to the task of cultivating "hardiness zones" for girls—that is, spaces of real engagement that allow girls to experience control, commitment, and challenge. Hardiness zones move the focus from the individual girl to the network of relationships with caring adults that create girls' social worlds and environments, giving girls access to skills, relationships, and possibilities that enable them to experience power and meaning. [47] But the Mansfield and Acadia girls are also "hungry for an us," and their group sessions point to the potential power of girls' interactions with one another.[48] While the dynamics of the group sessions were mediated by class and culture, both the Mansfield and the Acadia girls found in their group a sense of home—"a safe space, where one can weave whole cloth from the fragments of social critique and sweet dreams."[49]

From the very beginning of the study, the Mansfield girls conveyed the importance of their friendships and the group to their psychological survival. Their strong, supportive relationships helped to minimize the hurtful and oppressive aspects of both home and school.[50] The group gave them an opportunity to articulate their feelings and thoughts, and also a sense of their collective power to act on their own behalf.

Movement toward collective, constructive action depended on the girls' listening closely to and trusting one another and also Diane. Learning about each other's feelings and thoughts over the course of the year increased their solidarity. Their exterior toughness and defensive teasing yielded to a wider range of emotions and more open attempts to understand and identify with one another's feelings. The girls learned they had thoughts and feelings that were more complicated than they knew or expected. They became more reflective about their treatment of others and more sensitive to others' emotions.

Rachel, for example, began the group sessions voicing intense anger and assuming that the others felt comfortable with her aggressive behavior. Over the course of the year, however, she began to reflect on the impact her temper had on her relationships. Her friends, she discovered in the discussions, "thought I got mad easily and I didn't know that . . . They said they always had to be careful about what they said around me, because I always get so mad. I felt everybody was like, all of us were like that . . . but they said I was the worst." Rachel admits that as she first began to take in her friends' voices and to think before she spoke, she felt like she was not being herself.

> I did. I did at first, but I kind of understand because I noticed I got mad over stupid things . . . I noticed that nobody else—everybody else kind of took it, didn't get mad at those things . . . so I felt that I probably shouldn't . . . [things like] doin' somethin' or disagreein' with somethin' that was said. I didn't want it to be like that—but there's no way I'm gonna change them. So I have to change myself.

The group discussions gave Rachel an opportunity to see herself as her friends saw her. While learning not to get "mad over stupid things" by listening to her friends' advice may sound like white middle-class girls' propensity to take themselves out of relationship for the sake of relationship, such awareness of others' feelings opens the door to deeper communication and more genuine relationships among these working-class girls.[51]

Cheyenne, too, gained relational information that both surprised her and moved her to a closer, deeper examination of others' thoughts and feelings. She was amazed at how often her best friend, Donna, "said stuff that I didn't think she'd say, because she's like really quiet." "I felt like I knew what my friend was thinking," she said, but "after they said what their answers were to the questions . . . it felt like they were thinking something different." Meeting weekly in a group educated Sarah about relationships as well:

> I learned like what—I don't know how to explain it . . . like when you get in a fight with them, what makes them mad and what makes them realize your feelings, you know, how you can talk to them . . . Like if I knew something that I did they didn't like, I wouldn't do it anymore or like if I was in a fight with someone, I would talk to them more than I did before . . . I don't know. It made me feel like I should think before I said something.

Sarah is trying to stop her habit of yelling at her friends when she is in a bad mood. "I've been trying lately real hard to not get mad and try to just calm down and not take my anger out on other people so much." As a result, she has decided "not to get in the middle of" fights between her friends. "[Now] I really think about it," she explains, "and think if I really do want to be in a fight with them."

Along with this emerging appreciation of other voices and perspectives comes a more open acknowledgment of the emotional and physical jeopardy that accompanies such exposure, the potential of being suddenly all alone, "left with no friends." As the Mansfield girls became more aware of one another's feelings, their solidarity increased and they began to consider the possibility of collective action. As they came to acknowledge the complexity and range of their own feelings, they also became more articulate and open about the reasons they felt treated badly, and more invested in learning how to respond constructively and effectively. They came together around their support of Corrine and others who were hurt, as well as around unjust school policies and practices.

Most striking, the Mansfield girls' propensity to voice their feelings publicly as a group deepened their commitment to learning and to making school a place they wanted to be. Frustrated with their English class, for example, the girls decided to take their complaints to the administration. Surprisingly it is Rachel, who so doubts her academic abilities, leading the charge this day: "You know what we're going to do?" she asks, excitement in her voice. "Know what we're gonna do? There are a bunch of us that we think we need to know English for high school, so we're going to get English books and take them home, and look over 'em, so that we can learn something."

The move to collective action is particularly difficult for the Acadia girls, whose struggle to remain in connection is thwarted by a white middle-class ideology that espouses a profound distrust of the relational. These middle-class girls began their group sessions assuming not that they were all alike, but that, while they were similar in some obvious ways, they were distinct individuals. They believed that the intensity of their feelings around invisibility, their struggles with pressures to be perfect, and their anger at the popular boys and girls were experiences unique to them. Although the girls knew one another, some quite well, when the group began, and though they shared a common identification as the "smart," "middle-class" girls, they, too, were surprised at what their meetings revealed. Jane, who was a close friend of Elizabeth's, and had known Lydia "since fifth grade," and Kirstin "all my life, longer than anyone else," was amazed when she discovered that the other girls "thought like I did on a lot of things . . . think the same things I do on a lot of issues." Elizabeth saw the group as a place to say "personal" things the girls "wouldn't have normally talked about." For Lydia, the group sessions were a chance "to tell what our feelings were . . . I don't really have that many people to tell my feelings to," she continues, but then pauses, "and I actually have a lot of feelings to tell." The girls' discussions of their personal writings seem to attest to the extent of their emotional separation from one another, particularly with respect to anger and sadness.

Over the course of the year, these girls began to appreciate both the similarity of their experiences and the shared intensity of their feelings. They spoke of the pressures they felt to move their academic capabilities, as well as their social critique and strong feelings, underground in order to escape judgment by others, as well as to avoid embarrassment and exclusion. Their group became a safe place to express their anger and complain, as they did frequently and vociferously, about the power of the popular kids and their frustration about the frequent disregard for the rules of meritocracy. Their discussions spilled over into their nightly phone conversations and sleep-overs, creating other safe spaces for their social critique. Increasingly the sessions became a place to let go of what had been held in, to be outrageous and silly. The girls found support, encouragement, and shared resistance in the group meetings, as well as an opportunity to experiment with responses to the popular boys' behavior, to create "cool" ways to distinguish themselves from the popular girls, to disagree and argue, to complain about their siblings and friends, and to test their developing theories of life and politics.

In these moments they imagined different possibilities, played with forms of resistance, developed a shared language and an acceptable group image of themselves as witty, deep, and smart.

These middle-class girls did not, however, openly challenge the culture of the school or publicly dispute those others who held the power to constrain their expressions and movements; nor did they successfully confront the tension between expectations of conventional femininity and dominant notions of success. As the year progressed, the girls began to struggle with the contradiction between maintaining loyalty to one another and maintaining loyalty to the ideology of individualism and meritocracy that they so embraced. The relationships among the girls, initially a source, not only of genuine pleasure, but also of voice and underground resistance, became a liability as the girls struggled for recognition and visibility. Speaking through the voices of such a competitive system, they could not afford the risk that relationships would silence their individual voices and hold them back. By the end of the school year, the Acadia girls were struggling to stay in touch with those aspects of their relationships that had, in fact, encouraged their individual voices as well as their collective critique of the school structure and social scene.

These distinctions between the Acadia and the Mansfield groups suggest not only how differences in culture and class affect the girls' understandings of themselves and their relationships, but also how such understandings create openings for or barriers to collective, political action. They also point to the critical nature of this developmental period in the girls' lives—how the capacity for abstract thought, so important and so liberating in one sense, also "allows the mind to travel further from experienced reality" and makes girls vulnerable to societal ideals.[52]

Such a vulnerability is more apparent for the Acadia girls. Their closeness to one another is threatened by, because it is threatening to, individualistic and competitive ideals, even as their desire for recognition is tamed by idealized femininity. And yet it is clear that the Mansfield girls, in their increased attention to others' feelings and thoughts, are also undergoing profound changes, both cognitively and emotionally. Their struggles, however, seem to be not so much with a white middle-class culture of competition and individual achievement as with an emerging appreciation of others' perspectives and what this means for their constructions of self, for their relationships with others, and for how they imagine their futures. As the Mansfield girls explore the range of their feelings, particularly the subtlety and nuance of their anger, they open themselves to the sadness and fear that underlie the invulnerability they project. While their openness deepens their connections with their close girlfriends, it can also leave them feeling defenseless and frightened in relation to more powerful others.

Perhaps sensing both the possibilities and the dangers of this emerging vulnerability, the Mansfield girls came to define themselves as an "oppositional culture" within their school.[53] Although their opposition was not grounded fully in a coherent "cultural frame of reference," they began to experience and voice the power of their collectivity. This sense of groupness took shape, not only as a result of their increased support of one another, but also as a result of their successful political action.

These girls, both middle and working class, thus offer us strategies for educating the resistance, even as they warn us of the roadblocks we might expect to encounter in our attempts to do so. The Acadia girls point to the transformative power of language, especially for those educated into the culture of power, and thus comfortable enough to reappropriate the meanings of unjust or divisive words and actions.[54] They underscore the importance of the active underground as a safe-house for the resistance—a place for girls to know one another, to explore the pressures to disconnect from themselves and other girls, and to examine critically the social and educational scene.[55] But these girls also speak to the compelling attraction of the culture of individualism and its distrust of relationship, and to the pressures they feel to conform to idealized notions of femininity that will ensure their safety and protection. Encouraging white middle-class girls at the edge of adolescence to stay with the reality of their experiences, to stay in touch with one another, and to bring their critique into the public world—just as these dominant cultural voices intensify—is an enormous challenge.

The Mansfield girls point to the personal and political power of experience, directly expressed and held in relationship with other girls and with women who remain in their presence during the long, difficult process of breaking through layers of invulnerability and toughness. The girls' relationships with Diane Starr and with the other "muses" in their lives suggest the importance of women who will listen with "open hearts and minds," who will allow the experiences of girls who are different from them to "edge themselves into [their] consciousness."[56] Their relationship with Diane, in particular, made room for strong feelings and opinions, out of which came their social critique and a useful explication of the expectations and norms of the culture of power. Without this explication and interrogation the girls would not and could not have acted effectively in their school. Out of such actions developed new voices and stories that, if they did not dissolve, then at least stood in tension with, the Mansfield girls' ventriloquation of themselves as "stupid" and their futures as "dim."

Girls' movement into patriarchal cultures is a complicated, layered process, so gradual as to be nearly imperceptible. Although "it is easy to slip into a parallel universe," Susanna Kaysen writes in her book *Girl, Interrupted,* "most people pass over incrementally, making a series of perforations in the membrane between here and there until an opening exists. And who can resist an opening?"[57]

The Acadia and Mansfield girls' class-related struggles with contradictory voices, desires, and needs threaten to expose the well-maintained fiction of idealized femininity. Their anger calls our attention to the increased regulation of their bodies and their minds. The differences between these two groups of girls, and their particular efforts to resist the constraints on their lives, disrupt the taken-for-granted polarity of conventionally gendered reality and reveal its place in a monolithic, symbolic order. The conflicting identities these girls try on contest the seemingly natural order of things and open the door to new possibilities, new constructions of womanhood.

As different as the Mansfield and Acadia girls are, their expressions of anger and outrage thus signify an opening. As a sign of self-respect, a signal that something is wrong in their world, their anger focuses our attention away from the psychological and toward the political. Such a shift in focus is critical if we are to foster an education for liberation.

Appreciating the ways in which girls from very different experiences and backgrounds capitulate to or resist appropriating the intentions of a patriarchal discourse about femininity is central to understanding not only girls' psychological health and development, but also the complexities of social reproduction. Girls at early adolescence, in the process of negotiating their connection to the wider culture, have the potential to contribute alternative visions and voices, but they have to recognize themselves as complete and whole beings, with a range of feelings and thoughts connected to their experiences. Teaching girls how to pinpoint what is causing them anger or pain and how to act on their feelings constructively provides a kind of warrior training for social justice. Out of such clarity, the outlines of creative action and the possibility for human freedom are born.

Notes

1. Stones in the Road

1. Basu, 1994.
2. Vold, 1993.
3. See, for example, AAUW, 1993; Stein, 1992; Stein, Marshall, and Tropp, 1993.
4. AAUW, 1991, 1992; Orenstein, 1994; Sadker and Sadker, 1986, 1994; Sadker, Sadker, and Klein, 1991.
5. See, for example, Allgood-Merton, Lewinsohn, and Hops, 1990; Attie and Brooks-Gunn, 1992; Harter, 1990; Peterson et. al, 1993; Pipher, 1995; Renouf and Harter, 1990; Steiner-Adair, 1986, 1991.
6. Fine, 1992, p. 178. (Italics in original.)
7. *Utne Reader*, no. 64, July/August 1994.
8. Ibid., p. 55.
9. *Newsweek*, August 2, 1993, p. 44.
10. See, for example, Campbell, 1984, and Harris, 1994. Girl gangs exist in small towns such as Acadia, but I have seen no attempts to explore white girls' experience with gangs.
11. Campbell, 1987, p. 452.
12. Klein, 1993, p. 7.
13. *Seattle Weekly*, August 5, 1992, p. 23.
14. Kagan, 1971; Haste, 1994.
15. Haste, 1994, p. ix; see Lloyd, 1984, for an in-depth analysis of the association of Western reason and rationality with masculinity.
16. Debold, 1996, p. 15.
17. Studies showing how parent-child interactions shift at early adolescence point to the ways in which girls are regulated and brought under control at puberty (Hill, 1988). Girls are interrupted and ignored more in their families, for example. Also, researchers find that mothers exert more power over their daughters at adolescence than they did when their

daughters were younger, and that mothers' use of power is associated with daughters' compliance and accommodation to appropriate gender roles. See Brooks-Gunn and Reiter, 1990.

18. Debold, 1996, pp. 88–89.
19. Kagan, 1971, p. 92.
20. Brown and Gilligan, 1992.
21. Haste, 1994, p. 23.
22. Ibid., p. xi.
23. See also Brown and Gilligan, 1992.
24. See Butler, 1991.
25. Fine, 1992, p. 177.
26. Bernardez, 1988; Lerner, 1985; Lorde, 1984; Miller, 1983; Miller and Surrey, 1990; Spelman, 1989; Tavris, 1982; Thomas, 1993.
27. Miller, 1983, p. 193.
28. Debold, Wilson, and Malave, 1993, p. 94. See Jagger, 1989, p. 161.
29. Pastor, McCormick, and Fine, 1996, p. 16.
30. Ibid., p. 20; Anyon, 1982.
31. See Markus and Kitayama, 1991; also, Cox et al., forthcoming.
32. Spelman, 1989, pp. 264, 267. See also Scheman, 1980.
33. Lyman, 1981, p. 61.
34. Lyman, 1981; quoted in Spelman, 1989, p. 272.
35. Belenky, Bond, and Weinstock, 1997.
36. Miller and Surrey, 1990, p. 2. See Brown and Gilligan, 1992, for a discussion of young girls' psychological development and their ability to experience and express the full spectrum of feelings, including anger and sadness as well as joy and love.
37. Brown and Gilligan, 1992.
38. Miller and Surrey, 1990, p. 2.
39. See Debold, 1996.
40. Although, again, the psychological literature on girls' anger is fragmentary and sparse. Most of the findings come from gender-difference studies focusing specifically on indirect and direct aggression.
41. Brown and Gilligan, 1992.
42. Bernardez, 1988, p. 1.
43. Brown and Gilligan, 1992; Gilligan, 1990.
44. Bjorkqvist, Lagerspetz, and Kaukiainen, 1992.
45. Such an interpretation no doubt arises out of gender comparisons. That is, compared with boys' tendency to express aggression in more direct, physical, or violent ways, such indirect expressions of aggression—less physically harmful and less impulsive—are interpreted as more mature. I want to shift the conversations away from such gender comparisons, however, and consider both the reasons girls, white middle-class girls especially,

tend to express aggression indirectly, and the consequences of such expression over time. In other words, my concern is with the shift from a capacity I recognize in young girls to express strong feelings like anger, to the tendency for young women to disguise these feelings or turn them into forms of indirect aggression.

46. Scheman, 1980, p. 178.
47. Bjorkqvist, Lagerspetz, and Kaukiainen, 1992, p. 126.
48. Lagerspetz, Bjorkqvist, and Peltonen, 1988, p. 413.
49. Underwood, Coie, and Herbsman, 1992, p. 376.
50. Rys and Bear, 1997, p. 89; see Crick and Grotpeter, 1995.
51. Eder, 1990, 1991, 1993.
52. Merten, 1997, p. 188.
53. Again, see Debold, 1996, as well as Kagan, 1971. See also Brown, 1991; Brown and Gilligan, 1992.
54. See Brown and Gilligan, 1992; Debold, Wilson, and Malave, 1993; Taylor, Gilligan, and Sullivan, 1995.
55. See, for example, Tavris, 1982.
56. Miller and Sperry, 1987; Underwood, Cole, and Herbsman, 1992, p. 377.
57. Henwood, 1997, p. 183. Tracking poverty rates across race and gender lines, Henwood finds that almost half—48.1 percent—of the poor are non-Hispanic whites. In addition, contrary to prevailing stereotypes, the 17.2 percent poverty rate of those living in rural areas is not a great deal lower than the 21.5 percent rate of those living in cities. "Rural single-mother families," Henwood adds, "are poor at a rate only marginally below that for urban families of that same maligned type (46.2 percent urban, 42.6 percent rural)" (p. 183). Henwood underscores the need to read and report poverty rates carefully, however. When one looks at the distribution of income within racial and ethnic groups one finds that, over the past twenty years, "the black poor have done miserably, falling further behind poor whites . . . Since the black poor did so much worse than the white poor, income distribution among blacks, which has always been more unequal than that among whites, has gotten more unequal and at a faster rate" (p. 179).
58. Walkerdine, 1990. The U.S. literature on class tends to focus more on sociological than on psychological processes; even the best-known psychological studies on class, written in the 1970s—Rubin's (1976) *Worlds of Pain* and Sennett and Cobb's (1972) *The Hidden Injuries of Class*—originate in sociology. Most of the more recent literature on girls and class is out of Britain, and much of this literature, such as the work of Angela McRobbie (1991) and Valerie Walkerdine (1990, 1997), focuses on girls and popular culture or cultural studies. I know of no in-depth studies of

U.S. girls and the reproduction of class similar to Jay McLeod's (1995) study of working-class boys' aspirations.

59. Willis, 1977.
60. Fine, 1988, 1992; Fordham, 1993.
61. Ogbu, 1989; see also Fordham, 1988.
62. Stevenson and Ellsworth, 1993, p. 269. See also Weis, 1990.
63. Steedman, 1987, p. 14.
64. Frankenberg, 1993, pp. 6, 9. See also Spelman, 1988.
65. Fine et al., 1997; Wray and Newitz, 1997.

2. Privileging Difference

1. Steedman, 1987, p. 22.
2. Starr, 1994.
3. See index.
4. Ibid., p. 59. At the time of this study, approximately 62 percent of Mansfield parents had received twelve years or less of education. Twenty-four percent of parents were unemployed, 26 percent were unskilled, and 20 percent were skilled laborers, while 20 percent described themselves as self-employed and 18 percent as professionals. Fifty-one percent of Mansfield students were signed up for the free-lunch program at their school.
5. Ibid., pp. 69–70.
6. See Hansot and Tyack, 1988, for a discussion of the relationship between school structures and community contexts. At the time of the study, however, Acadia School was just two years into a new, progressive middle-school philosophy and structure in which they introduced multi-age classrooms, team teaching, block scheduling, and heterogeneous grouping of students. Students were evaluated on the basis of accomplished skills and their performance on agreed-upon tasks; they had a say in the running of the school and helped choose the topics and issues they studied. This shift from a more conventional school structure had a profound effect on the relationship between school and community, primarily because a significant number of community members did not support such a transition, and felt their protests had not been addressed. During the year that the girls were involved in the study, controversy over the school's new philosophy—framed largely as a debate between liberal progressives and more conservative Christian traditionalists—reached a crisis point. The future of the new school structure looked uncertain at best.

The students themselves struggled with the changes, even though most I spoke with liked the increased openness and movement the new structure provided. Ironically, their outspoken critique of certain aspects of the new school policies and procedures, their interest in debating their pros and cons, their very level of involvement and awareness of the current climate, seemed to me a constructive outcome of the progressive approach. I credit this atmosphere, in combination with their trusting relationship with Diane, for the open, easy interactions among the girls during their group meetings.

7. Often the girls would greet me on tape, direct their comments to me, or wave good-bye to me at the end of their sessions. It was clear that I was an audience to their thoughts and feelings, although my "presence" was seemingly forgotten during their conversations.

8. See McLeod, 1995; Willis, 1977.

9. Luttrell, 1993, p. 511.

10. Starr, 1994, p. 55.

11. Ibid., pp. 68–69.

12. Ibid., p. 71.

13. In the late 1800s French-Canadians, primarily from Quebec, moved to Maine for employment in the growing number of wood mills that dotted the rivers. Willing to work long hours for low pay, they were a desired source of cheap labor and endured negative stereotypes and harsh treatment, not only because of their lower-class status, but because of their Catholic religion. Unlike most parts of the state, however, the Acadia area was home to French-Canadian immigrants of all class levels. While there was some prejudice, there was also great pride and community involvement. Still, this side of the city, close to the river, is historically French. I should also add that, though some of the girls from both Acadia and Mansfield are of Franco-American heritage, this fact had little or no significance to them.

14. Owing to her busy schedule, Robin—although in many ways the most critical and outspoken of the girls—attended the group sessions the least. Much of her contribution comes via individual interviews.

15. The fact that the Acadia girls' mothers were interested and engaged with the study and encouraged their daughters' participation is also important to note. The study became, in this sense, more public and formal, and the girls may not have wanted to embarrass their mothers by revealing family dynamics. This in no way negates the fact that such public-private boundaries are a function of white middle-class culture. On the contrary, the girls' increased surveillance would underscore the anxiety associated with threats to this structure.

16. I struggled a good deal with this difference in the way the Acadia and Mansfield girls spoke (or did not speak) about their private lives. While I think this is an important difference to highlight, not only because it represents constructions of reality grounded in class, but also because it has implications for the way girls are perceived and treated in school, I did not want to expose or exploit the Mansfield girls. Nor did I want to sug-

gest that, simply because the Acadia girls did not speak of their private lives, they did not experience any of the struggles the Mansfield girls described. Other than a few specific incidents, disguised and chosen to make larger points, I limit my discussion of the Mansfield girls' home lives.

17. "The concerns of white elite women are represented as *the* concerns of this age cohort [adolescents]," Fine and Macpherson (1992) argue. "The very construction of [the literature on adolescent females and their bodies] is positioned largely from white, middle-class, nondisabled, heterosexual, adult women's perspectives" (p. 176).

18. Bakhtin, 1981, p. 340.

19. Lather, 1991, p. 116.

20. Brown et al., 1988; Brown et al., 1991; Brown and Gilligan, 1991, 1992; Brown et al., 1989.

21. Reid, 1993.

22. Campbell, 1987, p. 452.

23. Wertsch, 1991, p. 59.

24. Miles and Huberman, 1984.

25. Campbell, 1987, p. 452.

26. Butler, 1991.

27. Allison, 1994, p. 9.

28. Ibid., pp. 9, 10.

29. Ibid., p. 12.

30. Walkerdine, 1990, pp. 196–197.

31. Ibid., p. 198.

32. Ibid., p. 195.

33. Ibid., pp. 199–200.

34. See Harvey, 1992, p. 142.

3. Mansfield: Living outside the Lines

1. Allison, 1995, p. 54.

2. In their study of focus groups of girls from six different cultural communities, Taylor and Ward (1991) find that this is not a polarity recognizable only in white culture, but a distinction they heard, to various degrees and in various ways, within each group.

3. Deborah Tolman writes extensively about adolescent girls' "dilemmas of desire" and the different discourses they use to speak about sexual experiences and romantic relationships (1992, 1994a, 1994b). She writes against a psychological literature that presents girls' experiences of desire as pathological and views their sexual decision-making as individual risk-taking behavior; she argues instead that sexuality and desire are a central part of girls' relationships (Tolman and Church, 1998).

4. Fine, 1988.

5. Ibid., pp. 38–39.

6. Debold, Wilson, and Malave (1993) refer to such a stance of invulnerability as "fronting," a term used by adolescent girls in Boston.

7. Although there are more pages of video transcription for the Acadia girls, the Mansfield girls used verbs such as "want" and "need" three times more often. More important, perhaps, the objects of the Acadia and Mansfield girls' longing differed dramatically. The middle-class girls' less frequent expressions of want tended to underscore their desire to be more outspoken and honest in their relationships, that is, to have the courage to say more directly what they felt and thought, particularly when they were treated badly or unfairly; or, more mundanely, they simply wanted more of what they already had—to travel more, go to different places, and do and see more things.

8. This contrasts with Walkerdine's (1990, 1997) findings and with suggestions from other British researchers writing about working-class girls' lives (McRobbie, 1991; Steedman, 1987) that such ideals of beauty represent escape from the limits and drudgery of working-class life. This may be a function of the girls' ages. That is, unlike younger girls, who are not yet captivated by such distinctions, or older adolescent girls, who have appropriated or bought into cultural ideals, these girls at early adolescence are seeing and sorting out the realities and possibilities more clearly. More likely it points to differences in the experience and expression of working-class culture in the United States and Britain.

9. See Way, 1990.

10. Stevenson and Ellsworth, 1993, p. 270.

11. Here Stevenson and Ellsworth are quoting Ogbu, 1989, p. 189.

12. Way, 1995, p. 113.

13. Ibid., p. 125.

4. Acadia: The Conventions of Imagination

1. Over the course of the year this shifts somewhat for the two girls whose parents move toward divorce.

2. "Wiggas" is a short-hand reference to white students who identify with black hip-hop culture, who wear baggy pants low on their hips, listen to rap music, and so on. In this way, these students represent a distinct counterculture in their school and are better described as actively rejecting the dominant school structure, rather than as cast out by the popular students.

3. Friere, 1970/1992, p. 48.

4. In *Mother-Daughter Revolution* (1993), Debold, Wilson, and Malave discuss in more detail how the hierarchy of school and individualism pushes girls toward achievement at the expense of relationship.

5. Taylor, Gilligan, and Sullivan, 1995, p. 24.
6. Brown and Gilligan, 1992; Fine and Macpherson, 1992; Gilligan, 1990, 1991.
7. Fine and Macpherson, 1992, p. 188.
8. Brown and Gilligan, 1992; Gilligan, 1990.
9. See Cox, Bruckner, and Stabb (forthcoming).
10. Fine and Macpherson, 1992, p. 193. See also Pastor, McCormick, and Fine, 1996.

5. Voice and Ventriloquation in Girls' Development

1. Sheldon, 1992, p. 95. See also Bakhtin, 1981.
2. Sheldon, 1992, p. 98.
3. I conducted this small study with Mark Tappan at the request of the school principal, who was concerned about the students and how they were making sense of this incident. We observed the children over the course of a week and interviewed each individually, along with a number of their classmates, about a range of topics.
4. One might even go so far as to suggest that while such an experience and its re-telling would underscore the connection between boys' bodies and voices as the boys see the power of their words on the girls and in the culture, the incident would seem to disconnect the girls' voices from their bodies, pulling the girls away from themselves.
5. Wertsch, 1991, p. 59.
6. Bakhtin, 1981, pp. 293–294.
7. Ibid., pp. 341, 345, 346. See also Day and Tappan, 1996.
8. Ibid., p. 348.
9. Brown and Gilligan, 1992; Gilligan, 1990, 1991.
10. Brown and Gilligan, 1992; see also Gilligan, 1991.
11. Taylor, Gilligan, and Sullivan, 1995, p. 39.
12. Sachs, Lieberman, and Erickson, 1973; see also Graddol and Swann, 1989.
13. Brown et al., 1973; Apple et al., 1979.
14. Gilligan, 1993, p. xvi.
15. Ibid.
16. See Gilligan, 1990.
17. Bakhtin, 1981, p. 294. See also Tappan and Brown, 1996.
18. In this way Robin, a white middle-class seventh-grader in public school, sounds remarkably like twelve-year-old Anna, a white working-class resister who attended Laurel, a private girls' school in the Midwest. See Brown and Gilligan, 1992.

19. See Harvey, 1992. Harvey uses the term "ventriloquistic cross-dressing" to describe men speaking women's voices; that is, using their power and position to speak about women or on behalf of women and thus to mute women's voices. In my use of the term, girls speak a male discourse about women or speak through patriarchal voices about femininity. In other words, they are girls who speak as men would speak of women. When doing so, girls unwittingly contribute to the muting of their own voices.

20. Increased use of the phrase "I don't know" at early adolescence (see Brown and Gilligan, 1992; Gilligan 1991) signifies this interpretive moment and points to girls' struggles to stay connected with their thoughts and feelings.

21. Hudson, 1984, p. 35. "Thus," Hudson argues, "the girl playing a lot of sport is doing something which is still conceived of as essentially masculine . . . Girls displaying competitiveness, or 'adolescent' aggression, will be displaying qualities thought of as masculine." Hudson, who is from Britain, notes the female football player who is "accorded headlines in the popular press such as 'playing the boys at their own game' " (p. 35). More recently, as it has become acceptable for girls in the United States to excel in sports, anxiety over appropriate gender behavior has taken a somewhat more complicated form. This is illustrated by the ambivalent attention given to the professional hocky player Manon Rheaume in magazines and on talk shows—her talent is nearly always nervously acknowledged in combination with comments on her beauty; or the 1993 *Sports Illustrated* story on Lisa Lesley, a star women's basketball player, entitled "A Model Role Model," complete with a picture of her in miniskirt and full make-up.

22. Fine and Macpherson, 1992, p. 197.

23. Ibid., p. 176.

24. Ibid.

25. Campbell, 1987, p. 452.

26. Thompson 1994, p. 228. Thompson's sample included African American, Puerto Rican, Chicana, and white adolescents—middle class and poor, lesbian, bisexual, and heterosexual from the northeastern, midwestern, and southwestern United States.

27. Ibid., p. 245.

28. Freire, 1970/1992, pp. 48–49.

29. Thompson, 1994, p. 230.

30. See Campbell, 1987.

31. "Ho" is an idiomatic reference to "whore" that the working-class girls have appropriated from popular black rap music. It is a term that has its own popular cultural manifestations within this music genre—a genre still considered, like the working-class girls, marginal and problematic within

dominant white middle-class culture. The term is polyvalent to the girls, and their use of it depends on the person they are talking about, the situation, and the audience. Although their use of "ho" is not fully disconnected from its popular cultural meanings, it has its own power and significance within their group and community. The girls appropriate its misogynic overtones when they use the term as a form of threat or to denigrate other girls and women they dislike. (In other words, the girls use "ho" much the way boys use the term "slag," according to Sue Lees [1993]. Thus, in these moments, they speak through or ventriloquate male voices.) The term is also used playfully, however, and can serve as a linguistic marker of intimacy; that is, a word whose layers of meaning are understood only by the initiated (hence their response to Diane Starr when she queries them about the term: "Hoe? . . . It's just a garden tool"). "Ho" can also be used to threaten those who have been disloyal to the group or may indicate the girls' rejection of someone who has, in some way, challenged their understanding of what is appropriate treatment of those in the group or appropriate behavior for girls like them. Hence the term is drenched in intentions, some parodic and some subversive.

32. Harvey, 1992, p. 142.
33. Foucault, 1980, p. 119.
34. Walkerdine, 1990, p. 143.
35. Ibid., p. 144.
36. Bakhtin, 1981, p. 293.

6. Resisting Femininity

1. Reynolds, 1992.
2. See also Brown, 1989, 1991; Brown and Gilligan, 1992; Gilligan, 1991; Gilligan, Brown, and Rogers, 1990.
3. Bakhtin, 1981.
4. Butler, 1991, p. 21.
5. hooks, 1994, p. 167.
6. Ibid.
7. This show is a favorite of the girls. Because MTV continually re-runs the episodes, the girls know each nearly by heart.
8. hooks, 1994, p. 169.
9. Scheman, 1980, p. 178.
10. Gilligan, 1991.
11. Butler, 1991, p. 24.
12. Ibid.
13. It is perhaps significant that a gesture around the feet generates the girls' reactions and changes the course of the conversation. The girls seem to

imply that regulating perfection down to the feet reveals how absurd the whole enterprise is.

14. Butler, 1991, p. 21.
15. Ibid., p. 24.
16. Fine, 1992, p. 193.
17. Butler, 1991, p. 21.
18. Walkerdine, 1990, p. 198.

7. The Madgirl in the Classroom

1. See, for example, AAUW, 1992; Sadker and Sadker, 1986, 1994. Peggy Orenstein's *SchoolGirls* (1994) is a notable exception. And yet, though Orenstein relays the complexity and range of girls' experiences in junior high, her reliance on the overall framework of psychological loss at the hands of gender bias causes her at times to downplay the resistance and critique of the girls to whom she listens.
2. Given that *Beavis and Butthead* is a parody of the immaturity of adolescent boys, it is, of course, ironic both that the boys identify with the cartoon, and that the girls take the boys' imitation seriously.
3. King and Emmons, 1990.
4. Jack, 1991; Jack and Dill, 1992.
5. Valerie Walkerdine (1990) makes this point in *Schoolgirl Fictions*.
6. See Delpit, 1988, 1995.
7. Here I refer specifically to Donna Eder's research on white working-class girls' friendships and peer relations (1985, 1993). See also Peggy Miller (1986).
8. See Luttrell, 1993, p. 539.
9. See Gilbert and Gubar, 1984.

8. Educating the Resistance

1. Walkerdine, 1990, p. 165.
2. Winterson, 1985, p. 158.
3. Ibid., pp. 44–45.
4. Ibid., p. 45.
5. Paul Willis argues this point in *Learning to Labour* (1997). See also Way, 1995.
6. Fine and Macpherson, 1992, p. 196.
7. Walkerdine, 1997, p. 4.
8. Ibid., p. 134.
9. Luttrell, 1993, pp. 524, 525.
10. hooks, 1994, p. 178.

11. Luttrell, 1993, p. 519; Delpit, 1988.
12. I am indebted to Paul Willis's (1977/1981) analysis of the experiences of working-class schoolboys in Britain for this interpretation. Although there are a great many differences between these girls and his "lads," I find most helpful Willis's emphasis on the cultural tension between school ideology and the boys' lives, and his exploration of the processes by which the boys' opposition to school authorities serves to reproduce their working-class standing.
13. While here I draw on Wendy Luttrell's (1993) perceptive analysis of the meaning of teacher's pets for working-class white and black women recalling their school experiences, it is interesting to note that in this study such distinctions are made by the middle-class and not the working-class girls.
14. See Brown and Gilligan, 1992.
15. As shown, the Mansfield girls also practice such gestures and voices, but they do so more playfully; perfecting such personas is serious business for the Acadia girls—a way to ensure their protection and secure their place in white middle-class culture.
16. "Cultural capital," a phrase made popular by the French sociologist Pierre Bourdieu (1984) and used by critical or resistance theorists in education, "refers to the general cultural background, knowledge, disposition, and skills that are passed on from one generation to another. Cultural capital represents ways of talking, acting, and socializing, as well as language practices, values, and styles of dress and behavior" (McLaren, 1989, pp. 197–198). Delpit, 1988, p. 24.
17. Delpit, 1988, p. 34.
18. hooks, 1994, p. 179.
19. Ibid., p. 177.
20. Frankenberg, 1993, p. 6.
21. Frankenberg, 1993, p. 70.
22. Walkerdine, 1997, p. 31.
23. hooks, 1994, p. 155.
24. See Belenky, Clinchy, Goldberger, and Tarule, 1986. Note especially their discussion of the shift from "received" to "subjectivist" knowing.
25. McIntosh, 1983, p. 10.
26. Ibid., pp. 14, 10.
27. Debold, 1996, p. 20.
28. Dorney, 1991; Harris, 1988.
29. Belenky, Clinchy, Goldberger, and Tarule, 1986; Dorney, 1991.
30. Belenky, Clinchy, Goldberger, and Tarule, 1986.
31. Goldberger, 1996, p. 5.
32. Clinchy, 1996, p. 218.
33. Dorney, 1991, p. 170. The particular power of girls' relationships with

adult women at this stage in their lives has been argued repeatedly. See, for example, Brown and Gilligan, 1992; Debold, Wilson, and Malave, 1993; Gilligan, 1991; Taylor, Gilligan, and Sullivan, 1995.

34. Dorney, 1991.
35. Ibid., p. 242.
36. Sullivan, 1996, p. 227.
37. Ibid., p. 246.
38. Taylor, Gilligan, and Sullivan, 1995, p. 155.
39. Hartman-Halbertal, 1996, p. 227.
40. Ward, 1996, p. 94.
41. Robinson and Ward, 1991; Ward, 1996. Robinson and Ward are talking about racial socialization; specifically about the strategies African American mothers use to ensure their daughters' survival in a racist culture. Given that class is either invisible or openly denied in our culture, class-related experiences are often fragmented and not spoken about in schools. As a result, I suspect that these white women teachers are less conscious of their own anxieties and their fears for their students, and thus of the ways their feelings would move them to develop such strategies.
42. McLeod, 1995, p. 263.
43. Hartman-Halbertal, 1996, p. 232; Dorney, 1991.
44. Sennett and Cobb, 1972.
45. Delpit, 1995, pp. 46–47.
46. Winterson, 1985, p. 171.
47. See Debold et al., 1998. See also [Ouellette] Kobasa, 1979, 1982, 1993.
48. Fine and Macpherson, 1995.
49. Pastor, McCormick, and Fine, 1996.
50. Angela McRobbie (1991) also reports that friendships and supportive networks provide such a role for working-class girls in Britain.
51. Brown and Gilligan, 1992.
52. Debold, 1996, p. 91; see also Brown and Gilligan, 1992.
53. Ogbu, 1989.
54. Donna Eder, 1995, makes this point in her book *School Talk*.
55. Gilligan, 1991.
56. Delpit, 1995, pp. 46, 47.
57. Kaysen, 1993, p. 5.

References

Allgood-Merton, B., P. Lewinsohn, and H. Hops. 1990. Sex differences and adolescent depression. *Journal of Abnormal Psychology* 99(1): 55–63.

Allison, Dorothy. 1994. *Skin: Talking about sex, class, and literature*. Ithaca, N.Y.: Firebrand Books.

———. 1995. *Two or three things I know for sure*. New York: Dutton.

American Association of University Women. 1991. *Shortchanging girls, shortchanging America*. Washington, D.C.: AAUW Educational Foundation.

———. 1992. *How schools shortchange girls*. Washington, D.C.: AAUW Educational Foundation.

———. 1993. *Hostile hallways: The AAUW survey on sexual harassment in America's schools*. Washington, D.C.: AAUW Educational Foundation.

Anyon, Jean. 1982. Intersections of gender and class. In Lois Weis, ed., *Issues in education: Schooling and reproduction of class and gender inequalities*. Buffalo: State University of New York.

Apple, W., L. A. Streeter, and R. M. Krauss. 1979. Effects of pitch and speech rate on personal attributions. *Journal of Personality and Social Psychology* 37: 715–727.

Attie, I., and Jeanne Brooks-Gunn. 1992. Development issues in the study of eating problems and disorders. In J. H. Rowther, S. E. Hobfoll, M. A. P. Stephens, and D. L. Tennenbaum, eds., *The etiology of bulimia: The individual and familial context*. Washington, D.C.: Hemisphere.

Bakhtin, Mikhail. 1981. *The dialogic imagination*. Austin, Tex.: University of Texas Press.

———. 1990. *Art and answerability*. Austin, Tex.: University of Texas Press.

Basu, Rekha. June 4, 1994. Girls give a hoot about free speech. *USA Today*.

Belenky, Mary, Lynne Bond, and Jacqueline Weinstock. 1997. *A tradition that has no name*. New York: Basic Books.

Belenky, Mary, Blythe Clinchy, Nancy Goldberger, and Jill Tarule. 1986. *Women's ways of knowing: The development of self, voice, and mind*. New York: Basic Books.

Bernardez, Teresa. 1988. Women and anger—Cultural prohibitions and the feminine ideal. Working paper no. 31. Wellesley, Mass.: Center for Research on Women, Wellesley College.

Bjorkqvist, Kaj. 1994. Sex differences in physical, verbal, and indirect aggression: A review of recent research. *Sex Roles* 30(3/4): 177–188.

Bjorkqvist, Kaj, Kirsti Lagerspetz, and Ari Kaukiainen. 1992. Do girls manipulate and boys fight? Developmental trends in regard to direct and indirect aggression. *Aggressive Behavior* 18: 117–127.

Bourdieu, Pierre. 1984. *Distinction: A social critique of the judgement of taste.* Cambridge: Harvard University Press.

Brooks-Gunn, Jeanne, and Edward Reiter. 1990. The role of pubertal processes. In S. Shirley Feldman and Glen Elliott, eds., *At the threshold: The developing adolescent.* Cambridge, Mass.: Harvard University Press.

Brooks-Gunn, Jeanne, and M. Zahaykevich. 1989. Parent-child relationships in early adolescence: A developmental perspective. In K. Kreppner and R. M. Lerner, eds., *Family systems and life-span development.* Hillsdale, N.J.: Erlbaum.

Brown, B. L., W. J. Strong, and A. C. Rencher. 1973. Perceptions of personality from speech: effects of manipulations of acoustical parameters. *Journal of the Acoustical Society of America* 59: 29–35.

Brown, Lyn Mikel. 1989. Narratives of relationship: The development of a care voice in girls ages 7 to 16. Unpublished doctoral diss., Harvard University.

———. 1991. A problem of vision: The development of voice and relational knowledge in girls ages 7 to 16. *Women's Studies Quarterly* 15: 52–71.

Brown, Lyn Mikel, Dianne Argyris, Jane Attanucci, Betty Bardige, Carol Gilligan, Kay Johnston, Barbara Miller, Richard Osborne, Mark Tappan, Janie Ward, Grant Wiggins, and David Wilcox. 1988. *A guide to reading narratives of conflict and choice for self and relational voice.* Monograph no. 1. Cambridge, Mass.: Project on the Psychology of Women and the Development of Girls, Harvard Graduate School of Education.

Brown, Lyn Mikel, Elizabeth Debold, Mark Tappan, and Carol Gilligan. 1991. Reading narratives of conflict and choice for self and moral voice: A relational method. In William Kurtines and Jacob Gewirtz, eds., *Handbook of moral behavior and development: Theory, research, and application.* Hillsdale, N.J.: Lawrence Erlbaum.

Brown, Lyn Mikel, and Carol Gilligan. 1991. Listening for voice in narratives of relationship. In Mark Tappan and Martin Packer, eds., *Narrative and storytelling: Implications for understanding moral development.* New Directions for Child Development, no. 54. San Francisco: Jossey-Bass.

———. 1992. *Meeting at the crossroads: Women's psychology and girls' development.* Cambridge, Mass.: Harvard University Press.

Brown, Lyn Mikel, Mark Tappan, Carol Gilligan, Barbara Miller, and Dianne Argyris. 1989. Reading for self and moral voice: A method for interpreting narratives of real-life moral conflict and choice. In Martin Packer and Richard Addison, eds., *Entering the circle: Hermeneutic investigation in psychology.* Albany: State University of New York Press.

Butler, Judith. 1991. Imitation and gender insubordination. In Diane Fuss, ed., *Inside/out: Lesbian theories, gay theories.* New York: Routledge.

Campbell, Anne. 1984. *The girls in the gang.* New York: Basil Blackwell.

———. 1987. Self-definition by rejection: The case of gang girls. *Social Problems* 34(5): 451–466.

Clinchy, Blythe. 1996. Connected and separate knowing: Toward a marriage of two minds. In Nancy Golberger, Jill Tarule, Blythe Clinchy, and Mary Belenky, eds., *Knowledge, difference, and power.* New York: Basic Books.

Cox, Deborah, Karin Bruckner, and Sally Stabb. Forthcoming. *Women's anger: A developmental perspective.* Washington, D.C.: Taylor and Francis.

Crick, N. R., and J. K. Grotpeter. 1995. Relational aggression, gender, and social-psychological adjustment. *Child Development* 66: 710–722.

Day, James, and Mark Tappan. 1996. The narrative approach to moral development: From the epistemic subject to dialogical selves. *Human Development* 39: 67–82.

Debold, Elizabeth. 1996. Knowing bodies: Gender identity, cognitive development and embodiment in early childhood and early adolescence. Unpublished doctoral diss., Harvard University.

Debold, Elizabeth, Lyn Mikel Brown, Susan Weseen, and Geraldine Kearse Brookins. 1998. Cultivating hardiness zones for adolescent girls: A reconceptualization of resilience in relationships with caring adults. In Norine Johnson, Michael Roberts, and Judith Worell, eds., *Beyond appearances: A new look at adolescent girls.* Washington, D.C.: American Psychological Association.

Debold, Elizabeth, Marie Wilson, and Idelisse Malave. 1993. *Mother-daughter revolution.* New York: Addison-Wesley.

Delpit, Lisa. 1988. The silenced dialogue: Power and pedagogy in educating other people's children. *Harvard Educational Review* 58: 280–298.

———. 1995. *Other people's children: Cultural conflict in the classroom.* New York: The New Press.

Dissed, mythed, and totally pissed. July–August 1994. *Utne Reader,* no. 64.

Dorney, Judith. 1991. "Courage to act in a small way": Clues toward community and change among women teaching girls. Unpublished doctoral diss., Harvard University.

Eder, Donna. 1985. The cycle of popularity: Interpersonal relations among female adolescents. *Sociology of Education* 58: 154–65.

————. 1990. Serious and playful disputes: Variation in conflict talk among female adolescents. In A. D. Grimshaw, ed., *Conflict talk: Sociolinguistic investigations of arguments in conversations*. Cambridge, England: Cambridge University Press.

————. 1991. The role of teasing in adolescent peer culture. In Spencer Cahill, ed., *Sociological studies of child development* 4: 181–197.

————. 1993. "Go get ya a french!" Romantic and sexual teasing among adolescent girls. In Deborah Tannen, ed., *Gender and conversational interaction*. Oxford: Oxford University Press.

————. 1995. *School talk: Gender and adolescent culture*. New Brunswick, N.J.: Rutger's University Press.

Fine, Michelle. 1988. Sexuality, schooling, and adolescent females: The missing discourse of desire. *Harvard Educational Review* 58: 29–53.

————. 1992. *Disruptive voices*. Albany, N.Y.: State University of New York Press.

Fine, Michelle, and Pat Macpherson. 1992. Over dinner: Feminism and adolescent female bodies. In Fine, *Disruptive voices*.

————. 1995. Hungry for an us. *Feminism and Psychology* 5(2): 181–200.

Fine, Michelle, Lois Weis, Linda Powell, and L. Mun Wong, eds. 1997. *Off white: Readings on race, power, and society*. New York: Routledge.

Fordham, Signithia. 1988. Racelessness as a factor in black students' school success: Pragmatic strategy or pyrrhic victory? *Harvard Educational Review* 58(1): 54–84.

————. 1993. "Those loud black girls": (Black) women, silence and gender "passing" in the academy. *Anthropology and Education Quarterly* 24: 3–32.

Foucault, Michael. 1980. *Power/knowledge: Selected interviews and other writings, 1972–1977*, ed. Colin Gordon, trans. Gordon et al. New York: Pantheon.

Frankenberg, Ruth. 1993. *White women, race matters: The social construction of whiteness*. Minneapolis: University of Minnesota Press.

Freire, Paulo. 1970/1992. *Pedagogy of the oppressed*. New York: The Continuum Publishing Company.

Gilbert, Sandra, and Susan Gubar. 1984. *The madwoman in the attic: The woman writer and the nineteenth-century literary imagination*. New Haven: Yale University Press

Gilligan, Carol. 1982. *In a different voice*. Cambridge: Harvard University Press.

————. 1990. Teaching Shakespeare's sister. In Carol Gilligan, Nona Lyons, and Trudy Hanmer, eds., *Making connections: The relational worlds of adolescent girls at Emma Willard School*. Cambridge, Mass.: Harvard University Press.

———. 1991. Joining the resistance: Psychology, politics, girls, and women. *Michigan Quarterly Review* 29: 501–536.

———. 1993. Letter to readers, 1993. *In a different voice.* Cambridge, Mass.: Harvard University Press.

Gilligan, Carol, Lyn Mikel Brown, and Annie Rogers. 1990. Psyche embedded: A place for body, relationships, and culture in personality theory. In A. Rabin, R. Zucker, R. Emmons, and S. Frank, eds., *Studying persons and lives.* New York: Springer.

Girls will be girls. August 2, 1993. *Newsweek,* p. 44.

Goldberger, Nancy. 1996. Looking back, looking foward. In Nancy Goldberger, Jill Tarule, Blythe Clincy, and Mary Belenky, eds., *Knowledge, difference, and power.* New York: Basic Books.

Gradol, David, and Joan Swann. 1989. *Gender voices.* Oxford: Basil Blackwell.

Greene, Maxine. 1988. *The dialectic of freedom.* New York: Teachers College Press.

Hansot, Elisabeth, and David Tyack. 1988. Gender in American public schools: Thinking institutionally. *Signs* 13(4): 741–760.

Harris, Linda, Robert Blum, and Michael Resnick. 1991. Teen females in Minnesota: A portrait of quiet disturbance. *Women and Therapy* 11(3/4): 119–135.

Harris, Maria. 1988. *Women and teaching.* New York: Paulist Press.

Harris, Mary G. 1994. Cholas, Mexican-American girls, and gangs. *Sex Roles* 30(3/4): 289–301.

Harter, Susan. 1990. Self and identity development. In S. Shirley Feldman and Glen Elliott, eds., *At the threshold: The developing adolescent.* Cambridge, Mass.: Harvard University Press.

Hartman-Halbertal, Tova. 1996. Mothering in culture: Ambiguities in continuity. Unpublished doctoral diss., Harvard University.

Harvey, Elizabeth. 1992. *Ventriloquized voices.* New York: Routledge.

Haste, Helen. 1994. *The sexual metaphor.* Cambridge, Mass.: Harvard University press.

Henwood, Doug. 1997. Trash-o-nomics. In Wray and Newitz, eds., *White trash.*

Hill, John. 1988. Adapting to menarche: Familial control and conflict. In M. R. Gunnar and W. A. Collins, eds., *Development during the transition to adolescence,* vol. 21. Hillsdale, N.J.: Erlbaum.

hooks, bell. 1984. *Feminist theory from margin to center.* Boston, Mass.: South End Press.

———. 1990. *Yearning: Race, gender, and cultural politics.* Boston: South End Press.

———. 1994. *Teaching to transgress.* New York: Routledge.

Hudson, Barbara. 1984. Femininity and adolescence. In Angela McRobbie and M. Nava, eds., *Gender and generation*. London: Macmillan.

Jack, Dana. 1991. *Silencing the self: Depression and women*. Cambridge, Mass.: Harvard University Press.

Jack, Dana, and D. Dill. 1992. The silencing the self scale: Schemas of intimacy associated with depression in women. *Psychology of Women Quarterly* 16: 97–106.

Jagger, Allison. 1989. Love and knowledge: Emotion in feminist epistemology. In Allison Jagger and Susan Bordo, eds., *Gender/body/knowledge*. New Brunswick, N.J.: Rutgers University Press.

Jones, Andrea. Spring 1993. "They get right in your face": Are girls turning meaner? *YO! (Youth Outlook)*.

Jordan, Judith, Alexandra Kaplan, Jean Baker Miller, Irene Stiver, and Janet Surrey. 1991. *Women's growth in connection*. New York: Guilford Press.

Kagan, Jerome. 1971. A conception of early adolescence. In Jerome Kagan and Robert Coles, eds., *Twelve to sixteen: Early adolescence*. New York: W. W. Norton.

Kaysen, Susanna. 1993. *Girl interrupted*. New York: Random House.

King, L., and R. Emmons. 1990. Conflict over emotional expression: Psychological and physical correlates. *Journal of Personality and Social Psychology* 58: 864–877.

Klein, Melissa. February 1993. Riot grrrls. *Off Our Backs*.

Lagerspetz, Kirsti, Kaj Bjorkqvist, and Tarja Peltonen. 1988. Is indirect aggression typical of females? Gender differences in aggression in 11- and 12-year-old children. *Aggressive Behavior* 14: 403–414.

Lather, Patti. 1991. *Getting smart: Feminist research and pedagogy with/in the postmodern*. New York: Routledge.

Leadbeater, Bonnie, and Niobe Way. 1996. *Urban girls: Resisting stereotypes, creating identities*. New York: New York University Press.

Lees, Sue. 1993. *Sugar and spice: Sexuality and adolescent girls*. London: Penguin Books.

Lerner, Harriet Goldman. 1985. *The dance of anger*. New York: Harper and Row.

Lloyd, Genevieve. 1984. *The man of reason*. Minneapolis: University of Minnesota Press.

Lorde, Audre. 1984. *Sister outsider*. Freedom, Calif.: The Crossing Press.

Luttrell, Wendy. 1993. "The teachers, they all had their pets": Concepts of gender, knowledge, and power. *Signs* 18(3): 505–546.

Lyman, Peter. 1981. The politics of anger. *Socialist Review* 11: 55–74.

Markus, H. R., and S. Kitayama. 1991. Culture and the self: Implication for cognition, emotion, and motivation. *Psychological Review* 98(2): 224–253.

McIntosh, Peggy. 1983. Interactive phases of curricular re-vision: A feminist perspective. Working paper no. 124. Wellesley, Mass.: Center for Research on Women, Wellesley College.

McLaren, Peter. 1989. *Life in Schools*. White Plains, N.Y.: Longman.

McLeod, Jay. 1995. *Ain't no makin' it: Aspirations and attainment in a low-income neighborhood*. Boulder, Colo.: Westview Press.

McRobbie, Angela. 1991. *Feminism and youth culture*. Boston: Unwin Hyman.

Merten, Don. 1997. The meaning of meanness: Popularity, competition, and conflict among junior high school girls. *Sociology of Education* 70: 175–191.

Miles, Matthew, and A. Michael Huberman. 1984. *Qualitative data analysis*. London: SAGE.

Miller, Jean Baker. 1983. The construction of anger in women and men. Working paper no. 4. Wellesley, Mass.: Center for Research on Women, Wellesley College.

Miller, Jean Baker, and Janet Surrey. 1990. Revisioning women's anger: The personal and the global. Working paper no.43. Wellesley, Mass.: Center for Research on Women, Wellesley College.

Miller, Peggy. 1986. Teasing as language socialization and verbal play in a white working-class community. In Bambi Schieffelin and Elinor Ochs, eds., *Language socialization across cultures*. Cambridge: Cambridge University Press.

Miller, P., and L. Sperry. 1987. The socialization of anger and aggression. *Merrill Palmer Quarterly* 33: 1–31.

Ogbu, John. 1989. The individual in collective adaptation: A framework for focusing on academic underperformance and dropping out among involuntary minorities. In L. Weis, E. Farrar, and H. G. Petrie, eds., *Dropouts from school: Issues, dilemmas, and solutions*. Albany, N.Y.: State University of New York Press.

Orenstein, Peggy. 1994. *Schoolgirls: Young women, self-esteem and the confidence gap*. New York: Doubleday.

Ouellette, S. 1993. Inquiries into hardiness. In L. Goldberger and S. Breznitz, eds., *Handbook of Stress: Theoretical and Clinical Aspects* (2nd ed., pp. 77–100). New York: The Free Press.

[Ouellette] Kobasa, S. 1979. Stressful life events, personality, and health: An inquiry into hardiness. *Journal of Personality and Social Psychology* 37: 1–11.

———. 1982. The hardy personality: Toward a social psychology of stress and health. In J. Suls and G. Sanders, eds., *Social Psychology of Health and Illness*. Hillsdale, N.J.: Erlbaum.

Pastor, Jennifer, Jennifer McCormick, and Michelle Fine. 1996. Makin' homes: An urban girl thing. In Leadbeater and Way, eds., *Urban girls: Resisting stereotypes, creating identities*.

Peterson, A., B. Compas, J. Brooks-Gunn, M. Stemmler, and K. Grant, 1993. Depression in adolescence. *American Psychologist* 48(2): 155–168.

Pipher, Mary. 1995. *Reviving Ophelia.* New York: Ballantine.

Reid, Pamela. 1993. Poor women in psychological research: Shut up and shut out. *Psychology of Women Quarterly* 17: 133–150.

Renouf, A. G., and Susan Harter. 1990. Low self-worth and anger as components of the depressive experience in young adolescents. *Development and Psychopathology* 2: 293–310.

Reynolds, Simon. February 9, 1992. Belting out that most unfeminine emotion. *New York Times.*

Robinson, Tracy, and Janie Ward. 1991. "A belief far greater than anyone's disbelief": Cultivating resistance among African-American female adolescents. In Carol Gilligan, Annie Rogers, and Deborah Tolman, eds., *Reframing resistance: Women, girls, and psychotherapy.* New York: Haworth Press.

Rogers, Annie, Lyn Brown, and Mark Tappan. 1994. Interpreting loss in ego development in girls: Regression or resistance? In Amia Lieblich and Ruthellen Josselson, eds., *The narrative study of lives,* vol. 2. Newbury Park, Calif.: Sage.

Rubin, Lillian. 1976. *Worlds of pain.* New York: Basic Books.

Rys, Gail, and George G. Bear. 1997. Relational aggression and peer relations: Gender and developmental issues. *Merrill-Palmer Quarterly* 43(1): 87–106.

Sachs, J., P. Lieberman, and D. Erickson. 1973. Anatomical and cultural determinants of male and female speech. In R. W. Shuy and R. W. Fasold, eds., *Language attitudes: Current trends and prospects.* Washington, D.C.: Georgetown University Press.

Sadker, Myra, and David Sadker. 1986. Sexism in the classroom: From grade school to graduate school. *Phi Delta Kappan* 68: 512–515.

——. 1994. *Failing at fairness: How America's schools cheat girls.* New York: Charles Scribner's Sons.

Sadker, Myra, David Sadker, and S. Klein. 1991. The issue of gender in elementary and secondary education. In G. Grant, ed., *Review of research in education,* 17. Washington, D.C.: American Educational Research Association.

Scheman, Naomi. 1980. Anger and the politics of naming. In Sally McConnell-Ginet, Ruth Borker, and Nelly Furman, eds., *Women and language in literature and society.* New York: Praeger.

Seattle Weekly, August 5, 1992.

Sennett, Richard, and Jonathan Cobb. 1972. *The hidden injuries of class.* New York: Vintage.

Shaull, Richard. Foreword to Freire, *Pedagogy of the oppressed.*

Sheldon, Amy. 1992. Conflict talk: Sociolinguistic challenges to self-assertion and how young girls meet them. *Merrill-Palmer Quarterly* 38: 95–117.

Spelman, Elizabeth. 1988. *Inessential woman*. Boston, Mass.: Beacon Press.

———. 1989. Anger and insubordination. In Ann Garry and Marilyn Pearsall, eds., *Women, knowledge, and reality: Explorations in feminist philosophy*. Boston, Mass.: Unwin Hyman.

Starr, Diane. 1994. *Voices of rural adolescent girls*. Unpublished master's thesis, Goddard College.

Steedman, Carolyn Kay. 1987. *Landscape for a good woman*. New Brunswick, N.J.: Rutger University Press.

Stein, Nan. 1992. *Secrets in public: Sexual harassment in public (and private) schools*. Working paper no. 256. Wellesley, Mass.: Center for Research on Women, Wellesley College.

Stein, Nan, N. Marshall, and L. Tropp. 1993. *Secrets in public: Sexual harassment in our schools*. Wellesley, Mass.: Center for Research on Women, Wellesley College.

Steiner-Adair, Catherine. 1986. The body politic: Normal female adolescent development and the development of eating disorders. *Journal of the American Academy of Psychoanalysis* 14: 95–114.

———. 1991. When the body speaks: Girls, eating disorders and psychotherapy. *Women and Therapy* 11(3/4): 253–266.

Stevenson, Robert, and Jeanne Ellsworth. 1993. Dropouts and the silencing of critical voices. In Lois Weis and Michelle Fine, eds., *Beyond silenced voices: Class, race, and gender in United States schools*. Albany, N.Y.: State University of New York Press.

Sullivan, Amy. 1996. From mentor to muse: Recasting the role of women in relationship with urban adolescent girls. In Leadbeater and Way, eds., *Urban girls: Resisting stereotypes, creating identities*.

Tappan, Mark, and Lyn Mikel Brown. 1996. Envisioning a postmodern moral pedagogy. *Journal of Moral Education* 25: 101–109.

Tavris, Carol. 1982. *Anger: The misunderstood emotion*. New York: Simon and Schuster.

Taylor, Jill, Carol Gilligan, and Amy Sullivan. 1995. *Between voice and silence: Women and girls, race and relationship*. Cambridge, Mass.: Harvard University Press.

Taylor, Jill, and Janie Ward. 1991. Culture, sexuality, and school: Perspectives from focus groups in six cultural communities. *Women's Studies Quarterly* 19: 111–137

Thomas, Sandra, ed. 1993. *Women and anger*. New York: Springer.

Thompson, Sharon. 1994. What friends are for: On girls' misogyny and romantic fusion. In Janice Irvine, ed., Sexual cultures and the construction of adolescent identities. Philadelphia: Temple University Press.

———. 1994a. Doing desire: Adolescent girls' struggles with/for sexuality. Gender & Society 8: 324–342.

———. 1994b. Daring to desire: Culture and the bodies of adolescent girls. In J. Irvine, ed., Sexual cultures: Adolescent communities and the construction of identity. Philadelphia: Temple University Press.

Tolman, Deborah, and Sarah Church. 1998. Female adolescent sexuality in relational context: Beyond sexual decision-making. In Norine Johnson, Michael Roberts, and Judith Worell, eds., Beyond appearances: A new look at adolescent girls. Washington, D.C.: American Psychological Association.

Underwood, Marion, John Coie, and Cheryl Herbsman. 1992. Display rules for anger and aggression in school-age children. Child Development 63: 366–380.

Vold, Mona. January–February 1993. Queengate! Teen fights for truth, justice —and her crown. Ms. Magazine.

Volosinov, Volosinov. 1929/1986. Marxism and the philosophy of language. Cambridge, Mass.: MIT Press.

Vygotsky, Lev. 1978. Mind in society. Cambridge, Mass.: Harvard University Press.

Walkerdine, Valerie. 1990. Schoolgirl fictions. London: Verso.

———. 1997. Daddy's girl. Cambridge, Mass.: Harvard University Press.

Ward, Janie. 1996. Raising resisters: The role of truth-telling in the psychological development of African-American girls. In Leadbeater and Way, eds., Urban girls: Resisting stereotypes, creating identities.

Way, Niobe. 1990. Social class and time perspective: A critique of the literature. Unpublished Qualifying Paper, Harvard University.

———. 1995. "Can't you see the courage, the strength that I have?" Listening to urban adolescent girls speak about their relationships. Psychology of Women Quarterly 19: 107–128.

Weis, Lois. 1990. Working class without work: High school students in a deindustrialized economy. New York: Routledge.

Wertsch, James. 1991. Voices of the mind. Cambridge, Mass.: Harvard University Press.

Willis, Paul. 1977. Learning to Labor. New York: Columbia University Press.

Winterson, Jeanette. 1985. Oranges are not the only fruit. New York: Atlantic Monthly Press.

Wray, Matt, and Annalee Newitz, eds. 1997. White trash: Race and class in America. New York: Routledge.

Acknowledgments

First and foremost I want to thank the girls who so eagerly embraced this project and moved it in directions I could never have anticipated. They are a brave and hardy bunch. Their individual and collective voices offer new possibilities and underscore the need to appreciate how class and culture affect white girls' understandings of themselves, their relationships, and the social world. I'm so grateful to Diane Starr and Valerie Pettit, both remarkable women teachers and muses, for introducing me to the girls and for generously giving of their time and skill as group facilitators. Diane, in addition, helped me to understand the small Mansfield community in ways crucial to my analysis and to my presentation of the girls' voices.

My early ideas for this book came from interviews made possible by a small grant from the Interdisciplinary Studies Council at Colby College. Support for the study presented here came from a National Academy of Education Spencer Postdoctoral Fellowship, for which I am extremely grateful.

Colby's commitment to interdisciplinary studies has made it possible for me to conduct research and write in ways that cross boundaries and borders. Thanks to my "Women, Girls, and the Culture of Education" students over the years for their many insights. Their questions, social critique, and playfulness never fail to move me to new levels of awareness. A special thanks to Grace Von Tobel for her generous and excellent help, to Hollis Rendleman for her video skills, to Kori Heavner and Amy Ostermueller for their expert transcriptions of the videos, and to Abby Wolfson for assisting me with background research.

I am grateful to so many people for their insights, challenges, and responsiveness to this work. Angela von der Lippe nurtured me through the early stages of this project. Elizabeth Knoll patiently and firmly brought the book to fruition. Christine Thorsteinsson edited with clarity and vision. Special thanks to Mary Belenky, Pam Buffington, Elizabeth Debold, Carol Gilligan, Dana Jack, Betty Sasaki, Deborah Tolman, Niobe Way, and Sarah Willie, as well as to two anonymous peer reviewers, for reading draft forms of the book, offering invaluable critique, and suggesting minor and major revisions. Also, I want to express my deepest appreciation to Carol Gilligan for her guidance and friendship, and to the women and men with whom I worked for so many years on the Harvard Project on Women's Psychology and Girls' Development. If our subjectivities are truly constructed from the many loving, disparate, and competing voices we have taken in, you are ever present and powerful influences. I am so grateful for the invisible threads that connect us across time and space.

In those moments when I could not write, when life entwined with work to create patterns that caught me off guard, my family and closest friends were there. I could not have written this book without the generosity and care of my parents, Diane and Lindy Brown, my brothers, Bill and David Brown, my sister, Susan Christy, my friends Sarah Willie, Betty Sasaki, Elizabeth Debold, Pam Thoma, Deborah Tolman, and Sandy Grande, and without the deep love and support of my husband, Mark Tappan. They encouraged me, helped me name my fears, offered me room to maneuver and space to explore and imagine. As if that were not enough, Mark created a way of living fluid and wide-open enough to ensure our daughter's central place in our life. She is my joy and my inspiration.

Index

Abstract thinking, 7, 221
Abuse: of authority/power, 155, 183; physical, 26, 51–53, 56, 95, 120–121, 141, 192, 196, 207, 208; resistance to, 54, 55–56, 57, 67, 69; sexual, 47, 56, 120
Acadia, town of, 27
Acadia girls: betrayal by teachers, 161–165; competition with friends, 84–85, 102, 195; conflicts of loyalty, 221; double binds of, 158–159, 161, 167–168, 205–206, 221–222; effects of group on, 220–221; expressions of anger, 99–102, 156–157; families of, 29, 95; group characteristics of, 18, 21–22, 28–30, 38, 71–72; and idealized femininity, 148, 151–152, 154, 221; individualistic resistance strategies, 160, 166–175, 195; invisibility of, 165–168, 195; lack of collective action, 219–220; lack of gender analysis, 163–166; privileges of, 71–72, 99, 130, 133, 134; and public-private split, 94–99, 152, 195
Acadia Junior High, 27; class structure of, 72–73, 77, 80, 81; hierarchical nature of, 85; institutional boundaries of, 29
Adolescence: developmental changes of, 7–9, 12; as masculine construct, 115; pre-, 14, 17. *See also* Cognitive development; Early adolescence; Girls' development
Aggression, 13, 16; vs. anger, 11; and class, 16, 203; development of, 13; direct, 13, 15; gender differences in, 13; indirect, 13–14, 15; and movement into the dominant culture, 15; as play, 41; relational, 14. *See also* Teasing
Allison, Dorothy, 36–37, 40
Amber, 24, 42, 62, 63, 67, 119, 135ff., 142, 143–146, 181, 186, 187, 189, 192, 212
American dream, 65, 160, 177, 195. *See also* Meritocracy
Anger, 3, 4, 13, 15, 40, 58, 67, 124; at abuse, 51–57; and aggression, 14; vs. aggression, 11; and class, 16, 65–70, 99–102; control of, 192–194; as creative force, 9, 134; as defense against feelings, 65, 68; as disruptive, 131–132; as emotional touchstone, 132; at friends, 67–68; and girls' development, 11–13, 209–210; healthy, 11; indirect expressions of, 100–101; at injustice, 11–12, 68, 69, 101–102, 183; listening for, 33–34; and lucid thinking, 11; and mental health, 176–177, 224; and move into the culture, 15; and personal authority, 11, 12; physical manifestations of, 66; as political emotion, 11, 224; and political resistance, 10, 13, 16, 101; politics of, 196–197; at regulation of voice, 124, 132; and school, 155; as sign of self-respect, 11, 12; and social critique, 209–210; as source of power, 5, 10, 16, 19, 65, 102, 210; suppressed, 176–177; as threat to status quo, 8, 11; at unearned privileges, 101; and violence, 67; and women, 10–11. *See also* Resistance; Schools; Teachers
Angry girl movement. *See* Riot Grrrls